From
The Reich
to
Rhodesia

Peter Sternberg

TSL Publications

First published in Great Britain in 2018
By TSL Publications, Rickmansworth

Copyright © 2018 Peter & Hermoine Sternberg

ISBN / 978-1-912416-15-8

The right of Peter Sternberg to be identified as the author of this work
has been asserted by the author in accordance with the UK Copyright,
Designs and Patents Act 1988.

All rights reserved. No part of this publication may be reproduced,
stored in a retrieval system or transmitted, in any form or by any
means without the prior written permission of the publisher, nor be
otherwise circulated in any form of binding or cover other than that in
which it is published and without a similar condition being imposed on
the subsequent buyer.

Cover design: Tamara Sternberg

This book is dedicated to my wife and soul mate
Hermoine,
who proved the inspiration and guiding light
behind this project.

THANK YOU

I should sincerely like to thank various good
friends for giving so freely of their advice
and assistance during the compilation of
From the Reich To Rhodesia, especially John
Fox (Harare) and Gwynne Robins (Cape
Town). Their assistance has been greatly
appreciated. And special thanks to my dear
wife Hermoine for typing out endless
manuscripts and correcting spelling errors!

1935 ⚜ 1936 ⚜ 1937

I was born on Wednesday 27 February 1935 in Dortmund, Germany. My parents were Robert and Irmgard Sternberg, and I was their firstborn child. I gather that the rest of the immediate family, relatives and friends all rejoiced in seeing a new addition to the family, although my mother, some years later, confided in me that several of their relatives had expressed their reservations at the time, for they felt, and not without reason, that it was not too wise to start a new family, especially a Jewish one, in Nazi-dominated Germany. For this was pre-World War Two Germany that we were living in. Adolf Hitler had been in power for two years, Jew baiting was on the rise and anti-Semitic feelings and laws were gathering swift momentum.

And perhaps they were right in expressing those opinions. For at the time that I came into this world, concentration camps had already been built, Jewish business concerns were being actively boycotted, Jews had been deprived of German citizenship, and in the summer of 1935 notices appeared at the approaches of many towns and villages which quite blatantly stated "No Jews Allowed". Many shops, restaurants and hotels had already banned Jewish patronage from their establishments. And much worse was to follow in the few remaining years leading to the outbreak of World War Two.

However, a brief few weeks respite for the Jewish population occurred during the two week period that the summer Olympic Games were staged in Berlin in 1936 – for the Nazis ordered that all anti-Jewish notices should be taken down, Jew baiting articles should not appear in the newspapers and anti-Semitic attacks and references to Jews in general should be toned down

Poster blaming the Jews

as much as was possible. This in order not to "upset the sensitivities" of athletes and spectators visiting Germany from various countries around the globe. So everything was toned down and, in order to placate Hitler and not to offend him, a number of participating countries went the whole mile and more and chose to exclude Jewish athletes from their teams altogether despite the fact that these athletes had already qualified to represent their countries at the forthcoming Olympic Games. Of course the Jews of Germany realized well enough that this move amounted to no more than a temporary respite, and that is exactly how it turned out to be. For once the Olympic Games were over it was back to business as usual. Down with the Jews! I had indeed been born in precarious times, to say the least.

Helene Sternberg

Julius Sternberg

For the record, a few details about my parents. My father, Robert, was born on 11 January 1904 in Erwitte, Germany, to Julius Sternberg and his wife Helene (née Lebach). There were five children, two sons and three daughters. Eldest son Otto had been born in 1897 and the three daughters were Grete (born 1899), Herta (born 1901) and Mathilde (born 1910). Both Grete and Mathilde were fated to perish in Nazi concentration camps during the years 1943/1944, exact dates unknown. Their mother, Helene (my grandmother) perished on 8 June 1943 in the Theresienstadt Concentration Camp.

Just prior to my father's thirteenth birthday, and his imminent barmitzvah, his father Julius passed away and the barmitzvah proved, in the circumstances, to be a celebration tainted by grief. My father however conducted the entire service that Saturday morning in the little synagogue in Erwitte — quite a remarkable feat for a youngster in his early teens. He had a strong belief and interest in religion which would stand him in good stead throughout his life.

In due course he graduated from high school with top marks in the Abitur (matric) examinations and thereafter joined a bank. Times were extremely difficult in Germany following that country's defeat in World War One and unemployment throughout the country was rife. This was at the time of the Weimar Republic, and

Robert Sternberg circa 1930

political instability had spread throughout the land whilst levels of social discontent attained a new high.

Jeanette Loewenstein

My mother, Irmgard, was born on 22 September 1912 in the town of Wittmund to parents Wilhelm Loewenstein and Jeanette (née Gutkind). Her father was a butcher by trade, and had served as a motor cycle despatch rider in the German army during the Great War. My mother was the second of three daughters, the eldest sister being named Marta and the youngest Ruth. My grandfather in later years managed to leave Germany for Northern Rhodesia shortly before World War Two broke out, and Marta and Ruth both emigrated to Africa, Marta to Southern Rhodesia and Ruth to South-West-Africa. However, my maternal grandmother Jeanette, through a series of administrative delays, did not manage to leave Germany in time and was trapped when war broke out. She likewise perished in Theresienstadt Concentration Camp — date unknown.

My mother in her late teens

My parents first met each other on 15 March 1930 – the "Ides of March" as they always liked to remind one another! My father had at that time left the bank and had found employment with his cousin Julius Weinberg, proprietor of a cigar factory, and he met his future wife (my mother to be) at the home of his eldest sister Grete, where Irmgard, then aged 17, and recently out of school, had found employment as a junior governess for the children. Apparently, my parents to be both took an instant liking to one another which soon blossomed into love. However, they decided against an early marriage, as times were extremely difficult from the financial point of view – the world wide Great Depression had affected Germany badly – but agreed that if matters improved they would then be in a position to "tie the knot". Whilst they were still courting my father was appointed agent for the entire Ruhr area for the popular brand of cigars manufactured by Julius Weinberg, and this move opened up the field for a lucrative agency covering a densely populated sector of the country.

On 1 July 1932 he moved to Dortmund, having found himself a comfortable apartment to rent at Gneisenaustrasse 40. Wedding plans were announced thereafter and a date set. The civil

wedding ceremony took place on Friday 23 December 1932 and the wedding proper (the religious service) a few days later on Monday 26 December. Rabbi de Haas performed the ceremony at 11 o'clock in the morning at the home of the bride's parents in Oldenburg.

Unfortunately so-called "normal" times lasted barely a month as on 30 January 1933, Adolf Hitler took power in Germany. Within a few months he urged the German public to boycott all Jewish businesses, thereby launching his first attack upon the Jewish citizens of the country. The assault on the Jews had begun, and very soon gained momentum. In April 1933 pupils at schools throughout the country were compelled to use the Hitler salute – and the formation of the Hitler Youth Movement was well under way.

New bride in her kitchen

Jewish adults and children became instant targets for Nazi indoctrinated thugs of all ages – and the victims soon discovered that they had virtually no recourse to the country's justice system.

My parents continued to live at Gneisenaustrasse for the next six years and despite government led boycotts and numerous other problems, my father's agency prospered. But when in September 1938 a law was passed that Jews would no longer be permitted to trade, my father and countless others were compelled either to abandon their businesses, or sell them for a mere pittance. Not only did he now find himself out of work but worse still, stood no reasonable hope of ever finding employment again in a country which had now become extremely hostile and paranoid towards members of the Jewish faith.

As mentioned earlier, I was born in 1935 and restrictions on Jews had at that stage already extended into all walks of life. Jews were refused entry to state owned hospitals and it was only through the good offices of the family (non-Jewish) doctor that

Myself in Dortmund

my mother was allowed into the delivery ward of a hospital situated in Dortmund's Friedenstrasse. So much for my start in life...

Raising a Jewish family in Nazi Germany at that time must have taken some courage, but the chances were that very few parents could possibly have envisaged the horrors that were yet to unfold.

I was but a few years old when I developed a middle ear infection which worsened rapidly. German doctors were by then strongly discouraged from treating Jewish patients. Finally, in desperation, my mother phoned the family doctor who had delivered me and pleaded with him to come over to the apartment to examine me as this infection appeared to be gradually turning into an emergency case. By that stage I was screaming uncontrollably as ear infections of this nature can be extremely painful.

After much persuasion he agreed to pay us a visit – choosing to arrive after midnight in order that his presence would hope-fully not be noticed by any of the neigh-bours in the apartment building. For some of them may well have been in-clined to report him to the authorities for continuing to treat Jewish patients. He arrived in the early hours of the morning to find two distraught parents and a sobbing child and I was told in later years that the doctor actually per-formed a minor operation on my ear whilst I was being held down on the

Aged 3 years

kitchen table by my desperately worried parents. The doctor had no choice in the matter, for he dared not take me to either his surgery or to a hospital for the operation that I in actual fact required, for in doing so he could well have lost his medical licence and possibly even have faced imprisonment for his deeds.

What anxiety I must have caused my parents at that time – perhaps those who doubted the wisdom of Jewish parents bringing children into the world during the period of the Third Reich had a very legitimate point!

Fortunately I survived the ordeal and was given the book *Der Struwwelpeter* (a classic German children's story) by my Aunt Ruth to help me get over my recent trauma. I still have this book which was inscribed by her and this would have been one of the first books I ever received. It became one of my favourite reads in the years to follow, as was *Max und Moritz*, another classic children's tale and likewise graphically illustrated.

Max und Mortiz

1938

Kristallnacht (the Night of the Broken Glass) occurred during the night of the 9th/10th November 1938 and had the most terrible consequences for Jewish families throughout the land. No less than a thousand synagogues were either set alight, badly damaged or vandalized throughout the land, some two hundred and seventy being completely destroyed. Approximately seven thousand Jewish owned shops and businesses throughout Germany had their plate glass doors and windows shattered whilst the contents of the buildings were often trashed, looted and in many instances also set alight. Pedestrians were attacked as were many homes and Jews were kicked, beaten up and grossly humiliated by mobs and many, especially the elderly, were beaten to death in the process, almost 100 deaths being reported. Although fire brigades were called out the fire fighters were under strict instructions from the authorities simply to hose down those buildings which adjourned burning synagogues and shops in order to safeguard any non-Jewish owned properties from being affected by the flames – but the fire fighters were to make no attempt whatsoever to save the blazing synagogues or Jewish owned shops!

As for the police – they simply stood by and watched all this unfolding – neither arresting, nor for that matter preventing, murderous gangs of thugs throughout all corners of Germany from committing arson, wanton destruction of property, or worse still, causing serious assault, grievous injury or even death to many innocent and defenceless members of the Jewish community.

The following morning my father, who was, not at all surprisingly, still out of work, took me out for a walk to enable my mother to clean the apartment. However, we soon returned home after having seen the all too obvious destruction around us and, ashen faced, he told my mother that "all appears to be lost – we are surely doomed!" He then proceeded to describe the terrible scenes he had just witnessed – not only relating to the damaged, burnt and still smouldering buildings but also to the great number of bloodstains, shattered spectacles, items of ripped clothing and other appalling evidence stemming directly from the assaults and mayhem which had occurred several hours earlier.

In addition, rumours were rife within the Jewish community that all Jewish men and youths were to be arrested and incarcerated by the Nazi authorities. The entire Jewish community throughout the land was absolutely stunned by what had happened.

In the possible event that this frightening rumour should indeed prove to be factual, my parents had, a few days earlier, discussed the impact that this would have on our lives. They agreed that my mother, rather than remaining in the apartment in Dortmund, would travel with me to Cologne and stay with my father's sister Herta and her husband Paul in their home until, hopefully, the position had improved.

Shortly thereafter the "rumour" regarding the round-up of Jewish males proved to be all too chillingly correct. There was a pounding on the front door and two Gestapo officials presented themselves in order to arrest my father. Thankfully, these two men surprisingly displayed a spark of humanity and acted in an almost apologetic manner in having to perform their obviously obnoxious duty. In fact, they allowed him a few moments of privacy in order to bid farewell to my mother and myself, and also permitted him to change into a suit which he had requested. Then, instead of brutally pushing or kicking him down the stairs, which fate he later heard had befallen many other detainees, they allowed him to walk unaided down the stairs, out of the front door and into the street.

My mother sat at the kitchen table – her mind must have been in complete turmoil, whilst I sat on the floor under the table next to her feet. Would she ever see her husband again – dead or alive – or would he simply vanish off the face of the earth, especially in the light of the atrocities he had so recently witnessed, chillingly taking into account his prediction of impending doom? Was this to be the end of their marriage and their lives together?

She remained seated in the kitchen of the now silent apartment for some considerable time, deep in personal thought, with only the ticking of the kitchen clock breaking the silence. Finally she arose, packed a suitcase for our journey to Cologne and scooped me up from the kitchen floor. She locked the apartment door behind her, possibly for the last time for all she knew. Together we walked to the railway station to catch the express train to Cologne.

The train journey was well underway when my mother noticed that a fellow passenger sitting opposite her had begun to munch on a bar a chocolate. It was then that my poor mother suddenly realized, with all the trauma of the previous few hours thrust upon her, that she had completely forgotten to provide me with either breakfast or lunch. And for that matter, neither had I requested anything to eat, which in my case was rather out of character! Perhaps the events of that morning had proved almost as traumatic for me as it

He who buys from Jews is a traitor

had been for her. It was only now, seeing the chocolate being consumed right in front of her that she was reminded of her oversight. As she had likewise forgotten to take any food with her for the journey she now found herself in a quandary. Deciding to swallow her pride, she asked the fellow passenger whether she would let her have a small piece of her chocolate bar so that she could feed a little to her son. The woman duly broke off a small piece as requested and that single piece of chocolate kept me going until we eventually arrived at our destination some hours later.

It was upon our arrival at her sister-in-law Herta's house in Cologne that my mother received the news that her own father had likewise been arrested at his home in Oldenberg by the Gestapo. He too had been taken to an unknown destination. First her husband, and now her elderly father. When and how would this nightmare end?

Having spent some days in Cologne with my aunt and uncle, my mother decided that the two of us would probably be better off returning to our apartment in Dortmund to await information on my father's fate, and to ascertain the outcome regarding the applications for emigration which had been submitted in the weeks prior to Kristallnacht. And so we returned to Dortmund and in the uncertain and agonizing weeks following my father's arrest, we both anxiously awaited his hoped for release. My father had, via the good offices of the Red Cross, managed to keep in touch with us from Sachsenhausen, a notorious concentration camp situated north of Berlin. This was one of the three concentration camps into which Jewish males had been incarcerated on the day following Kristallnacht – the other two camps used in this operation being Dachau and Buchenwald. Some 30,000 Jewish men between the ages of 16 and 60 had been arrested throughout the land, joining Jews already imprisoned there. Conditions in the camps proved terrible and the *Manchester Guardian*, a British newspaper, reported that the inmates were subjected to "great barbarities".

It was during this agonizing period of waiting for his hoped for release that the good news was received by my mother that permission had been granted by the authorities in Southern Rhodesia, a British self-governing colony situated in south-central Africa, allowing us entry to that country. My parents had, some time before, applied to emigrate to Southern Rhodesia (which at that stage was still a virtually "unknown" country in Africa, certainly to the majority of continental Europeans) for the simple reason that my mother's elder sister Marta, together with her husband Julius, had emigrated there a year previously. In our particular circumstances we required a resident of the country to sponsor us in order that we could be accepted for residency in Southern Rhodesia, and my uncle and aunt were fully prepared to do that. Sponsorship proved vitally necessary, as we would otherwise have been denied permission to leave Germany had we not been able to produce official permission, in writing, from the Southern Rhodesian immigration authorities authorizing us to both enter and thereafter reside in this African country. Such rules and regulations, which likewise applied to many countries, proved to be a great stumbling block to families intending to emigrate. Thus, should the necessary paperwork not be available, the unfortunate individuals often found themselves trapped within Germany's borders when war eventually broke out. With official permission in hand to confirm that our immigration status was legal, my mother went to the offices of the German East African Line (Deutsche Ost-Afrika-Linie) and purchased steamship

DEUTSCHE OST-AFRIKA-LINIE

FAST SERVICE via the WEST COAST
ROUND AFRICA SERVICES via the
EASTERN AND WESTERN ROUTE

tickets to the port of Beira, Portuguese East Africa (Mozambique) – the nearest port to Southern Rhodesia. It was now a case of patiently waiting, hoping and praying for my father's release.

Six weeks after his arrest, my father was finally released from Sachsenhausen concentration camp, as too was my grandfather, my mother's father, who had, by coincidence, been sent to the same camp. Upon arriving back in Dortmund after his horrific experiences behind barbed wire, my father was indeed gratified to receive the good news of our impending departure from Nazi Germany and all that our country of birth now stood for. Ironically, within the space of a few weeks, permission was also granted by the United States embassy for us to settle in America. But the American waiting list was virtually filled to capacity with the names of tens of thousands of other hopeful would-be emigrants to the U.S.A. – all forming part of a lengthy quota system to gain entry to the United States. Because of the delays experienced with the American application, my parents had at the same time forwarded an application to emigrate to Southern Rhodesia, and now this small African country had extended its hand of assistance to desperate refugees – way ahead of the all powerful and extremely cautious United States. At this stage, any change in destination would have meant cancelling the already paid for steamship tickets to Africa, then attempting to obtain bookings on a liner heading for America. As the great majority of the country's Jewish population seemed intent on making their way to the United States, there was unfortunately no guarantee that a booking would become available for some considerable time to the "land of the free". It had likewise become patently obvious that the sooner one departed Germany the better, for time appeared to be fast running out. Choice of country now became of secondary importance, it was a case of departing as soon as was humanly possible and heading for any friendly country that would hopefully provide reasonable shelter.

Leaving Germany and emigrating to safer climes must have been uppermost in most people's minds, but on the whole most countries were not at all keen to accept German-Jewish refugees, crisis or no crisis! The question has been asked many times – why would the Nazis let German Jews depart the country a scant year prior to the outbreak of war? The answer appears to be that Jews were actually being encouraged to leave because the policy at that time was to expel as many of them from Germany as was possible. This would no doubt help to "purify" their beloved Third Reich of this despised race, while at the same time being in a position to confiscate all the assets that the Jews would be compelled to leave behind upon their departure. We all know what befell those Jews who remained in Germany – once war broke out they were well and truly trapped. And this in fact is what happened to both my grandmothers, uncles, aunts, cousins and so many other relatives and friends. The great majority disappeared into concentration camps – and were simply never seen or heard of again ...

Apart from the fact that it was extremely difficult to obtain visas from foreign embassies in pre-war Germany, and long queues attested to this, the emigration policy of the Nazi regime brought into effect the most intricate and formidable bureaucratic procedures that virtually robbed refugees of everything that they possessed.

Firstly, the Tax Authorities froze all bank accounts belonging to would-be emigrants. Household furniture, effects and personal belongings were however permitted to be shipped to the country of destination in a container (usually a large wooden crate) which was known as a "lift". Thereafter an exit levy had to be paid. Finally, those fortunate enough to be able to leave the country were severely restricted in taking out any currency – the maximum allowed was ten Reich Marks per person on departure from Germany – a minimal amount indeed.

However, the problems did not end there. Financial obligations very often awaited the battered emigrant (now hopeful immigrant) upon arrival at destination, as reflected in the Immigration Regulations as issued by the German African Lines for the benefit of passengers in December 1938.

These regulations applied to passengers travelling to various African countries.

Extracts, primarily as applied to Southern Rhodesia, follow:-.

ZANZIBAR

Travellers to Zanzibar must be in possession of a passport, duly visaed by a British Consulate.

Subjects of any country named in Section 11, B I do not require a visa.
See also paragraphs 1 to 5.
The amount of the landing deposit, if any, is £37.10 Sterling.

III RHODESIA & NYASALAND

The decrees for the conditions of Immigration in South-Rhodesia are laid down in the law: "Immigrants Regulations, ordinance 1914 amended". Similar conditions are in force for North-Rhodesia and Nyasaland (see paragraph 1-5). In general, for South-Rhodesia and Nyasaland a British visa is required for subjects without nationality and for those under French protectorate.

The passport is not to be limited in time, thus enabling the holder to return to the country of origin at any time. In general, the Consulates grant visas only to such persons who can prove the possession of sufficient means, in order to assure their own support and that of their family in accordance with their social position.

The granting of the visa does not necessarily guarantee the permission to land, nor is the possession of cash only, sufficient to obtain a permit of landing. On arrival, each passenger will be thoroughly examined by the Immigration Authority, as to whether he and also the documents comply with the Immigration Regulations. On principal a permit of landing will not be granted in advance. Therefore, each passenger has to undertake the voyage to one of the Rhodesian boundary towns at his own risk and it depends on the Immigration Officer there, whether or not the passenger after examination receives a landing permit. Any costs for Hotel etc. during the time of examination are for the account of the immigrant.

The sole exception is made for wives and children under age of such persons who may be considered as definitely settled in Rhodesia, i.e., having resided in Rhodesia for 3 subsequent years, without interruption. In such cases the Rhodesian Authorities can confirm to the applicant that his family will be granted a permit of landing, provided the family does not fall under the law forbidding the immigration.

Passengers to Rhodesia and Nyasaland travelling via Beira or Lourenco Marques require a Portuguese visa in transit through Portuguese East Africa (see also 12, B I for deposit in transit). Passengers entering Rhodesia and Nyasaland through territory of the South African Union require a transit visa for the South African Union (with the exception of those mentioned under 18, D I) and in general have to deposit £50.- on landing, being refunded to them immediately after their permit of landing for Rhodesia and Nyasaland has been granted. Furthermore, they have to observe the Regulations for tourists travelling through South Africa.

IV. BRITISH COLONIES IN WEST AFRICA

Passengers to British Colonies in West Africa (Gambia, Sierra Leone, Gold Coast and Nigeria) require a passport duly visaed by a British Consulate. Passengers are advised to provide themselves with extra passport photos.

Subjects of any country named in Section 11, B1 do not require a visa.

In the meantime, matters were heading from bad to worse on the home front. The German government had by now placed severe restrictions on the publication of even minor Jewish newspapers, having already banned all the major ones. This further deprived thousands of readers of vital information which they sorely thirsted for in those strife-ridden and forbidding times. Shortly thereafter the publication ban was extended to Jewish interest magazines, and even affected local community bulletins.

Jewish identity card

These decrees virtually deprived the Jewish population of any last remaining sources of information and communication in a world that was fast collapsing all around them. The net was fast closing in.

Life in Germany was becoming completely intolerable for the distraught and terrified Jewish population. Having been virtually ostracised from public life, yet another new proclamation came into effect in order to drive home the fact that Jews had been declared "non-persons" residing in a Nazi paradise. The proclamation stipulated that no Jew was permitted to own a radio. To be found in possession of one was strictly "verboten" (forbidden) and punishable by arrest. A further ban on telephones followed. Subsequent laws included the following: Jews were barred from using public swimming bath facilities. Jews were prohibited from owning any domestic pets. Jewish midwives were no longer allowed to attend to non-Jewish births. Jews were only allowed to sit on park benches that had been designated for them – benches that had been marked by a yellow sign. Jews were now obliged to carry identity cards stamped with the letter "J" on the cover, indicating the bearer's Jewish identity. And, hard as it is to believe, a further law was passed in 1938 which proclaimed that Jewish and non-Jewish children were no longer permitted to play together – any fraternization was strictly disallowed. The noose was drawing tighter and the outlook became bleaker and more dangerous by the day.

The Nazi hailstorm on the Jews continues

1939

The weeks that followed were filled with extreme trepidation as conditions appertaining to Jews deteriorated at an alarming rate. Restriction after restriction followed, all being extremely negative. Jewish doctors and dentists were now stripped of their medical licences and barred from any further practice, as were Jewish lawyers and those belonging to other professions. All Jewish children were expelled from state schools. Succeeding weeks saw Jews barred from entering any theatres, cinemas and other places of entertainment.

In order to raise funds to clean up the chaos and destruction caused by their own Nazi thugs and hooligans on Kristallnacht when synagogues and Jewish owned businesses were desecrated, burnt and destroyed, the German government now had the audacity to impose a fine of no less than one thousand million Reich Marks on the country's Jewish population – the innocent party in this infamous disgrace, thus efficiently eliminating the Jews of Germany from all economic life.

My parents continued to live and somehow survive through these frightening and turbulent times and no doubt fervently prayed that the permission granted them to leave the country would not be withdrawn by the German authorities at the last moment – for anything could and did happen in a land that was clearly running amok.

As departure day approached, farewells to relatives and close friends were said – both parties no doubt wondering whether they would ever get a chance to see each other again. Although an uncertain future might well be facing those who were departing – what sort of future lay ahead for those poor souls who remained behind? Many tears of despair were shed at the sheer hopelessness of the situation. In 1933 it was estimated that there were approximately half a million Jews living in Germany.

By 1939 almost half that number had somehow or other managed to leave the country. The Jews who now remained behind were mainly too old, infirm or for various reasons had been unable to obtain visas to settle in other countries. These poor folk virtually all perished over the next six years in the terrible holocaust that was to follow.

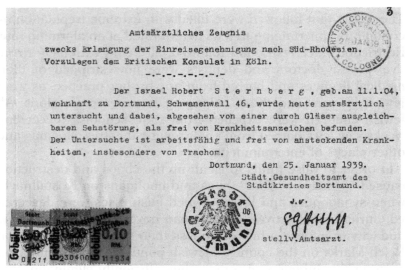

Health Certificate issued to Robert Sternberg for immigration purposes

Departure day finally arrived and we caught the train from Dortmund to the port city of Hamburg, travelling via Cologne, Munster and Bremen. Prior to boarding the train, and several times during the rail journey our travel documents were thor-

SS Ussukuma

oughly scrutinized by on-board railway police and were thankfully found to be in order, no doubt much to my parents' intense relief. On arrival in Hamburg we made our way to a hotel situated close to the railway station where we spent our last night in the land of our birth, embarking the following day, Friday 24 February 1939, on the German passenger liner

S.S. *Ussukuma*, which was to serve as our home for the next six weeks. We were assigned Cabin 130 and at 10 o'clock that evening the ship set sail.

The liner headed for England and we spent Monday 27 February in the English port of Southampton – which day happened to coincide with my fourth birthday. The large wooden container commonly known as a "lift" and which contained our furniture, crockery, glassware, clothing, linens, books and other household effects had been safely lodged in the ship's hold and the realization finally sunk in that we had, despite all our previous doubts and fears, finally managed to escape the Nazi tyranny. Nevertheless, there was also the distinct feeling amongst passengers that a very precarious and uncertain future awaited the German/Jewish refugees aboard the *Ussukuma*. Most of them, whether they admitted it or not, were now sailing into an unknown and unpredictable new chapter of their lives which they hoped would turn out to be vastly preferable to the appalling life that they would undoubtedly have faced had they remained in the so-called German "Fatherland".

The *Ussukuma* belonged to the Deutsche-Ost-Afrika Linie (German East Africa Lines). This fairly modern 7,834 tonne liner had been built by Blohm & Voss in Hamburg in 1920 and was powered by four steam turbines which managed to attain a speed of fourteen knots. Manned by a courteous captain and crew, the ship carried a total complement of 264 passengers and the *Ussukuma* proved to be both comfortable and popular with the passengers. Amongst those on board were a fair number of children who now found themselves revelling in warm sunshine and fresh sea breezes in contrast to the cold and wet European winter they had just left behind. The food aboard ship was good and plentiful and a sea voyage of this nature could only have helped ease the trauma and stress that the majority of passengers had experienced over the past number of years. Despite all this, the chances were high that a degree of tension would neverthe-

Sailing for Freedom

less have remained, for no matter how much the refugees may have endeavoured to enjoy the current voyage, they were still, after all, sailing on a German liner whose flag very prominently displayed the hated Nazi swastika ...

On occasional evenings my parents arranged for a "babysitter" to keep an eye on me, usually in the form of a young fellow-passenger, so as to give themselves the opportunity to relax on deck after dinner and chat with newly found friends. I was told that on one occasion when they returned to the cabin they found the babysitter, who happened to be in his early twenties, stretched out fast asleep on the cabin floor whilst I in turn had taken over the responsibility allocated to him and was most engrossed in watching this young man, from the raised vantage point of my bunk, slumbering deeply!

As the voyage progressed and the ship drew closer to the African continent, passengers' apprehensions may well have returned because, with possibly only a handful of exceptions, the Jewish refugees now heading for Africa would never have left Germany in the first place had the Nazis not come to power and forced the issue. Africa to them represented an unknown factor and few would have chosen the "dark continent" to emigrate to had they been given an alternative destination. For the refugees were now heading for countries that had different customs, different cultures and different languages to the ones they were accustomed to and had been brought up with, and as for those holding university or technical degrees, be they medical, legal or mechanical, such degrees for a variety of reasons were most often not recognized or accepted in the majority of African countries. Many of the refugees on board were therefore compelled to earn a living starting virtually from grass roots level, with absolute minimal resources to their name and very often without any back-up system awaiting them at destination. And anti-German feelings were running high in the latter stages of the 1930s, especially in many parts of the British Empire. But despite the odds stacked against them, the majority of these refugees succeeded in their chosen field regardless of the handicaps that they would face upon arrival.

Jewish immigrants were, in many cases, not exactly welcomed with open arms in their new countries of abode. It may have been partially appreciated by the populace that the Nazis in Germany were brutally persecuting the Jews and that alone should have explained the reason that they (the Jews) were now being forced to flee their home country but despite this, these refugees were likewise of German nationality, held German passports ... and many could only converse in German – or speak a poor English laced with a strong German accent. It was not that easy to fit into the general community. And apart from their personal problems these refugees, now hopefully heading for freedom, must have likewise been giving a lot of thought to the current position of relatives and friends left behind in an extremely oppressive Germany. What would happen to those who had remained behind and how were they managing to cope given the environment in which they were now virtually prisoners?

Aunt Ruth

En route the ship docked at Luanda in Angola (Portuguese West Africa) and in due course proceeded to Walvis Bay in South West Africa (a former German colony – where German was still one of the major languages) and where we were welcomed by my Aunt Ruth, my mother's younger sister who had herself left Germany a year or so previously. She was newly married to Hans Isenberg who had also fled Germany and the couple now lived in Windhoek, capital of South West Africa. When World War Two broke out Hans joined the South African Air Force and served in the North African campaign, thus becoming one of the many who helped drive General Rommel and his Afrika Corps from the African continent. It must have lifted my parents' spirits to be

Uncle Hans Western Dessert c1942

re-united with Ruth, even if only for a few brief hours. The ship then pulled anchor and headed for its next port of call – the South African harbour city of Cape Town, situated close to the southernmost tip of the African continent.

Cape Town has the well deserved title of being one of the most beautiful coastal cities in the world with its spectacular backdrop of Table Mountain which overlooks both city and harbour. As the tugboat manoeuvred the *Ussukuma* into dock we could clearly see vendors positioned at the quay side holding boxes of magnificent Cape grown fruit, including grapes – the latter selling for all of sixpence a box! Although greatly tempted to purchase the delicious fruit on offer – for my father loved grapes – my parents nevertheless declined the temptation – every penny was being carefully budgeted for in order to meet the formidable expenses that still lay ahead.

However, together with other passengers from the liner we were taken for a drive up a section of Table Mountain and were shown around various parts of Cape Town by members of the local Jewish community who rallied around to show their solidarity, a gesture greatly appreciated by the now somewhat travel weary passengers.

Dad (left), Mom (right) and myself on sightseeing drive around Cape Town

During the six week voyage, one of the ship's lounges had been regularly set aside each Friday evening and Saturday morning for religious services and here it was that my father led the congregation of fellow passengers in Sabbath prayers, himself reading from the Torah scroll that he had brought with him from Germany – a Torah scroll that had been donated to the Erwitte Hebrew Congregation by his paternal grandfather Herz Sternberg in 1856 on the occasion of his (Herz's) marriage that year. The services on board ship were well attended and towards the end of the voyage the passengers presented my father with a letter of appreciation thanking him for his efforts in ensuring that Sabbath services were regularly held throughout the voyage and wishing him and his family well for the future. One can safely assume that not too many Jewish religious services were being held at that time under the auspices and permission of the German authorities, yet for the entire voyage these services were held on a regular basis, whilst at the same time the Nazi flag fluttered away in the breeze a small distance from where the worshippers were gathered. Strange times indeed ...

Testimonial of Appreciation by passengers to my father for conducting prayer services on board ship

Herrn Robert Sternberg, aus Dortmund sprechen wir hiermit herzl.
Dank aus, daß er uns während der sechswöchentlichen Seereise einen
solch schönen und andachtsvollen G'ttesdienst bereitet hat. Er fungie:
te hier als Vorbeter, und hat er durch seinen angenehmes Organ und
Wissen in den alt-jüdischen Gesängen sich die Achtung aller erwor-
ben. Herr Sternberg ist fähig, das Amt eines Vorbeters zur Zufrie-
denheit eines jeden auszufüllen. Wir wünschen ihm und seiner Familie
für ihren ferneren Lebensweg nur das Beste.

An Bord der U s s u k u m a im März 1939.

From Cape Town the ship sailed around the South African coastline and approximately a week later docked at Lourenço Marques, the capital of Mozambique, a Portuguese colony on the east coast of Africa. Following a short stopover we now embarked on the final stage of the voyage, our destination being Beira, Mozambique's second largest port. Situated a few hundred miles further north of Lourenço Marques, Beira was the closest sea-outlet/harbour to Southern Rhodesia, a land-locked country. Six weeks after departing Germany our long sea voyage had finally come to an end!

After the Rhodesian bound passengers had disembarked at Beira the *Ussukuma* sailed up the East African coast, through the Suez Canal and into the Mediterranean and back to Germany. With war clouds looming she may well have chalked up a few further voyages around the African continent but in early December 1939, some three months after World War Two had broken out, she was found steaming off the southeastern coast of South America, a Nazi ship in international waters.

At that time the German pocket battleship *Admiral Graf Spee* was busy launching attacks on commercial vessels plying the South Atlantic Ocean, and her formidable firepower had already sunk ten cargo vessels, thus sending over 50,000 tonnes of shipping to the

Movements of Steamers

DEUTSCHE OST AFRIKA LINIE.

HOME VIA THE EAST COAST.

S.S. WATUSSI, from Beira 18th February, arriving at Southampton on the 26th March.

S.S. WAGONI, from Beira 8th March, arriving at Southampton on the 16th April.

S.S. USSUKUMA, from Beira 7th April, arriving at Southampton on the 14th May.

S.S. UBENA, from Beira 22nd April, arriving at Southampton on the 28th May.

HOME VIA THE WEST COAST.

S.S. NJASSA, from Beira 21st February, front Cape Town 6th March, arriving at Southampton 2nd April.

S.S. PRETORIA, from Lourenco Marques 18th March, from Cape Town 25th March, arriving at Southampton 9th April.

S.S. USAMBARA, from Beira 22nd March, from Cape Town 6th April, arriving at Southampton 1st May.

S.S. WINDHUK, from Lourenco Marques 15th April, from Cape Town 22nd April, arriving at Southampton 7th May.

S.S. ADOLPH WOERMANN, from Beira 29th April, from Cape Town 11th May, arriving at Southampton 5th June.

bottom of the ocean. Such state of affairs could obviously not be allowed to continue and the British Royal Navy therefore dispatched a sizeable number of warships to the South Atlantic to hunt down this dangerous raider. Forming part of "Force G" and known as the South American Hunting Group, the cruisers HMS

Exeter, Ajax and *Achilles* (the latter a New Zealand warship) set sail in search of the battleship. A fourth cruiser, the powerful HMS *Cumberland* remained to cover the Falkland Islands region. On Tuesday 5 December 1939, the *Cumberland* sighted the *Ussukuma* on the high seas sailing north from Bahia Blanca in Argentina towards Montevideo in Uruguay. This was the very port that the *Admiral Graf Spee* was to be holed up in following the Battle of the River Plate which took place on Wednesday 13 December, barely a week later. The report issued by the *Cumberland* at the time of her engagement with the *Ussukuma* stated that the German vessel had been identified as a cargo vessel, no mention of her previous status as a passenger liner was mentioned.

It transpired that the *Ussukuma* had been converted into a supply ship for the Kriegsmarine (German Navy). In place of passengers, she now carried a cargo of ammunition, explosives, torpedoes and food supplies destined for Nazi submarines and surface raiders operating in the South Atlantic.

HMS *Ajax* had also arrived on the scene. On sighting this cruiser heading towards his ship, the captain of the *Ussukuma* ordered that the sea ventilators be opened up, with the result that this once fine passenger liner, rather than be allowed to fall into enemy hands, sank to the bottom of the ocean within hours. The ship was scuttled approximately 60 miles off the mouth of the River Plate in Argentina in Position 39"24°S57"15°W. The German crew members survived the sinking, took to their lifeboats and all of the 107 crew were taken aboard the *Ajax* and made prisoners of war. They were then transferred to the *Cumberland,* which transported them to the Falkland Islands, before sailing to Montevideo, Uruguay, where the *Admiral Graf Spee* lay anchored.

A watery grave for yet another victim of World War Two and a sad ending indeed for the ship that had so ably carried us to freedom a scant eight months earlier.

In our case, having now disembarked at the port of Beira, we caught the next passenger train to Umtali, Southern Rhodesia's border town with Mozambique. Upon arrival in this picturesque town nestling in the foothills of the Vumba mountain range, we booked into a hotel until the final paperwork granting us perma-

nent entry into Southern Rhodesia had been processed and
approved – a procedure which took a few days.

Permission having now been granted by the Southern Rhodesian Immigration Department to officially reside in the country,
we were permitted to catch the Rhodesia Railways passenger
train to Salisbury, travelling on a railroad track that had been
laid barely 40 years earlier through the wildest of bush, mosquito infested swampland and, at the time of its construction, a land
still teeming with all sorts of game, including a healthy propor-
tion of lions!

On arrival at Salisbury Railway Station, a far larger terminal
than anticipated, we were met on the platform by our relatives
and taken to their home at 75 Second Street – a semi-detached
residence on the corner of Second Street and Livingstone Avenue.

Julius Phillipson and his wife Marta (my mother's older sister)
had, as previously mentioned, undertaken to sponsor our initial
stay in Southern
Rhodesia and my
parents were most
relieved and grate-
ful to have a "family
support   system"
available to them.
We now had a roof
over   our   heads
until we were in a
position to find our
feet   in   this   new
land   which   was
destined to become
our home.

75 Second Street, Salisbury

Within a few weeks the container with our furniture and
belongings arrived by train from Beira, and duties and transport
charges were required to be paid. The "lift" was collected from
the Salisbury railway goods depot by the well known transport
firm of George Elcombe Ltd. Total transport charges amounted
to £34.11.0p. (thirty four pounds and eleven shillings) plus a
charge of 12/6d (twelve shillings and six pence) being customs

duty levied on my father's typewriter. If there were any breakages, they must have been minimal.

Southern Rhodesia at the time was a country still in its formative years – yet already relatively developed considering

Customs No. 50C.

BILL OF ENTRY.—Duty Paid for Warehoused Goods.

6d. STAMP.

Port of ....SALISBURY... ....R. STEPHENS.................... Importer.

Ex Train which arrived .....28.4.39............... From........BEIRA..............

Truck No. ....21400.............. EX SHIP Railway Advice Note No.........................

Customs Advice Nos. (For Customs Office use only)	Packages		Tariff No.	Particulars of the Goods				Duty		
	Marks	Number of and Description		Country of Manufacture, or Production	Nature and quantity	Weight Tale or Gauge	Value £	£	s.	d.
	ADD	1c/s	73	GERMANY	H.Hold Ctn. Goods		11	–	–	–
	12		269	"	Wooden Furniture		25	–	–	–
			63	"	Carpet	1	15/-	–	–	–
			160 b	"	Sewing Machine	1	12	–	–	–
			172	"	Glassware		7	–	–	–
			99	"	Cutlery		5	–	–	–
			360 b	"	Clocks	2	15/-	–	–	–
			143 d	"	Elect. Kettles	2	2	–	–	–
			116	"	Lampware		1	–	–	–
			108	"	Holloware		1	–	–	–
		a 149		"	Typewriter		2.10.-	–	12	6

I declare that these goods are my own personal property which were in use by me prior to shipment and are not for sale or disposal to any other persons, and further, I also declare that I have entered this Colony with the intention of taking up permanent residence herein.

SIGNED.................................WITNESS....... ....

Beira R.I.B. 428/2108

Advice 2832/5901 – 1

| Total No. of Packages | 1 | | | | Totals ... | | £68. | – | 12 | 6 |

Less Approved Credit Note No...........................annexed hereto ... ...

Net amount ... ...

I, the undersigned, ...G. J. RICHTON.............................for the Importers do hereby declare that the above is a true description and complete return of all the goods contained in the abovementioned packages, removed from ....BEIRA...under Bond, as per Advices above noted, and now entered for consumption, and that the values given of the same are the true current value of the same as defined by law, including the cost of packing and packages, and the cost of carriage thereon to the port of shipment.

Witness my hand the.............1st............day of......MAY.............193..9..

fifty years had barely lapsed since whites had settled on the land and created its villages, towns and the two fledgling cities of Bulawayo and Salisbury. The country's soil proved fertile and farms were being developed, hewn from virgin bush. In 1904 there were estimated to be some 300 farms owned by whites, some ten years later these had already increased to no less than 2,000 – the majority of farmers concentrating on crops such as tobacco and maize and the cattle ranching industry was beginning to come into its own. Building construction was in full swing, the original pole and dhaka huts (mainly small round buildings constructed of mud and poles/tree trunks and covered with a thatched conical roof) where new farmers, prospectors and small time gold miners and their families resided were being replaced by homesteads constructed of bricks with corrugated iron roofs, with mosquito-gauzed window frames and surrounded on all sides by wide verandah's that were intended to keep the interior of the houses cool. It was a land under intense development – the railroad had reached Bulawayo from South Africa in 1897, although it was to take another five years to complete the last three hundred miles of track to Salisbury. A comprehensive road system had been laid out to link all towns, using the unique strip road system, and by the late 1930s the country was already connected by air links to South Africa, a number of other regions of Africa and a few centres in Europe.

The land was rich in minerals – asbestos, chrome, coal, and above all, gold. The climate was, by African standards, extremely moderate. A referendum had been held in 1922 to decide on whether Southern Rhodesia should amalgamate with the Union of South Africa in order to effectively become a fifth province of its larger neighbour to the south, or else to "go it alone" and form a Responsible Government of its own. The majority of voters chose the latter course and Southern Rhodesia thus became a self-governing colony with its own House of Parliament and representative members.

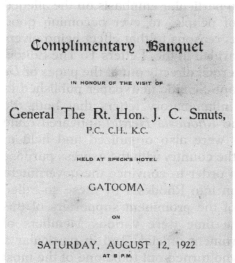

Menu – Referendum Dinner – Specks Hotel

Complimentary Banquet

IN HONOUR OF THE VISIT OF

General The Rt. Hon. J. C. Smuts,
P.C., C.H., K.C.

HELD AT SPECK'S HOTEL

GATOOMA

ON

SATURDAY, AUGUST 12, 1922
AT 8 P.M.

By 1939 the entire European (white) population of the country stood at 60,000 and its black population at around 1,400,000. Salisbury, the country's capital city had an estimated population of 12,500 whites while Bulawayo's white population exceeded Salisbury's by approximately a thousand.

For the now newly arrived immigrants from Germany life in Southern Rhodesia must have seemed peaceful and tranquil in comparison to the turmoil and ever increasing Jew-baiting and hatred they had left behind them in Nazi Germany but, as I was to discover to my extreme surprise in later years, both Southern and Northern Rhodesia had in the latter part of the 1930s their own share of Jew haters, Nazi Party sympathizers and supporters of fascism.

Although we were fortunate enough to have been accepted into the country, and would forever remain most grateful for this blessing, for indeed that is what it most certainly was, many would-be immigrants had had their applications for residence refused and in the late 1930s the country's major newspapers published countless letters debating the pros and cons of granting residential status to those who wished to flee Hitler's tyranny and seek refuge in Rhodesia. Many residents felt that these would-be immigrants should not be allowed to enter into either of the two Rhodesias, placing particular emphasis on the alleged unsuitability of this "type of people" to ever becoming good citizens, a variety of spurious reasons to that effect being given. And some of the reasons provided in the "Letters To The Editor" columns could well have emerged directly out of the pages of *De Stürmer* – the violent Nazi anti-Semitic newspaper published in Germany. Apart from the inflammatory letters that both the *Bulawayo Chronicle* and the *Rhodesia Herald* appeared quite happy to publish, meetings were also organized and held in various centres throughout the country with the express purpose of gaining public support in order to convince the government to halt any further migration into Rhodesia by these so-called "non-British" aliens. Some of the prominent supporters of this "Anti-Jewish Brigade" at the time were various Members of Parliament, some top government officials and in particular a future Mayor of Salisbury, who turned out to be one of the most scurrilous and anti-Semitic correspondents of them all.

In the circumstances fewer than five hundred Jews who wished to flee Nazi Germany in the years 1936-1939 were permitted to settle in Southern Rhodesia. In early 1939, with the position in Europe looking more and more ominous by the day, further applications for refuge from approximately one thousand Jews from Austria, Czechoslovakia, Germany and Hungary were received by the government of Southern Rhodesia. They were all turned down – and the chances were that the great majority of these poor souls whose applications had been refused landed up in the gas chambers of Nazi occupied Europe. However, when compared to many other countries, Southern Rhodesia could hold its head high regarding its attitude to taking in refugees from a war-imminent Europe, of that there was no doubt.

In the meantime my father had been offered employment by a firm situated in Bulawayo, some three hundred miles distant, but I understand that this firm was quite prepared to relinquish its offer should he prefer to find a suitable position closer to his family in Salisbury, which in fact is what transpired. He now received an offer to work in Eiffel Flats, a small gold mining township built around the Cam & Motor Mine, the then largest gold mine in the country and situated a few miles from the town of Gatooma, approximately a hundred miles from Salisbury. Job vacancies were certainly not plentiful in 1939, and new immigrants could count themselves fortunate to find employment. He readily accepted the offer.

Cam Trading, Eiffel Flats

The Cam & Motor Mine so dominated that little township that the village of Eiffel Flats was often referred to as "The Cam". Virtually all the men in Eiffel Flats were employed by the mine which was owned by the Lonhro Group, the mine employing some 300 whites and an even larger number of black Africans. Together with their families, well over 2,000 people lived in this community, which in turn was surrounded by rich farmland and many other gold mines varying in size. Eiffel Flats boasted a sizeable sports club which included a large swimming pool, a number of tennis courts, bowling greens, a golf course, rifle club, hockey field and last, but by no means least, one of the meanest and strongest rugby teams in the country! These afore-mentioned sporting facilities were all sponsored by the Cam & Motor

Mine. In addition, a small government public junior school catered for the children of the area and Eiffel Flats also possessed a post office and an airfield suitable for light aircraft.

My father was employed as a shopkeeper by the Cam Trading Company, a general trading establishment owned by wealthy businessman cum farmer Behor Samuel (B.S.) Leon, a Sephardi Jew originally from Rodos (Rhodes) Island in the Agean Sea.

He was a bachelor who generally resided in Salisbury, and proved to be a most generous philanthropist in his own right. Situated on Eiffel Flat's main street, opposite the main entrance to the mine, the Cam Trading Co. provided employment to a number of Jewish men who had recently left Germany and Czechoslovakia, and who were all relieved to have found employment in their new country of adoption. The business in Eiffel Flats was managed by a Mr David Alhadeff, proud owner of a recently purchased shiny new 1939 Graham Supercharger sedan (dubbed the "Sharknose" Graham) a somewhat radically designed American automobile sporting unusual styling cues that impressed me greatly from the very first moment I saw the car. My father and some of the other shop assistants were accommodated in the nearby Eiffel Flats Hotel which was owned by a Jewish couple, Mr A.B. Joffe and his wife Janey. This hotel, the only one in Eiffel Flats, consisted of 15 single bedrooms, a dining room and a public bar which did a rip-roaring trade once the miners came off their respective shifts at the end of the day –

and generated an even bigger trade on Saturday nights!!

My mother in the meantime had found employment in Darwendale, a prosperous farming area situated north-west of Salisbury, where she took over the position of governess to the young child of a Mr &

Eiffel Flats Hotel

Mrs Pichanick. I in turn remained behind in Salisbury under the care of my uncle and aunt who, both being master butchers by profession, were employed by a local butchery that was situated in the city centre. An African servant was left in charge of the house and its contents during the day whilst they were at work and their four year old nephew was likewise left in this servant's care on weekdays – Monday to noon on Saturdays. At this stage of my life I had made no friends and, for that matter, had probably not even met anyone in my age group since our arrival in the country, besides, I was only just beginning to learn the rudiments of the English language. And so, not surprisingly, I found myself spending the major part of my day sitting on the kerbside outside the house watching the traffic pass by – be they motor vehicles, cycles, mule drawn carts, motorcycles, taxis, heavy trucks or traders pushing barrows filled to the brink with fruit or vegetables for sale, plus a goodly number of pedestrians walking by. Second Street was, and for that matter still is, one of the city's main thoroughfares and I therefore had all the time in the world to watch cars and trucks of all sizes and vintages drive past on their way to and from the city's business centre which lay in fairly close proximity to the house at No. 75.

I soon learned to identify one motorcar from another, learning to tell a Chevrolet from a De Soto, a Chrysler from a Hudson, a larger American Ford from a smaller British built Ford and before long I could name the majority of these vehicles, not only recognizing them by their various shapes and sizes but in a number of cases even being able to identify them by the sound of their engines. There were many different makes of cars on Rhodesian roads in those days, the majority being American built vehicles. They included such automobiles as the Packard, Plymouth, Graham, Nash, Hupmobile, La Salle, Oldsmobile, Willys and Studebaker, makes that have all disappeared from the market in the years that followed. The ubiquitous Model "A" Ford with a hooter (horn) that produced a very distinctive "oooh-ah-oooh-ah" sound when blown was still widely in use in the late 1930s. American Fords and Chevrolets dominated the market at the time. Of course there were also many smaller British cars on the road, amongst them the Austin, Morris, Hillman, Standard, Vauxhall and the British Dagenham built Fords but these were outnumbered by the American vehicles which proved far more robust and better suited to the conditions posed by the country's fairly rough and ready rural road system

Model "A" Ford

at that time. It was a well known fact that American built motor transportation was considered first choice by the majority of farmers and miners in the outlying areas, as these vehicles were far more robust and ruggedly constructed and, depending on the time of the year, dozens of these mud splattered (rainy season) or dust covered (dry winter months) coupe imps (vehicles usually owned by farmers), light pick-up trucks (named "vanettes" in Rhodesia) together with a goodly variety of larger trucks were seen driving up and down Second Street on a daily basis carrying all manner of produce.

Two wheeled rickshaws seating two passengers side by side with space behind for a few suitcases were also still in use at the time. These vehicles always provided a colourful sight, being pulled by Black Africans who were known as "rickshaw boys" and were often dressed in gaudy clothing topped off by large and imposing feathered headgear. The rickshaws were lined up at the entrance to the Salisbury railway station and this mode of transport proved especially popular with tourists. As already mentioned, horse and mule drawn carts were still in common use on the roads and one had to be careful when crossing streets not to have the unfortunate and messy experience of stepping into a pile of dung deposited by these animals! Spans of oxen pulling heavy carts laden with bags of maize appeared from time to time and the cattle often left even greater piles of dung so one needed to be wary when crossing the road!

The obvious interest I displayed in motor vehicles (I probably talked on this subject ad nauseam to my uncle and aunt when they arrived home after a hard day's work cutting up and selling meat) prompted my uncle to very generously purchase an old worn-out "non-runner" saloon car for me to play in. He had this vehicle towed in from some junk yard and parked it in the narrow driveway of the property. I am sure he hoped this would lure me away from my daily kerbside seat and help keep me away from the gasoline fumes that were emitted by endless streams of vehicles driving by. He purchased nothing less than a large imposing Cadillac of early 1920's vintage, which he found at a local scrap dealers and for which he paid the then princely sum of £5 (five pounds). The car was left standing in the driveway, which ran alongside and between his house and the dividing wall that separated his neighbour's residential property.

I was indeed most grateful for this unexpected gift and enjoyed playing in this ancient vehicle, opening and closing the rusted and creaking square shaped doors, sitting behind the large black steering wheel and letting my imagination take me on journeys along make-believe highways. However, even playing in the ample space of this "king sized" toy had its limitations and I became somewhat bored after a few weeks, and whether it turned out to be the influence of Guy Fawkes' night coming up or not, I decided to pull the plug on the Cadillac. Over the next few days I gathered up fallen leaves and twigs off the driveway where my Cadillac was parked, piling them onto the vehicle's seats and floor, in addition to old newspapers and magazines that I knew were not going to be missed. I recall also requesting the African employee to assist in sweeping up the leaves from all around the house, which he willingly and cheerfully did, and helped me to place them into the car's trunk and interior. Little did he realize the dastardly deed I had in mind ... When finally satisfied that the car contained enough combustible material to produce a good bonfire, I carefully closed all four of the car's doors. It was easy to find a box of matches – for I knew exactly where my aunt used to "hide" them from me. Striking a few, I threw them through a partially opened window into the old vehicle. Having done that, I stood back at a safe distance in order to admire the outcome of my handiwork ...

I was told (after the event) that my "handiwork" had in fact proved to be a roaring success, for after the relatively still well upholstered car seats had caught alight a great plume of smoke arose into the air, followed thereafter by the fierce crackling sound of blazing twigs and dry leaves. This alarming sight no doubt prompted the neighbours on the other side of the wall to hurriedly summon the Salisbury Fire Brigade to come and douse the flames, an added bonus for me as I could now see a real fire brigade in action right on my doorstep! But later I had to admit that it was very fortunate that the fire had only engulfed the car and not my uncle's house as well, for the driveway was so close to the house that the slightest shift in the direction of the prevailing wind could easily have sent the flames heading towards the bedroom windows which were situated only a few feet away from the fiercely blazing automobile! The bedroom curtains too could quite easily have billowed out and caught alight and these in turn could well have set off the beds and then it would definitely have been curtains for me!! I guess four year old children do not take these frightening possibilities into consideration when playing with matches!

Once the fire brigade had completed its task they departed, leaving the car totally gutted and reduced to a smouldering wreck, the metal rims of the four wheels having partially melted and sunk into the now blackened and blistered driveway. The driveway looked a sorry sight, awash with dirty water, partially burnt and sodden leaves and sundry other debris. I do not recall my aunt and uncle's reaction when they arrived home – I must have successfully blocked that out of my mind at the time! In due course the car was hauled away much to my relief as it had now become a daily and very visual reminder of what a bored child with time on his hands could get up to ... How was I ever going to live down this deed which had originally only been intended to serve as a deviation from my daily routine?

Unfortunately not only was I once again reduced to sitting on the sidewalk "watching all the cars drive by" but the sight of the scorched driveway remained as a constant reminder to everyone, and I mean everyone, that a small but dangerous child dwelt within the four walls of my long suffering uncle and aunt's house ... It would not have surprised me at all to have been introduced to the visitors at their home by the words "I would like you to meet my nephew – the arsonist"!

Despite all this, I have always retained an interest and affection for the 1930's era cars – and this appears to have been prompted by the fact that I was surrounded by automobiles from this decade on a virtually daily basis from a very early age. Even to this day, whilst out walking, I will quite happily cross the street and study an automobile dating back to that particular vintage!

A few weeks later I was sent to join my mother in Darwendale for a short visit and it was my luck that during the few days I happened to be in that small farming town the circus also arrived. During that era two South African circuses, Boswell's Circus and Pagel's Circus dominated the circus scene in Southern Africa and they regularly paid visits to Rhodesia on an annual basis. One year Boswell's made the journey north and the following year it would be Pagel's turn. And so, as a special treat, my mother took me one morning, together with her little charge, to the grounds where the visiting circus was encamped, very close to the town's railway station, for the circus travelled around the country by train. Not only did the circus visit the cities and larger towns but many of the smaller places were also paid a call which gave nearly everyone in the country an opportunity to visit "the big top" on an annual basis! We spent some considerable time strolling around the area, marvelling at the lions in their cages, the circus ponies grazing in an adjoining field near where the giant circus tent was in the process of being erected and we were transfixed by a number of massive elephants who seem to have been left to their own devices whilst wandering around the surrounding circus ground.

All too soon it was time to head back home for lunch and after we had checked on the lions "just one last time" the three of us set off along a narrow pathway leading from the railway station towards the direction of the Pichanick homestead. We had hardly set off down this path when we became aware of yells, screams, shouts and cries of warning from some distance behind us, which in turn were followed by a sound of mad trumpeting. Turning round to see what all the commotion was about we saw, to our absolute horror, one of the circus elephants pounding down the very pathway that we were using and, what was more, heading straight in our direction!

My mother told me later that her heart virtually stopped at the sight of this gigantic creature rushing towards us but somehow she managed to grab us both and hastily veered off into the surrounding bushes, thus leaving the path clear for the elephant to continue its charge, trunk held high, followed in turn by its keeper and other circus employees in hot pursuit! The adventurous elephant was captured soon after and we had some exciting tales to tell over lunch! Unfortunately my short but very exciting visit to Darwendale came to an end all too soon and I returned once more to my uncle and aunt's home in Salisbury.

Daily living soon returned to its normal boring routine and, once the incident of the roasted Cadillac had been forgiven (but I am sure not forgotten!) my uncle Julius allowed me once more to sit on his lap after dinner in order to read me a bedtime story.

He obviously enjoyed smoking cigarettes (the majority of adults appeared to smoke during that era – no doubt greatly influenced by the myriad of cigarette advertisements which appeared in newspapers and magazines at that time) and once in a while he even indulged himself by smoking a cigar. One evening I timidly requested to be allowed to take a few puffs on the cigarette he was smoking in order, as I put it to him "to just try it out a little bit". His immediate reply was that four year old children were strictly forbidden to smoke but no doubt I must have continued to pester him with my requests because a few evenings later he most unexpectedly informed me that he would indeed let me have my wish – but only on the condition that I smoked a whole cigarette from start to finish – a few puffs alone would not suffice – it had to be either the whole cigarette or no cigarette at all. Take it or leave it!

I must have been surprised by his sudden change of heart and, without thinking of the possible consequences, foolishly decided to take him up on his offer. Placing a cigarette between my lips I confidently struck a match (I was good at striking matches ...) lit up and then settled back to relish my first ever smoke. No doubt I enjoyed the first few puffs but after some time began to feel, not at all surprisingly, somewhat queasy. Thereupon I intimated to my uncle that I would be more than happy to continue smoking the rest of the cigarette, provided that this would take place on the following evening. "Oh no" was his reply – "the arrangement agreed upon was that you smoke the entire cigarette in ONE sitting. So just sit back and carry on smoking"! So I sat back and continued to puff away – feeling decidedly more nauseous with each succeeding drag on this infernal piece of weed clutched between my by now perspiring little fingers ...

I must have smoked approximately three quarters of the cigarette when I suddenly began to feel quite bilious, the next moment my stomach heaved and a few moments later I became violently sick, the unfinished part of the cigarette landing up on the carpet in front of me together with the contents of my evening meal. No doubt about it – my uncle had most certainly proved his point that cigarettes were not intended to be smoked by four year old children! I had learnt my lesson. Ten years must have elapsed before I was again tempted to try another cigarette, and on this occasion enjoyed it no more than I had the first one, thus prompting me to "give up" smoking once and for all! To this day I am grateful to my uncle for granting me my original request, for it is indeed true that cigarettes can be detrimental to one's health, especially when one attempts to commence smoking at such a relatively young age.

At some point during the year my Aunt Marta decided to learn how to drive and in due course procured the services of a professional driving instructor, who turned up regularly each Sunday morning in his 1934 Ford coupe, a car fitted with a rumble seat (or dicky seat as they were better known in Rhodesia) built into the rear of the vehicle whose occupants were left at the mercy of the elements. This dicky seat could accommodate two passengers provided they sat in fairly close proximity to one another. I remember feeling quite envious as I watched her set off every Sunday morning as I so longed to be taken for a drive in a car, any car, no matter how short the journey might turn out to be! And one weekend my wish came true, for my aunt, no doubt feeling in a charitable mood that particular day, invited me to accompany the instructor and herself for that morning's lesson. I jumped at this opportunity and was doubly thrilled to be permitted to sit in the dicky seat which, as mentioned previously, was open to the elements. Strict instructions were issued that I was not permitted, under any circumstances whatsoever, to either stand up or move around in my isolated perch in the rear but was to remain firmly seated at all times – for in those days no seat belts existed for drivers or passengers to strap themselves in and remain securely seated. In 1939 the chances were that probably the only seat belts available for drivers and their passengers were fitted to grand prix racing cars of that era ...

My aunt must indeed have been in a pretty confident and generous mood that morning for she then proceeded to drive the short distance to the home of a friend, a Mr Rosenthal, who lived a few streets away. Bernard and Hedwig Rosenthal ran a small boarding house on the corner of Jameson Avenue and Third Street, patronised mainly by German Jewish refugees, and the couple likewise provided meals for the very reasonable sum of one shilling. He too was invited to come along for the ride, to which he readily agreed after first consulting with his wife, who gave us a friendly wave from her front door as he proceeded to clamber up and into the rear of the Ford, settled himself into the already confined area and in the process taking up most of the available space. That however did not bother me much, for we were now heading off into the somewhat sparse Sunday morning traffic of downtown Salisbury and I was relishing every moment of this wholly unexpected treat! Before long we were making our way towards Salisbury Kopje (hill) which could be accessed by a

fairly narrow gravel road which led to the summit overlooking Salisbury, and provided a magnificent view of the city's skyline spread out down below. This is where most of Salisbury's learner drivers found themselves at some stage or another in their quest to obtain a driver's licence and my aunt obviously felt confident enough to attempt this feat – otherwise why would she have invited two passengers along to witness her attempt at reaching the summit of this hill? It was quite possible that she had already mastered this feat during the course of a previous lesson and was now about to demonstrate her driving skills to members of her family and to her friends ...

Under the instruction of her tutor the car was brought to a halt. First gear was then engaged and slowly but surely the Ford V8 began to wind its way up the fairly steep gradient, the engine revving as we gathered momentum. With small stones being dislodged by the spinning rear wheels it was soon time to change into second gear as the car gained momentum. But for whatever reason the engine stalled, the car ground to a halt and the very next moment we proceeded to roll backwards!

Hysterical shouts of "use your brake, use your brake, use your damned brake" could be heard coming from the driving instructor sitting next to my aunt, yet somehow the car steadily kept on rolling backwards and it was at this point that Mr Rosenthal decided to jump ship. Completely belying a man of his age and apparent frailty, he rose up beside me and literally flung himself out of the moving vehicle, landing on the edge of the gravel road and appeared to tumble over once or twice before I lost sight of him in a cloud of dust. Eventually my aunt managed to locate the brake pedal and brought the car to a gradual halt but how on earth she had managed to keep the vehicle from veering off the narrow road and into the bush remains a mystery to me. It was likewise extremely fortunate that there happened to be no other motor vehicles following us at that particular time, as a collision of some sort would surely have been unavoidable.

A few moments later a somewhat shaken Mr Rosenthal came stumbling down the road, sporting several cuts and grazes, whilst both his trouser legs looked somewhat the worse for wear. Stiffly he climbed into the seat beside me and after my aunt had managed to turn the car around, we set off back in the direction of home in a rather melancholy silence. Salisbury Kopje was not conquered that day – at least not by my aunt! After dropping Mr Rosenthal off at his house where he was received by his very startled wife, we drove on to 75 Second Street where the keys of the car were handed back to the driving instructor, thus concluding the driving lesson for the day. But nevertheless my aunt persevered with her lessons and in due course obtained her driver's licence, but following this incident I was never again invited to accompany her whilst she was undergoing driving tuition – perhaps she might have felt – with some justification – that my answer would likely to have been a very polite but nevertheless firm "nein danke" which, translated into plain English meant "thanks, but no thanks!!"

Whilst still in Darwendale my mother required medical treatment but due to financial constraints decided to postpone visiting a doctor. Due to this decision her condition worsened and she was referred to Dr I.R. Rosin, one of Rhodesia's leading medical practitioner/surgeons. She duly presented herself at his surgery, which at the time was situated at N.E.M. House in First Street, Salisbury. She felt most embarrassed at having to explain to him that she would only be able to settle his bill for treatment in instalments.

Dr Isidore "Kipps" Rosin, a wise and learned scholar and physician, assured her that this would present no problem whatsoever. Prior to leaving the surgery she requested the receptionist to let her have the doctor's account for treatment, but was informed at the time that the bill would be mailed to her "in due course". However, no request for payment was ever presented – this turned out to be Dr Rosin's personal and generous contribution towards assisting immigrants who had fled oppression and danger and were at that stage of their lives still in the process of finding their financial feet in their new country of adoption.

Dr IR Rosin

In the years to come Dr (later Mr) Rosin and his wife Muriel (who in the 1950s was to become a Member of Parliament) became good and sincere friends of my parents – a friendship that lasted until the death of all concerned.

Towards the latter part of the year a place was found for me in the infants' class at the Dominican Convent for Girls, a prestigious Roman Catholic school in Salisbury. At that time the kindergarten section of this esteemed school still accepted young boys in their classes, a practice that came to an end a few years later. Thus one day I arrived at my very first school and the nun's discovered that they had a little Jewish kid on their hands who spoke and understood German a lot better at that particular stage of his life than he understood English. I am sure that this did not present them with a problem of any kind because the majority of the nuns themselves were German speaking, most having originated from Germany. But I discovered soon enough that the pronunciation of the English language by my new teachers could and did pose certain problems ... They spoke "Cherman" (German) to me in a pronounced accent because most of them had originated from "Chermany" (Germany). So it took me "chust" a little longer to get my pronunciation right!

I came home from school one day and asked my mother (who had come into Salisbury that day with her employers and who had dropped her off to visit me whilst they in turn had gone shopping) – "Mutti – wass sind cheeses?" (Mother, what are cheeses?) She replied that it was a food processed from milk that one ate on bread, but I was not satisfied with that explanation as the word "cheeses" was mentioned over and over again by the nuns, especially during the recitation of prayers, and sometimes even infant cheeses were included during the reciting of these prayers. My mother appeared somewhat puzzled by all this and asked me to elaborate on these various cheeses mentioned to which I replied that there seemed to be everyday cheeses and "baby" cheeses involved at other times. A little while later she figured out with a laugh that it was "Jesus" and not "cheeses" that the nuns were obviously referring to! Possibly just a slight matter of pronunciation??!!

One Sunday morning my uncle and aunt decided to spend a few hours at the local swimming pool which was situated in the well kept municipal gardens – the pride of Salisbury at the time. This was a popular venue for many of the younger folk to meet and where they could swim, sunbathe and generally socialise. A tea room within the grounds sold ice creams, cool drinks, teas, coffees and confectionery. On that particular Sunday we spent quite a number of hours at the pool and apart from getting in and out of the water a number of times I lay on my outstretched towel on the lawn and soaked up the warm sunshine. This was my first real experience of lying in the African sun and it certainly felt good!

It also soon became obvious that I had overdone my time in the sun – for when we left for home my skin had assumed a

definite rosy hue and by the time we arrived back at the house I was in considerable discomfort, felt nauseous and had developed a splitting headache. I was advised to get out of my clothes, climb into bed and try to sleep off my now relentlessly throbbing headache. It hurt considerably when I tried to take off my shirt and I yelled in sheer agony when my uncle attempted. Realising that something appeared seriously wrong, a doctor was called and on being advised that I had lain in the sun for some hours, immediately informed my worried relatives

Cultivating sunstroke

that I was suffering from a combination of severe sunburn and sunstroke! Taking a pair of scissors he cut the clothing off my body and saw that the skin on my back had already developed large blisters. The doctor advised that I should remain in bed until the blisters had subsided and I was told that under no circumstances was I to venture out into the sun again without applying adequate sunscreen lotion and to make sure that I always wore a wide brimmed hat when outdoors, especially during the summer months. A cooling and soothing lotion was prescribed for my skin and this somewhat helped diminish the pain.

After several days my skin started to peel in long swathes – I felt like a snake shedding its skin! It took me quite a while to recover from this ordeal which went to prove that a four year old child's tender skin, especially when he had recently arrived from Europe, is no match for the harsh African sun. This made me realize that from now on I should avoid being in the sun as much as possible.

Arrangements were now made that approximately once a month my mother and I would travel by train to Gatooma in order to spend some "quality time" with my father, who would then come into town from Eiffel Flats for the weekend, and on

these occasions he booked us all into Gatooma's Specks Hotel.
Compared to many of to-day's modern hotels, the hotels of the
1920s and 1930s, especially those situated in the smaller
centres, presented a
somewhat austere
nature, both in ap-
pearance and their
approach to com-
fort. Few rooms pos-
sessed even a wash
basin with running
water – there was in
its stead a large por-
celain jug of water
for washing one's
hands and face, the jug being placed in a porcelain bowl perched
on the dressing table. Private en suite bathrooms were virtually
still unheard of in the majority of Rhodesian hotels of that
period, especially so in the country districts. They were usually
found further down a long corridor whose creaking wooden
floorboards were usually overlaid with a somewhat worn and at
times threadbare carpet runner.

The communal bathrooms were fitted with large deep enamel
baths and it took a considerable amount of water to fill even half
such a bath. And if one tended to relax for too long in the bath
the door handle would invariably be rattled every five minutes
by impatient hotel guests queuing up on the other side of the
door waiting to take their turn in the bathroom! The water for
these baths was heated in either large coal or wood burning
boilers situated next to the hotel kitchen, and when taking a bath
late in the evening the hot water had by then generally turned
distinctly lukewarm – thus most guests tended to take early
evening baths in the handful of bathrooms available.

No elevators as a rule were installed in country hotels – as
hotels situated in smaller towns seldom exceeded two floors.
Radios or telephones were likewise not fitted in bedrooms,
however one could always find a bible placed on prominent
display on each bedside table. A glass and a jug of drinking
water, normally covered by a beaded doilie (cloth) to prevent

insects from landing in the drinking water was left on a small tray next to the bible.

Early morning tea or coffee would be served in the bedroom from around 5.30 a.m. onwards, the guest choosing the time of delivery whilst completing the hotel register upon arrival the previous day. Shoes could be safely left at night in the passage outside the bedroom door before going to bed, the shoes were cleaned and polished during the early hours of the morning by an employee whom the guest hardly ever saw or heard. The *Herald* daily newspaper would be slid under the bedroom door prior to breakfast. One night's accommodation, including meals cost 12/6 (twelve shillings and sixpence) at the time. Menus were typed out for all meals which were served in the hotel dining room, the day's date appearing thereon and placed on each individual dining room table.

As there were no telephones in the bedrooms, a phone booth

A typical breakfast menu would read as follows:

Stewed Fruit
Fresh Fruit
Mealie Meal Porridge
Maltabella Porridge
Corn Flakes
Eggs to Order
(Boiled/Fried/Scrambled/Poached/Omelette)

for the convenience of guests was usually found in the hotel lobby. Wall hanging telephones were then still in use and these were equipped with a small crank handle with which to ring through to the local telephone exchange. The operator at the exchange was then informed of the telephone number required and it was her job to make the connection. This method applied to both local and trunk calls and long distance trunk calls could sometimes take up to two hours or even longer to connect depending on how busy the lines were between towns at certain times of the day or night. And discreetness was required whilst using the telephone because, when lines were not particularly busy, telephone operators tended occasionally to listen in to calls in order to while away the hours ...!!

Night life in smaller towns (outside Salisbury and Bulawayo) for hotel guests had precious little to offer as a rule. After dinner one could take a walk around the limited business areas and view the shop windows, and this many did as it was perfectly safe to walk around after dark, for the streets were practically deserted after nightfall. Strict regulations ensured that no black Africans were permitted on the streets in town after 9 p.m. unless in possession of a letter signed by their employer. This letter needed to stipulate the precise reason for that particular employee to be around and about at night. And as there was a definite police presence on the streets, this law was strictly adhered to and muggings and hold-ups were virtually unheard of, both day and night.

Another choice for the hotel guest included a visit to the town's cinema but would be patrons of the Royalty Theatre needed to ascertain whether they had already seen the movie that was currently being screened, for films did not premiere simultaneously at cinemas throughout the country. New releases initially premiered in Salisbury and after approximately a run of a week or two the cans of 35mm film were dispatched by train to Bulawayo. After a run of a similar period the cans were then railed to such towns as Gwelo, Gatooma and Umtali where they were then shown for a few nights. This meant that it often took up to several weeks from initial screening in Salisbury until Gatooma finally received the movie for a brief screening. Three changes of programme per week were shown on the Gatooma screen. A feature film plus supporting programme on a Monday night, an entirely different programme on Wednesday night and a third and again different programme was screened on both Friday and Saturday nights, which also included a matinee (the week's only one) on Saturday afternoon.

The third alternative for the hotel guest to wile away an evening would be to pay a visit to the bar of either Specks Hotel or that of the competing Grand Hotel, the only two hotels in town. The bars of both establishments were well patronized by the locals each night, in those days both hotels employed only white barmaids (black Africans were not permitted in bars at the

time) and business as a rule was brisk. Specks Hotel was owned
and managed by a Mr Phil Levi, who was assisted by his wife and
a sizeable staff. Phil Levi hit the headlines when he placed a sign
above the hotel's main entrance which stated very prominently:
"All Rooms Face The Sea"!! Theoretically he was quite correct –
despite the fact that the nearest section of ocean happened to be
the waters of the Indian Ocean, on the Mozambiquean coastline – some 500 miles in distance from Specks Hotel!!

Sometime in 1939, my only surviving grandparent, my mother's father, Wilhelm Löewenstein, after having been released
from Sachsenhausen concentration camp, departed the shores
of Germany and managed to find refuge and a safe haven in

Wilhelm Loewenstein

Northern Rhodesia. He settled in Lusa-
ka, the country's capital, going into cattle trading, his butcher's background
standing him in good stead. He paid us
a visit in 1944, and I well remember his
stay with us, for he spent a lot of time
assisting his despairing daughter (my
mother) in cornering his grandson so
that I would finally accept my doctor's
advice and swallow a daily tablespoon
of liquid quinine! But more of that later
...

Towards the end of that year my father
managed to obtain some private accommodation in Gatooma with a local fami-
ly and sent for my mother and I to join him. And so we moved
to Gatooma where my parents settled down and made this town,
approximately the fifth largest in the country, their home for the
rest of their lives. I myself was destined to live in Gatooma (the
name later changed to Kadoma) for a total period of no less than
59 years (1939-1998) before moving on to Harare (formerly
Salisbury). But now, in late 1939, we were thankfully together
again as a family and living under one roof, even if the accommodation turned out to be but a single bedroom in the Pogrund
residence. Our landlord was a Mr Benjamin (Berel) Pogrund,
who owned a trading store twelve miles out of town which he
operated with the assistance of his wife, Chaike. The couple had

four children – all older than me, who attended the local school. Their house was situated in Brading Street, south of (below) the railway line and it was a good thing that traffic was sparse, as Brading Street was un-tarred and every time a vehicle drove past clouds of dust arose into the air and was often blown into the house. On the opposite side of the street a small maize growing farm was situated and on this farm an even smaller gold mine operated.

The mine's two stamp mills operated both day and night, the mill's mechanical "dumpeta-dumpeta – dumpeta-dumpeta – dumpeta-dumpeta" sound virtually became a part of one's thought process. For this mill never seemed to let up and it was only on the rare occasion when operations were briefly halted for purposes of repair or maintenance did one become aware that a deafening silence had descended upon the area. But it was never long before the familiar and compelling "dumpeta-dumpeta – dumpeta-dumpeta" sound of the mill was heard again. These sounds must have been in complete contrast to the sounds of everyday life that my parents had once heard in their apartment in Gneissenaustrasse back in Dortmund – but the sounds that we were now being subjected to must have felt a lot more reassuring ... for we were now situated a long and healthy distance away from Nazi Germany, a country at war with most of Europe and the entire British Empire.

The renting of a room and partial sharing of the house with the Pogrund family came to an end after a few weeks, as accommodation in the shape of two rondavels (circular corrugated iron huts roofed with thatched straw – the two huts in turn being connected by a single room) came up for rental on a good sized plot of land on the corner of Perry Street and Cam Road, Gatooma. The main road linking the cities of Bulawayo and Salisbury partially ran through Cam Road, likewise the road to Eiffel Flats also branched off from Cam Road. By the standards of the day, Cam Road was certainly considered a busy stretch of thoroughfare. In comparison to the previous Brading Street address, this new location provided more conveniently centred accommodation and finally became a home for the three of us in the sense that we were no longer compelled to share quarters with another family.

The grounds were very large in comparison to where we had previously lived, and a number of fruit trees grew on this property including mango and paw-paw, the property itself being partially ringed in by what was known as a rubber hedge. It was made quite clear to me at the outset that should a piece of this dark green coloured hedge ever snap off, I should steer well clear of the white milky fluid which generally tended to ooze from broken pieces of hedge, for this fluid proved to be highly dangerous if it came into contact with one's eyes, and could well cause blindness if the unfortunate eye was not treated immediately. As a result of this good advice I made quite sure that I always stayed well clear of this particular species of hedge, which was very prevalent at the time and surrounded many houses.

Eating and sampling all the exotic locally grown fruit which we found in the local fruit shops proved most exciting and we enjoyed the majority of them, especially mangoes, naartjies, lichis, pomegranates, granadillas, coconuts, guavas and paw-paws. The last named fruit caused us to laugh − for it rhymed with po-po, the German name for one's posterior! And as mango and paw-paw trees grew right next to our kitchen door the fruit was literally there for the picking. But I had also been warned that, prior to reaching out one's hand to pick fruit from the trees, one needed to carefully scan the branches in case there happened to be a snake lurking in the tree, this  not being an unusual occurrence in Africa. For that matter, Gatooma and snakes were synonymous, but thank goodness not all reptiles turned out to be poisonous, which was just as well!

My father was still employed at Cam Trading Company in Eiffel Flats and commuted to work daily on his bicycle. Cycling up Cam Hill proved somewhat strenuous but coming down the hill in the late afternoon after work was far simpler and the cycle tended to pick up quite a bit of speed in the process. However, like many rural roads the Gatooma-Eiffel Flats road consisted of a pair of bitumen strips that, like all other strip roads of the day, tended at times to have the sides of the tarmac crumble away due to the heavy flow of traffic. This often left jagged edges to the tarmac which regularly caused punctures to the tyres of both automobiles and cycles alike.

One late afternoon whilst cycling at a lively pace down Cam Hill he spotted a large snake wriggling its way across the road directly in his path — very possibly a cobra judging from its length, as it easily straddled both strips with room to spare. At the speed he was travelling it would have been both impractical and dangerous to suddenly veer off the section of strip road and onto the loose gravel, so he had little choice but to raise both legs as high off the ground as he possibly could — without losing his balance — and ride directly over the reptile. He felt two distinct bumps in succession as the wheels went over the snake but fortunately he managed to keep his balance and continued peddling in order to maintain a safe distance between himself and the writhing creature ...

And, as our first year in Rhodesia now drew to a close, all three members of our family had found ourselves in encounters with some interesting creatures — my father riding over a poisonous snake lying in his path and my mother and I with a rampant elephant following us on a narrow footpath. But why should we have been surprised — for this was after all Africa we were now living in!! Thank goodness we had all been fortunate enough to be spared unscathed — and were there to tell the tale! And perhaps I should also include my personal contribution to yet another possible disaster which could well have had dire consequences if things had gone wrong had the wind changed direction — the incident of the torched Cadillac ...

1940

Our new neighbours in Perry Street were Robert and Sylvia Fleischman and their two children, Becky and Maurice, whom I soon befriended. Becky was my age and her brother just a few years younger. Mr Fleischman, known to everyone as Bob, was tall and thin with a craggy face and seemed to possess a somewhat abrupt manner. Originally from Lithuania, he owned a small shop that went under the name of Hitit Store, situated several miles out of town on the Owl Mine road. This business, like so many others, catered largely for the needs of Black African workers employed on the surrounding farms and mines.

The country districts at that time were well served by a myriad of shops of a similar nature, many of them owned by Greek or Jewish shopkeepers. Some of the shops were situated barely a few miles from a town, others could well be up to fifty or more miles away from the nearest populated centres. A number of these store keepers resided in living quarters attached to the rear of their shops, while many others resided in town and made the journey to work by car on a daily basis, often as not on narrow gravel roads in poor condition.

During the year my father left the Cam Trading Company in Eiffel Flats, having been offered the position of bookkeeper with the Gatooma Trading Company. This business consisted of a grocery store with an attached liquor department (a liquor outlet was commonly referred to as a "bottle store") situated in Union Street, Gatooma. This firm also operated a butchery in Rhodes Street, Gatooma. The new job afforded a slight increase in salary – he now

Gatooma Trading & Bottle Store

received the sum of ten pounds sterling per month, plus a weekly meat ration, consisting of an ox tongue! In order to supplement his income, he would, after hours, assist a Mr Harold Behrens with his (Behrens) accountancy practice. When Mr Behrens passed away a year or two later, my father inherited a number of his clients, thus establishing himself, on a limited scale initially, within the town's accountancy field.

A few months later, better and more conveniently situated accommodation presented itself and so once more we moved house, to a semi-detached residence situated in Newton Street, this time "above the railway line". This house was owned by a Mr H.W. Campion, a wealthy gold mine operator who was one of the pioneers of the district. The monthly rental for this house amounted to £5.0.0d. (five pounds).

I was delighted to discover that the house was situated diagonally opposite the town's one and only bioscope (a cinema or movie house in those days was usually referred to as a "bioscope"). This establishment went under the somewhat grandiose title of "The Royalty Theatre" but was in actual fact a somewhat seedy and run-down looking building, sorely in need of urgent repair work and several coats of paint.

Edward Street in flood – side view of The Royalty Theatre

The town of Gatooma, founded around the turn of the century, derived its name from a local chief, Kutama, whose kraal was situated on a kopje (hill) which lay a few miles south from where the town is situated. Constituted a Village Management Board in 1907, the expanding township was granted Municipal status in 1917. Gatooma's altitude is 3,814 feet above sea level and the town lies at the geographical centre of the country. Gatooma was also the core of the gold mining area of Southern Rhodesia and relied heavily on the surrounding mines and farms for its existence. By 1939 the town was considered the fifth largest in the country (population wise) following Salisbury, Bulawayo, Gwelo and Umtali in that order, with near neighbour Que Que lying in sixth place. Several of the larger mines in the Gatooma area were owned by well established mining companies but many mines were operated by consortiums and by "smallworkers" – men who eked out a somewhat precarious living trying to extract gold from tonnes of crushed rock, a truly backbreaking existence for a "one man" business. These "smallworkers" were, however, assisted by a small gang of indigenous workers. Many of these grizzled miners still drove their old Model "T" and Model "A" Fords and I recall seeing these antiquated vehicles parked outside the Grand and Specks hotels whilst their owners sat at the bar quenching their thirst following a day's hard work.

A brief history of the town ... Gatooma began as a tent and "pole and dhaka" (mud) type settlement like all other Rhodesian towns and villages in the late 1890s. Initially, only one daily train passed through the then village in either direction – Gatooma being situated on the railway line between Bulawayo and Salisbury, the tracks having been laid through Gatooma in 1902. The train from Bulawayo travelled through the town at night and passengers intending to join this train very often lit a bonfire in the centre of the railway track in order to compel the train to stop. By the time the engine driver had clambered down from his locomotive and extinguished the flames these passengers had climbed aboard and were waiting to pay their fares to the conductor! Gatooma's water at the time was brought in by train twice a week from the Umsweswe river, some 12 miles distant – the very first well in the township was only sunk in 1908. Within a short while this well water became virtually undrinkable, and was therefore condemned. Investigation showed that a dead African lay in 35 ft. of water, and his body was pulled up. The body was placed next to the well overnight to await the arrival of a police surgeon from Salisbury to establish cause of death, but the next morning the body had disappeared – all that could be found in the sand surrounding the well was the spoor of a lone hyena ...

There may have been a shortage of water and other necessities in the area but the district was teeming with game. Elephants were a common sight and rhinos roamed the outskirts of the village. Stage coaches drawn by mules departed from the town's post office to outlying villages and carried both passengers and mail. And the occasional lion still roamed Gatooma's streets at night ...

With the discovery of gold in the district, Gatooma began to partially resemble the "gold rush" towns of America and Australia to a certain degree, and likewise boasted many characters of a similar nature. I read about one of these characters who went under the name of "Texas Jack" and who took to galloping through the town on his horse, twirling his lasso and riding into the bar of Specks Hotel where he proceeded to shoot corks from bottles displayed on the shelves! Another tale told is that of the town surveyor who, from his bar stool at one of the hotels, whilst clutching a drink in one hand, planned the street layout of the infant town. Judging by the odd angles of some of the streets, one can very well believe that particular story!

Mail coach for Chakari ready to depart from Gatooma Post Office - c.1920s

Specks Hotel, although in much altered form – one earlier version had burnt to the ground and an even earlier version had been demolished to make way for enlarged premises - remained an integral part of the town's fabric. In the years to come we frequented the dining room and lounge on many occasions for official dinners and dinner-dances, plus Round Table and Rotary Club lunches and functions. My sister Judy's wedding reception was held in the hotel's dining room many years later. A most popular venue.

I well recall visiting the showroom of Duly & Co., the local Ford dealers – and admiring the new 1940 American Ford V8 range of cars on display. Handsome looking vehicles they were too! This is my earliest recollection of visiting a motorcar showroom – many further visits to various car showrooms were to follow over the years to come! The manager of Duly's in Gatooma at the time was a Mr J.K. Handley and I wondered whether he was by any chance related to Tommy Handley, the British radio comedian and star of the popular ITMA show — a show which we regularly listened to over the airwaves!

Now this may or may not be of any major interest to readers but the great majority of houses constructed prior to the 1930s were built with exterior toilet facilities, toilets that at the time operated on a bucket system. These were known as "long drops". Specially laid out narrow gravel lanes (usually wide enough for a cart to travel in either direction) which were known as sanitary lanes, ran behind both residential and business properties, the rear hatches of these toilets faced the sanitary lane. This enabled the buckets to be extracted from under the seats through a flap in the rear of the small outhouse. In short, water born sanitation was still comparatively rare unless one lived in a lately constructed house, which the majority of townsfolk certainly did not do at the time. Many homes therefore, plus a fair number of the older shop premises, hotels, public buildings, hospitals and schools still required connection to the waterborne toilet system and this would still take several years to complete.

The majority of toilets in use were basically brick outhouses constructed to run parallel with the sanitary lanes and these toilets were known as "PK"s which stood for "piccanin kia' (small house). The PK had a wooden planked surface with just a circular hole to sit over. The night cart at the time usually arrived in the early hours of the morning and consisted of a trailer fitted with a stainless steel tank and pulled by either donkeys or mules and in later years by a tractor. The buckets were collected from the rear of the PK and replaced after the contents had been poured into the tank. It was, to put it mildly, somewhat startling to have this operation unexpectedly taking place when one was actually making use of the toilet at that particular moment!

It was also a little daunting to have to visit the outside toilet at night, especially so when it was raining. In this case an umbrella was taken in order to hold off the rain between house and toilet and such umbrella was then as a rule propped up against an inside wall of the toilet upon arrival. However, the water from the wet umbrella soon dripped onto the toilet's cement floor. This in turn often caused a multitude of insects and bugs to emerge from various cracks in the floor and lower walls and was in turn followed by their valiant attempt to climb up onto the seat right next to the occupant in order to save themselves from drowning in the puddles of water now forming on the floor!

These outside toilets were also the favourite haunt of a large variety of spiders, many of them claiming permanent residence therein. Although the majority of spiders were harmless it was nevertheless both discomforting and sometimes even quite terrifying to find a large spider scuttling towards one, whether from the direction of the floor, down the wall or poised directly overhead – or to have one dangling precariously in its web a few inches from one's head! Night time visits to toilets – and for that matter daylight visits as well – were not for the fainthearted but the call of nature required attention! And it was certainly also not unknown for the odd snake to seek shelter in the PK – especially on those properties bordering the verges of a town. And as to what inhabited outhouses situated on farms and mines – don't even think about it!!

As already mentioned, visiting the outside toilet after nightfall was always a challenge, especially for the ladies, who often pleaded with someone to accompany them in order to specifically check out the "spider situation" prior to the use of the facilities. Many outhouses were as yet not connected to electricity, therefore one needed to take a torch with at night. Should the torch battery prove to be weak or possibly faulty then one took a candle in its place – but a candle flame often attracted dozens of moths of various sizes that flapped their way into the toilet, circling the head of the occupant. Likewise, the flame tended to attract large preying mantis's at certain times of the year which in turn also flew around attempting to seize some of the smaller moths for personal consumption! It could get quite interesting sitting in this confined space during the night – and if by chance the candle flame went out for whatever reason the already hyped-up occupant would be left in utter darkness – which could well present an even scarier scenario! And as to what creatures might actually be lurking UNDER the wooden seat itself did not bear thinking about ... best to blot that thought right out of one's mind!

Visiting an outhouse at night was not for the faint hearted!!

It was literally with great relief (no pun intended) when indoor waterborne sanitation was finally introduced in the early 1950s to most of the older homes and buildings. People could now visit toilets at night without first having to lie in bed for half an hour or more in order to decide whether their visit to the toilet was really deemed a necessity!

At some stage during the year I recall seeing a troop train drawn alongside the platform at the Gatooma railway station and the coaches filled with soldiers kitted out in khaki uniforms.

What caught my attention however were the armoured cars and field guns lashed down on several flatbed wagons coupled between the locomotive and the passenger coaches. World War Two had been declared some months earlier and many Rhodesian troops were now heading for the war zone "up north" which was a euphemism for all countries in Africa situated north of the equator. Their task was to help liberate Ethiopia which the Italians had conquered in 1936 and likewise to wrest back Italian Somaliland.

It is worth recording that Southern Rhodesia was in fact the first country in the then British Empire (now Commonwealth) to send troops beyond its own borders in World War Two in defence of Great Britain and the British Empire. Likewise, the Second World War saw Southern Rhodesia provide more troops per capita than any other country in the British Empire. Of the approximate 10,000 white Rhodesians available for active service no less than 6,500 served overseas, mainly in the North African and European theatres of war. In addition, no less than 15,000 African troops were recruited and of these some 1,700 served outside the borders of Southern Rhodesia. An outstanding record for any country, and one to be justly proud of.

Gatooma was situated in one of the warmer parts of the country and winters experienced in the town were therefore relatively mild. The hottest month of the year, October, was known throughout the country as "suicide month" and everyone sweltered, hoping that the rains would fall once the month had drawn to a close. This wish was usually granted, for the rainy season fell between mid-November and mid-March and good rainfalls were thankfully recorded more often than not. The two most pleasant months of the year, temperature wise, were considered to be the months of April and May, which brought with them warm and sunny days with relatively cool nights.

Winter followed during the months of June and July and temperatures varied between cool and cold. Snow has never been known to have fallen in Rhodesia. August provided a relatively brief "spring" and by September, summer had returned. Thunderstorms could be violent but were usually of short duration in their intensity. We were warned never to cross fields or open spaces or stand under trees during a thunderstorm, for the chances of being hit by lightning were fairly high − Rhodesia has amongst the highest death rates by lightning strikes in the world − people and cattle being prime targets. Consequently we stayed well away from open spaces during thunderstorms − the vivid flashes of lightning and enormous peals of thunder which followed were best experienced under the safety of a secure roof over one's head!

The rains brought out a multitude of insects and one soon learnt which ones were harmless and which ones were best to avoid! Most harmless of all were the flying ants which, right after a shower of rain, emerged from their holes in the now wet soil and took to the air − and in the process became prime targets for flocks of birds which came winging in from all directions, seizing the slow flying ants in mid-air and making an easy meal of them. Many ants flew through open doors or windows where they shed their gossamer like wings and meandered helplessly across the floor, often ending up being consumed by the resident cat, who, more often than not, tended to play with them first before ending their misery!

African Millipedes − known to us by their indigenous name of "chongololo", crawled slowly around one's garden, driveway and veranda during the rainy season and often into one's house where, if they were not removed in time, would often get crunched underfoot, leaving a gooey black or grey mess to be cleaned up. The simplest way to get them out of the house was to tap them lightly with one's foot which caused them to curl up into a tight-knit ball, and they could then either be picked up or rolled out of the door and into the garden. There they uncurled themselves in due course and proceeded to continue their journey along the ground or up walls – and one hoped that they did not find their way back into one's house, for the procedure would have to be repeated all over again!

Christmas beetles, as the name implies, generally arrived on the scene during the month of December. A cicada, this was a winged insect that lived in trees, the male having a special membrane on the sides of the body which it vibrated and the resultant sound was then amplified by air sacs. Like moths, these beetles are attracted by light and those that flew into rooms at night droned their way around the four walls, often bumping into light fittings or furniture which action often caused their large and heavy bodies to crash onto the floor with a thud and invariably they landed up on their backs, legs waving feebly in the air, unable to regain their feet. They too were scooped up and deposited into the garden.

Fascinating to watch were the preying mantis's which often resembled a twig and sat patiently on a tree or bush waiting for an insect to pass by within striking distance. Preying mantis's came in shades of green or brown and could sit immobile for an extremely lengthy period of time whilst waiting for its prey to come within range of their extremely long, fast and accurate tongue.

Chameleons, a type of lizard adapted for living in trees and bushes, were often seen making their way shakily along the ground in a laboriously slow herky-jerky gait. It was quite nerve wracking watching them attempt to cross a road – seeing squashed bodies of chameleons flattened by car tyres was a common sight at certain times of the year.

Insects that one was advised to stay well clear of included hairy caterpillars, centipedes, wasps, wolf spiders, scorpions and water scorpions – we always checked the water very carefully before venturing into a swimming pool – for scorpion bites proved very painful. We always avoided walking near bee hives – for the African bee is a highly dangerous insect with a painful sting, far more so than the European and American bees. They can be most aggressive and I have personally known a number of people who have been attacked by a swarm of bees and as a result, lost their lives. Quite a few people tend to be highly allergic to bee stings, and for them, to be caught up in a swarm of African bees can, in some cases, result in a most agonizing death.

We soon settled down in our section of the semi-detached house in Newton Street and our neighbours on the other side of the common wall, whose names now escape me, were friendly and welcoming folk. In the evenings my parents and I often listened to the radio and tuned in to the latest news of the war in Europe. I well recall an evening programme called "Radio Newsreel" and George Formby with its distinctive signature tune entitled "The National Emblem March". Popular singers on radio at the time included Bing Crosby, Deanna Durbin, Judy Garland, Arthur Askey, Gene Autry, Gracie Fields, the Andrews Sisters and one of my favourites, George Formby, who always played the ukulele with the greatest of zest! George Formby at the time was voted one of Britain's most popular film comedians and a number of his movies were shown throughout the country, some of which I saw over the next few years.

Other songs and melodies of that period which featured regularly on radio, or "wireless" as it was commonly called, included *Coming Round The Mountain, Our Sergeant Major, Wish Me Luck As You Wave Me Goodbye, Seven Beers With The Wrong Woman, Buckingham Palace, Dicky Bird Hop, Christopher Robin, When You Wish Upon A Star, Sleepy Lagoon, Yours, Tangerine, Teddy Bears Picnic, Lords Of The Air, The Honey Bee, It's In The Air* and *You Are My Sunshine.* The latter became one of my favourites and proved to stand me in good stead several years later ...

1941

In January 1941 I commenced schooling in Gatooma at Jameson School and was placed in the Infants class, being a month short of my sixth birthday. The walk to school from our house in Newton Street was a brief one – even for a six year old! Exit out of the back gate, walk to the top of the sanitary lane, then turn left into Masters Avenue, followed shortly thereafter by a right turn into the school grounds – a ten minute stroll at the most. After being accompanied to school by my mother for the first few days, I felt confident enough to walk to and from school on my own.

At the end of the first three month term (semester) my teacher's report stated that I had settled down happily and had made a very good start to my schooling, having a good idea of numbers, that I read well and likewise expressed myself fluently and she also described me as a "bright and happy little person who was a pleasure to teach".

The following school term I progressed to the KG "A" class and in the third and final term of the 1941 school year found myself in the KG "B" class, my report card stating that "Peter's conduct is excellent" and that "he is a reliable and happy little pupil".

The only negative incident I recall from that first school year was that at one stage I must have committed some misdemeanour during lessons and as a result was sent out of the classroom for the remainder of the lesson. As my luck would have it, whilst standing outside the classroom door, the headmaster (Mr G.H. Tanser; later appointed Secretary for Education and later still elected Mayor of Salisbury) chanced to walk by and spotted me. He enquired as to why I was not in the classroom attending lessons and in my naivety I replied that I had been sent out having done whatever it was. "That" he told me "was a very naughty thing to do" and instructed me to follow him to his office where I promptly received a couple of smacks on my rear end!

My end of year report card stated I was a "happy little chap". However, on the day that I met Mr Tanser in his office, you can be rest assured that I was anything but!

I became friendly with Anthea Pugh, a fellow classmate and the daughter of the Anglican Church vicar, the Reverend Humphrey Pugh. They lived in the rectory situated in the church grounds which adjoined the rear of our house. Anthea invited me over for meals at her house a number of times and when the church staged a Nativity play that Christmas, an invitation was extended to me by my new friend. What I remember of this play in particular was that the male lead and head of the household spoke quite brusquely to his wife – "Woman, bring me my food", "Woman, don't talk back to me", "Woman, wash my toga". One soon got the gist of this man's attitude. This, I decided, was a most interesting and novel way to address the ladies and not one that I had ever experienced before ...

Next morning at breakfast my parents enquired as to whether I had enjoyed the previous evening's play, I answered that I most certainly had, and decided, on the spur of the moment, to try out this new method of talking to the lady of the house, as had been reflected on stage the night before. Looking directly at my mother I commanded, "Woman, get me my breakfast, and, woman, make it snappy!"

The next thing I recall is literally getting up off the floor as "my woman" must have clipped me across the ear after having been addressed in such manner by her "smart arse" six year old! I rapidly dropped this obviously dated and unacceptable form of biblical terminology – and everyday expressions such as "Mom", "please" and "thank you" promptly returned to current use ... normal services were thereafter resumed without any further comments!

My friendship with Anthea continued and when an invitation came to accompany her to a church service one Sunday morning it was readily accepted – it was something different for me to get involved in. And so, for a couple of weeks I became a church goer and enjoyed listening to some of the more melodious and stirring hymns sung by the congregation – *All Thing's Bright And Beautiful, Jerusalem* and *Onward Christian Soldiers* come to mind.

It was when I began to hum these tunes around the house that I was asked by my parents where I had picked them up, and I informed them that I regularly sang the songs whilst attending church services on Sunday mornings between the hours of 9 and 10 a.m. WRONG MOVE!! Thereafter I was strictly confined to barracks on Sunday mornings but future attendances at church services would in any case have terminated as Anthea's father was shortly thereafter transferred to another diocese and the family left the district. I never saw my good friend Anthea ever again and soon got out of the habit of humming tuneful hymns around the house!

My father conducted the Pesach (Passover) Seder home service each year at our dining room table and read from the Haggadah – the narration covering the story of the Children of Israel's enslavement by the Egyptian nation thousands of years ago. There they were subjected to extremely hard labour and were forced to construct the pyramids. And we likewise read about the ten plagues that were sent down to smite the Egyptians in order to convince Pharaoh to allow Moses to lead the Israelites out of Egypt and slavery.

Now one of the plagues sent down upon the Egyptians had turned the waters of the River Nile into blood, and at the time I must have wondered what a river of blood would possibly look like. I visualized a red hued sheet of water flowing colourfully along and which, I figured in my little mind, probably looked far more imaginative than an ordinary river filled with just plain, ordinary, colourless or even muddy water. And then I must have had one of my inspirational moments, for on one of the walls in our lounge hung a beautiful oil painting, a wedding gift to my parents, which depicted a mountain stream surrounded by lush green fields. And, as expected – the stream was filled with, well, very ordinary plain looking water ...

A few days later, being alone at home while my parents were out, and balanced very precariously on the edge of a chair, I managed to unhook the painting from its position on the wall – not an easy task for a six year old, and then, having already selected a crayon in a suitable shade of red, proceeded to colour in the water until the gushing mountain stream resembled, in my estimation, what the waters of the blood drenched Nile must have looked like all those years ago. The painting was then manoeuvred back onto its hook, the chair pushed back into place and I now awaited my parents' compliments and approval when they finally discovered what an artistic son (or possibly autistic son) they had produced ...

However, after some days had elapsed and no compliments or even comments were forthcoming, I began to feel let down that my artistry had neither been noted nor appreciated. I therefore asked them to come and stand in front of the painting and tell me what they thought was different about it. This proved to be another WRONG MOVE on my part!! After receiving a good spanking (which in later years I admitted as having been well deserved), my crayons were confiscated for a lengthy period of time and the painting was removed from its place and later sent away for cleaning and restoring. Although it was possible to remove most of the red stained "artwork", to this day the water itself still reflects a faint pinkish hue. I know this only too well, for in later years I inherited this painting and each time I walk past it I recall only too vividly the story of the ten plagues ... Some memories never fade ...

The school that I now attended had only recently been named "Jameson" after Sir Leander Starr Jameson, who had been one of Southern Rhodesia's pioneers and the right hand man to the country's founder, Cecil John Rhodes. The official naming of the school took place in October 1940. Prior to that point the school had been known as the "Gatooma Public School". These new school buildings which now housed us were partially still under construction, as were some of the playing fields that were in the process of being hewn out of thick surrounding bush. Warne House Hostel, named after Dr C.W. Warne, a local doctor of many years' standing and a former Mayor of Gatooma, housed the school's few dozen boarders, and had been built a few decades earlier. In later years many of us learnt to swim in Dr Warne's swimming pool – one of the very few privately owned pools in the town.

The original Gatooma Public School buildings were situated in Baker Street, just across the road from the Standard Bank. Despite the construction of the new school, these original buildings were still in use. In fact, during my second year at Jameson

School our particular class, together with a few other classes, were re-housed at the old Baker Street premises for the entire 1942 year. The following year we returned to the new school complex which had finally been completed.

The original school buildings in Baker Street had been constructed in 1908. One late weekday afternoon of that year, whilst the classrooms were still partially under construction and the corrugated iron roofing placed into position but not as yet nailed down, it began to rain heavily, The Black African builders employed on the job decided to spend the night in the unfinished building rather than return to their homes, due to the rain pelting down at that time. It proved to be an uncomfortable night for them and in the early hours of the morning they heard a snuffling sound and one of the workmen, braver than the rest, dared to take a look outside and came face to face with a lion! Fear gripped the occupants of the room and panic ensued as the men hammered on the corrugated iron roofing with their spades, in order to create as much noise as possible so as to frighten the beast away. Without warning the loose roofing sheets gave way and the whole structure collapsed onto the terrified occupants! The clamour achieved a positive result however, for in the pandemonium the lion fled and was seen no more! Next morning the foreman pointed a shaking finger at the pile of damp mortar outside their door. Clearly visible were the fresh paw prints of a large male lion! This was the school I was now attending – a school that just thirty-three years earlier still had lions roaming around in its grounds after sunset!!

The lion's paw print was preserved for posterity in the walkway outside one of the classrooms and remained there until 1943 when the Government PWD (Public Works Department) were tasked to clean up and repair certain sections of the old school. Headmaster Mr G.H. "Tony" Tanser implored the workmen not to touch the section containing the lion's carefully preserved paw print, for he felt it was of historical interest both to the town and to the school. But the "soulless PWD foreman", as he later described this man, simply overrode his pleas, and so the unique paw print, which had been preserved in cement for 35 years, was smoothed over and obliterated ...

The new school grounds and playing fields were still in a state of development in the early 1940s and the furthest ends of the grounds adjoining the kopje (hill) behind the complex were partially still covered in dense bush, low trees and vegetation. One day a warning was issued to all pupils that they should steer well away from the entire kopje area as a leopard had been spotted – an unusual sight as these creatures normally kept well away from towns. We were told that this sighting had been positively confirmed and visits to the furthest ends of the school grounds were strictly forbidden for several days.

I also recall two Afrikaans brothers arriving at school every day in a horse drawn trap (a light two-wheeled carriage). The horse was tethered to a long lead under a shady tree and was fed and watered during the morning tea break. When school ceased each day at 1 p.m. the boys un-tethered the horse, climbed into the carriage and the horse galloped off to return to their farm which was situated several miles out of town.

School uniforms had only recently been introduced and scholars were now getting used to wearing an official school uniform. Blue shirts and khaki shorts were worn by the boys and blue and white dresses by the girls. However, I also remember quite a number of children from poorer families coming to school minus footwear and wearing very obvious "hand me down" clothing – for this was the tail end of the world wide Depression era which had lasted throughout the 1930s.

Most evenings we listened avidly to the radio and one night in June 1941 it was announced over the news that Hitler had invaded Russia. "That" exclaimed my father "was very good news indeed", as he was of the firm opinion that the Nazis had now over extended themselves and would no doubt be decisively defeated in their quest to conquer that vast land. He felt that the Nazi war machine would eventually grind itself to a halt sooner rather than later. His analysis proved to be correct although it would still take another four long and agonizing years before the war finally ground to a halt in Europe.

Popular songs heard on the radio that year included *Deep In The Heart Of Texas, The White Cliffs Of Dover* and *Green Eyes* – the latter tune played during every interval at the local cinema! Some of the films I recall seeing at the Royalty Theatre that year were *Dumbo*, *Fantasia* and the epic *Sergeant York*, which starred Gary Cooper. I enjoyed *They Died With Their Boots On* starring Errol Flynn. This movie featured an excellent sound track which included a stirring melody which I hummed for years afterwards, but could never ascertain the title of that particular tune. However, many years later I came across an album of classic movie scores and there it was – *The 7th Cavalry: Garry Owen.* It still remains one of my favourite tunes from the movies – and finally I managed to put a name to it!

Business premises in Gatooma, and likewise throughout the country, closed on Saturdays at 1 p.m., and only re-opened on Monday morning at 8 a.m. Shops and offices closed between 1 and 2 p.m. during weekdays for lunch. The advantage of residing in a smaller town meant that virtually everyone could go home for lunch. With an increasing number of men now in the armed forces, it was felt that businesses and most certainly offices should now close on Wednesday afternoons to enable folk to take a break and get into the open air and play some sport. With a recently opened golf club in Gatooma, quite a number of town folk decided to take up the game and Wednesday afternoons soon became a traditional time to play golf, bowls and tennis. From then on Wednesday afternoon sport became a popular pastime in Rhodesia and has remained so to this day.

Both shops and cinemas remained closed on Sundays, so town centres became somewhat deserted. Restaurants and tea rooms remained open, thus permitting locals and passing motorists to at least obtain meals and refreshments. Likewise, petrol pumps at garages stayed open (no night-time facilities though) and with only limited facilities available to repair punctured car tyres, which in those days were a fairly common occurrence. Life remained firmly affixed in the slow lane during the 1940-1945 war period, or as the saying went at the time, "for the duration".

A vintage World War One cannon was displayed on a vacant piece of ground situated between the Grand Hotel and the Railway Station, but was removed at some stage and possibly melted down for the war effort.

1942

At the end of the first term of 1942 Mrs Caldicott, now my KG "B" class teacher, confirmed in her assessment that I was "mentally alert and took a keen delight in books, as well as being tidy, polite and helpful". Mr Tanser, the Headmaster, merely signed the report card, passing no comment of his own. Perhaps he recalled my previous year's "misdemeanour"!

On my seventh birthday I received one of the most enjoyable books I have ever had the pleasure of reading, namely *African Aesop* which included the "Kalulu The Hare" stories. The tales in this book, written and illustrated by Frank Worthington, were based on ancient African folklore, legend and culture. Some of the American "Uncle Remus" stories were likewise derived from these tales, being brought over to America by African slaves in later years. These stories had been related by tribal elders around camp fires at night and had been listened to by countless generations of audiences over many centuries. For when darkness fell, listeners eagerly gathered around the fire and sat spellbound as the tales unfolded, whilst in the background of the dark African night, the sounds of hyenas laughing, jackals barking or lions roaring could often be clearly heard. These stories gripped their imagination, and the enthralled audience could be safely assured that by the end of the tale the wise person or animal in the story would always prevail over his more brutish adversary – and a clear morality prevailed.

The Jameson School library at the time consisted of one small room filled wall to wall and floor to ceiling with shelves bent under the weight of the most interesting books that I had ever feasted my eyes on. Unfortunately the library was locked out of school hours and each class was allocated only a single visit per week under the supervision of their class teacher. I therefore made quite sure that I never missed the precious half hour that our class was allowed into that little den of treasures.

My sister Judy was born on 14 May 1942 and I guess must have been a good little baby – how many months old she was when she began to sleep right through the night I do not recall – but if her crying may possibly have kept my parents awake at night she certainly never seemed to disturb my slumbers! An interesting note here – many years later my parents told me that, as far as they knew, none of the other Jewish families who were our fellow passengers on the *Ussekuma*, and who may already have had one child when they departed Germany, ever had a second child – all those families remained either childless or one child families.

By now the Empire Air Training Scheme was well under way and I found it very difficult not to be distracted by the sound of low flying aircraft droning overhead during daily school lessons. This annoyed our teacher, for the sound of aircraft engines more often than not caused me to move to the nearest window in order to catch a glimpse of yellow de Havilland Tiger Moth biplanes, North American Harvards, Airspeed Oxfords or Avro Ansons flying over our school grounds, which complex lay directly under the flight path leading to the Gatooma airfield. Despite the fact that some seventy years have since elapsed, to this day the throaty growl of a Harvard's engine still sends goose bumps up and down my spine – in fact the sound of a Harvard flying overhead remains sheer music to my ears!

And then of course there was the bioscope (cinema); the only one in the town and situated, as previously mentioned, opposite our house in Newton Street and with three changes of programme per week. One movie was shown on a Monday night, another on a Wednesday night and the third film (as a rule a more family orientated movie and suitable for the whole family) was screened on Friday and Saturday nights, with a single matinee held on the Saturday afternoon, the only matinee of the week. The cinema was owned by one Joe Burke, who on warm nights (which meant virtually all year round) opened wide the cinema's front doors, pulled back the interior blackout drapes once the audience had been seated, then proceeded to settle himself comfortably into a deckchair which faced the screen. This chair was placed on the pavement (sidewalk) directly in line with the doors, thus enabling him to view the movie whilst

keeping relatively cool in the open air, whilst the audience
sweltered inside! Air conditioning was never installed in this
cinema but there were a few overhead fans in the auditorium's
high ceiling. These antiquated fans required at least ten minutes
or more in order to revolve sufficiently fast enough to mildly
circulate the tepid interior air. Once these fans revolved at their
"top speed" they wobbled, swayed and shook alarmingly so that
patrons were very loathe to sit directly under them. However,
should patrons find themselves unfortunate enough to occupy
any of these seats that were as a rule normally avoided like the
plague, the apprehensive cinema-goer kept furtively glancing at
the rickety fan spinning overhead to make quite sure that the
fans were still attached to their moorings and were not about to
spiral into the audience seated below with possible disastrous
consequences!

Thank goodness this never did happen but one night a whole
row of seats collapsed backwards into the row behind – depositing the row's sole occupant, a very stout and inebriated gentleman, flat onto his back – his legs waving in the air like an
upended beetle! He had been sleeping off the effects of his visit
to the Specks Hotel bar – part of his daily routine after locking
up his shop at closing time. Following this incident he was
helped to his feet, deposited into a seat in another row and
promptly lapsed once more into a deep sleep, later staggering
off into the night at the conclusion of the evening's programme.
The chances were that he probably never recalled the incident
and, being a bachelor, there was no wife to relate his tale to by
the time he reached home! He was one of the town's better
known characters – he walked everywhere, for he never owned
a car and never learned to drive. Ironically, he was killed in a car
accident some years later.

On weekday and Saturday nights I was permitted to sit on the
sidewalk next to Joe Burke (who also owned one of the town's
two local book stores in addition to its sole printing works, which
printed the town's only newspaper, the weekly *Gatooma Mail* –
of which he was also the editor and publisher). I received a gratis
viewing of the entire supporting programme screened prior to
the 15 minute interval – then I merely had to walk across the
road to return home. The feature film was screened after the

interval – by which time I was as often as not safely tucked up in bed!

Due to this generous "arrangement" with the owner of the cinema I became the only child in Gatooma who regularly caught up with the latest weekly British *Gaumont News* and *African Mirror* newsreels together with the rest of the supporting programme. This usually consisted of a cartoon (often Mickey Mouse, Popeye, Woody Woodpecker, Mr Magoo or Tom and Jerry) followed by a travelogue or occasionally, a Pete Smith speciality short. Every few weeks a Three Stooges comedy was screened as part of the supporting programme which featured their madcap adventures. You either loved them or heartily disliked them! The Gaumont newsreels brought to the screen the latest news of the world wide war front, scenes of bomb damage in the streets of London and other British cities, troops fighting in the deserts of North Africa. The British Royal Family were shown visiting bombed out areas, British Prime Minister Winston Churchill was seen delivering speeches, visiting various airfields in Britain and waving to aircrew as Allied heavy bombers took off on raids over Nazi occupied Europe. Ships of the Royal Navy in action hunting U-boats, tanks in battle and various other war news. The *African Mirror* showed the latest progress of the war with an emphasis on South African troops and airmen serving overseas, in addition to scenes from current events pertaining to the South African "home front".

Then of course there were the "forthcoming attractions" (known to us as "trailers") which featured the more exciting scenes from some of the movies that were booked to "hit our screens" within the next few weeks. These I especially enjoyed as I could get to see the highlights from some of the films that I was never going to be allowed to see due to the child age restriction in force – the thrillers, gangster movies, certain war films and last but by no means least, the Universal Studios horror movies that featured such frightening creatures as the Frankenstein Monster, Dracula, the scary Mummy and the ultra scary Wolfman. Plus an interesting variety of zombies and mad ghouls that were prone to scurry out of dark corners in order to pounce upon unsuspecting young ladies who, in turn, proceeded to faint on cue, but only after having first been given the opportunity to scream the house down!

It was a truly exciting time in the life of a seven year old! And what's more, I don't recall ever suffering a bad dream after watching these horror movie "trailers" – and I never ever requested the use of a "night light" to be kept on in my bedroom. I fully understood and accepted that the Universal Studio movie monsters resided only on the silver screen across the road – and NOT outside my bedroom door or window! No need to lose any sleep over them – but only to look forward to their next appearance at a cinema (very) near to where I lived!

As for my parents – neither were great movie goers. They seldom attended films on weekdays and for that matter not too often at weekends either. They never discovered what they were missing out on and for that matter what their young son was viewing in the company of Mr Joe Burke on the sidewalk outside the Royalty Theatre two or three times a week! As far as I was concerned it proved a win-win situation!

Saturday afternoon matinees at the Royalty Cinema featured highly in the social calendar of the town's youngsters. One needed to come fairly early in order to secure a good and safe seat – "safe" referring in this instance as to how far away one could possibly be seated from the whirling creaking fans overhead. Although the auditorium may have already been filled to capacity the matinee never commenced until one of the staff had first climbed a rickety ladder and placed squares of cardboard over the cinema's blacked out window panes in order to block out the sunlight. The majority of these panes were either badly cracked or missing altogether, thus allowing the bright afternoon sun to stream in and fall directly onto the screen, causing a considerable reduction in picture clarity. And without fail, some of these squares of cardboard managed to detach themselves during the performance and when this occurred the audience shouted, whistled and stamped their feet for several minutes before any notice of this commotion from the floor below was acknowledged by the projectionist sitting up in his little projection box. Eventually the projector was switched off, the film ground to a halt, the lights came on, the assistant brought in his ladder and commenced picking up the detached cardboard squares lying in the aisle and then proceeded to clamber up and attempt to re-affix the cardboard into its correct slot. This happened on average two or three times per performance and the damaged window panes were never ever replaced. We were a captive audience – for there was no competition of any kind to cause any concern to Mr Joe Burke ...

I was present, many years later when, during the course of an evening performance the film abruptly ground to a halt, the lights came on and the projectionist called out to the audience seated down below – "Has anyone got a screwdriver?" It was certainly a variation from the standard "Is there a doctor in the house?"!

Around this time I began to frequent the Gatooma Public Library visiting the public reading room whenever I found time. The library, being just five minutes walk from our house, was paid a visit on an almost daily basis and I remember reading the *Rhodesia Herald* and the *Sunday Times* (Johannesburg) newspapers on a regular basis, plus such magazines as the *National Geographic, Illustrated London News, Life, Punch, Wide World, Popular Mechanics* and my favourite magazine – the weekly aviation magazine *Aeroplane.* World War Two was in full swing and I followed the war's progress avidly, whether on radio, in the newspapers or in magazine articles, and of course via the weekly newsreels at the cinema.

Wide World Magazine – a monthly publication, was heralded as being the Twentieth Century's largest selling true adventure magazine. Exciting tales appeared in each issue accompanied by photographs and vividly drawn illustrations. Titles such as "A Lion Carried Me Off", "I Attempted To Climb Mount Everest Alone", "Buried Alive By A Dead Elephant", "Attacked By A Giant Octopus", "A Boa Constrictor In My Bed" and tales of a similar nature appeared in subsequent issues. Reading these gripping tales made me wonder how so many people had survived these ordeals yet managed to pen their adventures. I also recall being most upset when the library committee decided, some years later, to no longer renew the magazine's annual subscription. But by then I had graduated to *Time* magazine, so not all was lost ...

In later years a small children's section was introduced and I began reading the Doctor Doolittle series, the Biggles books and the Hardy Boys adventures. My favourite writer for quite a number of years was Richmal Crompton, author of the humourous "William" series of books, all of which I read avidly.

Another book that I enjoyed was *Emile and the Detectives* by Erich Kastner. Although basically restricted only to the junior section, I nevertheless often visited the art and film section and paged through *Picture Show* and *Film Pictorial* annuals – deciding there and then that Norma Shearer was the most beautiful film star in Hollywood!! These and other books were read and enjoyed over the years – there were of course no television sets, television games or computers to compete with reading during our leisure time – it was certainly a different world that we grew up in.

Count Curly Wee and all the other characters featured in the "Fur and Feather Land" comic strip – Gussie Goose, Colonel Bulldog, Belinda Bun, Cuthbert Colt and the arch villain of the strip, the crafty Mr Fox, were found in the daily *Rhodesian Herald* newspaper. I usually read this strip before turning to the newspaper's main headlines!

The librarian who allowed me to browse through the adult section was, I understood at the time, a Miss Page – which I figured was a very appropriate name for a librarian! It was only in later years that I discovered her name was in fact Miss Park, but by then she had long since retired from the library!

Our neighbours in the semi-detached house departed town and were replaced by the Woodrow family – Bill, his wife and their two sons, Clive and Rodney. My mother and Mrs Woodrow became friends, as did the two boys and I. Their eldest son Clive had been given a 1940 edition of *Aircraft Of The Fighting Powers* and I took the opportunity of leafing through this most interesting book whenever I visited my friends next door. I became fascinated with the many military aircraft that were flown by the warring nations. I looked up my father's large atlas (brought over in the lift) to find out where such countries as Belgium, Holland, Poland and Rumania were situated, as their aircraft and air forces were also embroiled in the conflict raging in Europe.

Bill Woodrow worked as a technician for the Electricity Supply Commission and drove a 1941 Ford coupe – this car was parked in the road right outside his front gate, for neither their house nor ours possessed a garage or a driveway. He would simply step into his car, close the door and within a split second he would drive off – the car always seemed to spring to life the very second he climbed in. By the time he closed the driver's door he would already be on his way – there never appeared to be any warming up of the engine at all. This feat always amazed me!

Meanwhile at school we were busy reading our way through the Beacon Infant Readers series of books and I recall one of the tales contained therein entitled *The Hobyahs!* – little creatures who tried to commit mayhem on an old man and his wife.

Other stories included *The Little Red Hen*, *The Ugly Boy and the Bear* and *The Cat and the Mouse*.

The dining room of the Grand Hotel had once served as the town's first makeshift cinema and had screened silent movies in the 1920s but this venue was eclipsed once the Royalty Theatre had been constructed and wired for sound. The dining room of the hotel however featured a stage and became the venue for most theatrical productions performed in Gatooma at the time. And occasionally a 16mm movie was still projected onto the old screen and I remember seeing two movies at that particular venue in the early nineteen forties.

The first was a British film documenting the exploits of R.A.F. Bomber Command during the early days of the war. *Target For Tonight* featured the epic story of a Wellington bomber crew that bombed Germany with great success. I still recall how we all cheered when the aircraft's bombs scored direct hits on their designated target, a railway station, and seeing the station buildings being blown to bits. Many years later I read that these buildings were in fact scale models detonated in a film studio, thus somewhat exaggerating the so called "pin point accuracy" as claimed by R.A.F. Bomber Command at the time. But in those early dark days of the war beleaguered Britain needed all the positive news it could get in order to boost the public's morale – and we certainly enjoyed the film!

The other movie we saw at the Grand Hotel was a feature film based on the true story of Nurse Edith Cavell, a British nursing sister who, during World War One, had administered to the medical needs of both Allied and German soldiers who had been wounded in action. The lead was played by Anna Neagle, an outstanding British actress and she played her role to perfection. Nurse Cavell was eventually arrested by the Germans, accused of spying and despite her pleas of innocence, was duly executed. At the end of the movie I doubt whether there was a dry eye in the audience; members of the young audience were seen sobbing quite openly as we filed out of the Grand Hotel doors into the late afternoon sunlight. It was, at our age, a very emotional film to have seen.

Some of my parents' friends ex-Germany still spoke with a very pronounced German accent, which often meant that when they pronounced an English word containing the letter "g", – the "g" was often pronounced as a "ch". Thus the word "German" would often be pronounced in such a way that it sounded exactly like "Cherman" or "Sherman". Some of them, for that matter, had similar difficulties with the letter "j" which they likewise pronounced as a "sh". Thus the line "just a minute, here comes a German" came out as "chust a minute, here comes a Sherman"!!

This being the case I found myself somewhat confused when, in 1942, the BBC Overseas News Service announced that the new American "Sherman" tanks now equipping Allied forces were beginning to face German tanks in battle and in most cases the Sherman tanks were proving superior to the German tanks ... Come again!!! It was only after my parents explained this position to me that I understood – for it almost seemed as if the Salisbury Convent "cheeses" were staging a comeback!

Popular songs heard on the radio in 1942 included "Jingle, Jangle, Jingle" and "This Is The Army, Mr Jones". One of the most haunting songs of the war turned out to be "Lili Marlene". Although this was a German song it proved to be highly popular with friend and foe alike and was heard on the radio over and over again.

A selection of the movies I saw at the Royalty Theatre that year included Johnny Weissmuller in *Tarzan's New York Adventure* (who could ever forget Tarzan's dive off the Brooklyn Bridge), Bud Abbott and Lou Costello in both *Rio Rita* and *Ride 'Em Cowboy*, Bob Hope and Bing Crosby in *Road To Morocco*, *Mrs*

Miniver, Wake Island, Captains Of The Clouds (featuring Harvard aircraft no less!!) and *Gentleman Jim*, the latter starring Errol Flynn. But the film of the year, as far as I was concerned, was Paramount's *Reap The Wild Wind*. This film told the tale of 19th century salvagers who descended beneath the waves in the still primitive diving suits of the day in order to salvage sunken treasure. The film's particularly exciting finale pitted a giant squid against John Wayne in a fight to the finish.

A friend in Salisbury told me years later that he had also seen the movie at the time, and had been talked into allowing his much younger brother to accompany him to the cinema, despite his better judgement. Arriving home after the matinee he found his mother entertaining some prim and proper ladies from the local church group to tea. This was 1942, when ladies were expected to be both prim and proper ... His younger brother, unable to contain his excitement any longer after having just seen the film, burst into the lounge where the ladies were sipping their tea and loudly proclaimed to all and sundry "I have just seen an exciting film where an enormous squid wrapped its testicles around a man and drowned him!!' These remarks, I was told, were met by gasps all round followed by a shocked and stony silence ...!

For most of his life my father would studiously avoid talking about his experiences in the concentration camp – the first time that I ever recall him talking publicly about this truly grim period in his life was when he gave a talk at a Rotary Club luncheon during the 1980s. Later I discovered that this was not the first time he had talked publicly on this painful subject for, when going through his papers following his death in 1992, I discovered the typewritten copy of a talk he had given to members of the Toc H Club in Gatooma in November 1942, just four years after his incarceration in Sachsenhausen Concentration Camp. A copy of this talk is reproduced exactly as he presented it at the time and in his own words, thus conveying his experiences with greater authenticity.

Herewith the address as presented to members of the Toc H Club in Gatooma in late 1942 by my father, Robert Sternberg.

Boys,

First I have got to thank you for the honour of having been asked to speak at this place and now, I like to ask you for one thing: In order to be able to understand what I am going to tell you please forget, during my address, that you are living in a country of democracy, lawfulness and decency, or to use a short term: that you consider it as the most natural right of a human being to be respected and to be treated as a human being. Forget all this, and, in substitute thereof, think in terms of brutal force and of nothing but brutal force which does not recognize any laws or rights or decency. Then, you may perhaps be in the position to follow me into a Nazi Concentration Camp of pre-war days.

Exactly four years ago, on the 10th of November 1938, the Gestapo made a big purge on German Jewry arresting within 24 hours no less than 54,000 male Jews through-out Germany. The reason they said was to punish the Jews for their being guilty of the murder of a German diplomat at Paris committed by a young Polish Jew. The real and sole reason was that we were just Jews.

The action started during the night and was accompanied by the destruction of nearly all Jewish shops and property and the burning down of all Synagogues in Germany. Many Jews were killed by the mob, members of the S.A. Brownshirts who, by command of their leaders, committed these atrocities. I was arrested by two Gestapo men at about 11 o'clock Thursday morning while being at home, and taken to the local Police gaol. There I met hundreds of more Jews and we were packed into small cells originally built for four, but 16 were in that cell of ours. We did not know what was going to happen to us. Two days later, early on Saturday morning, we were led to the railway station where a special train was waiting for us. There we were told that we were to be sent to a concentration camp. Off we went without having been able to see or even to notify our families. We were altogether over 600 people from 72 to 14 years old, all from my home town, Dortmund.

On the train we were treated quite well having been in charge of the ordinary police, but as soon as we had, after an eight hours journey, arrived at Sachsenhausen station and had been taken over by the S.S. Black Guards all hell broke loose. We had to jump off the train into a narrow ditch and were immediately beaten and kicked from all sides. As it was quite dark we could not see where to jump and many came to fall only to be trampled upon by their followers who could not see them. As we later learned three of our comrades met their death at this occasion while many more were hurt. And then we had to run two miles driven like cattle and constantly beaten with sticks, rifle butts etc. The old people were supported by their younger neighbours but two died during the following night of heart failure. It was the most dreadful reception one can imagine and served one purpose only, namely, to frighten all newcomers to such an extent that strict discipline and blind obedience ensued.

So we arrived at last at the camp and were lined up in a corner of an enormous square. The Commandant inspected us and at once sorted out 17 youngsters under 16 years of age whom even this cruel man had not expected to be arrested by the Gestapo. They were sent to a special barrack and one of us, the father of two of the boys, was made their special guardian. But, no fear, this was the only human feeling this commandant ever showed, we learned that quickly. And then we had to wait all the time standing lined up and not being allowed to move even one step. S.S. men came here and then kicking and hitting us and having, what they called, their fun with us. Some of us were sorted out and had to run round in a very narrow circle till they fell down. Others had to stand on one leg till exhausted only to get more kicks and beatings. Well, there were so many different ways of making "fun" that I can hardly describe them all.

And we were still standing and waiting all night without being given any food or water. We had had the last food at six o'clock in the morning before we left Dortmund and had only been given about half a pound of dry bread for underway. At six o'clock Sunday morning we had one after another to go into a barrack to be registered and then to go back to our place. And again to wait until about 2 p.m. to be marched to a barrack for bathing, haircutting and receiving camp clothing. Our own suits etc., were bundled and a number affixed, the same number we had received earlier when registering at that office. Under this number we were to be known in the camp, not under our names. My number was 11911. Each of us received a pair of socks, under-pants, a shirt and a special prisoner suit striped blue and grey and made of some ersatz material, probably wood fibre. Things did not fit, it was just a matter of luck to get something suitable and so we had to exchange as far as possible. The famous number printed on linen had to be affixed to both trouser and jacket. No caps or overcoats were issued in spite of the cold. Handkerchief and shoes of our own were left to us. All valuables, money and watches were taken, but, after our release, everything was returned to us. After that we had to wait and to stand for another two hours and, at last, were marched to our barracks. For exactly 25 hours we had been standing at the same place, without having had any food or water since early Saturday morning 36 hours before. We were absolutely exhausted, many of the old people having collapsed and taken to an empty barrack to be looked after by some orderly until being able to be sent to their barracks.

Before I go on with my tale I would like to give you a description of that camp.

The total area covered has been about one square mile surrounded by a brick wall 10 foot high. On top of this wall runs barbed wire loaded with high tension electricity and in front of the wall there is another barbed wire fence of the same kind. Then comes a path three foot wide made of white stones boarded by a grass path. Labels warned that whoever of the prisoners sets his feet on this white path would be shot without warning, his walking on this path being considered as an attempt to escape.

Every 100 yards there is a watchtower at that wall manned by several S.S. men and equipped with machine guns and powerful searchlights. One gate only, constantly guarded by a dozen Blackshirts with machine guns, forms the connection with the outer world. About 300 yards outside this fortress wall runs a second one, exactly alike but for fewer watchtowers. So, escape was impossible.

An enormous square extends over the whole front side of the camp. From there streets are leading lined by barracks. A little drawing will show you best how the camp has been built. Actually there are many more barracks, about 70 altogether. You see the two walls, the red circles showing the position of the watchtowers. There is no corner one could avoid the searchlights or, in case of revolt, the machine guns. That special walled part of the right upper corner is a special detention camp for special treatment. The famous Pastor Niemoeller was detained there. We have never seen him, as prisoners sent to that part of the camp never left it

How have the barracks been built? Each one is a doubled winged building made of bricks with a wooden roof. My little drawing gives you a fairly good picture. Each wing was designed for keeping 150 men but, caused by the sudden rush, 250 were packed in. For barracks or "Blocks" as they were called, were numbered, the left wing called "A" and the right one "B". I lived in 39B. There was a large dining room and dormitory in each wing, lavatories and washroom being for both sections in common. There were shower-baths and fountains in the washroom, sanitation was waterborne. Everything was spotlessly clean. Each wing had its leader, this being one of the old communist prisoners who had been in the camp for more than five years and had somehow obtained the confidence of the commandant. These men were our superiors and were in charge of their particular blocks. The actual head of the block was an S.S. man who could practically do with us whatever he liked. He, for his part, was responsible to and drew his orders from the Commandant or the officer in charge.

We entered our barrack at about 6 p.m. on Sunday and were given some food consisting of one pint of black fluid called coffee and a large piece of bread with a tiny piece of polony. Our hunger made us swallow this meal. Then we were told all the regulations concerning us and every second word was that we were to be severely punished if we broke one of those regulations. The main thing was blind and strict obedience to all orders given to us. Every S.S. man was entitled to shoot us on the spot in case of disobedience.

At last we were allowed to go to sleep. There were no beds, we had to sleep on the floor covered with straw. One blanket was given to each of us. As we were not allowed to keep our clothes on we felt rather cold during the night, November being a cold month in Germany. As the place was overcrowded we were packed like sardines. Our shoes covered with our trousers made the pillow and we used our jacket as additional cover for our feet, as we had to take off socks and underpants too, and it was very cold. One night there came a patrol of two S.S. men. Lights went on and we had to get up. About 20 of us were found with their socks and underpants on. Result – we all had to walk out without shoes or any clothing except for the shirt and had to stand motionless in front of our barrack for one hour. Then we could return to our sleeping place. I don't know how many of us caught a severe cold that night because everyone already had one anyway.

We had to get up at six o'clock in the morning, as it was winter, it was still quite dark until 8 a.m. In summer the prisoners had to get up at 4 a.m. After washing and dressing, breakfast had to be fetched by about forty men from the central kitchen. There was a sort of porridge, mostly oats or sago cooked in thin milk of which we got one pint each, and a piece of bread. Sundays some black coffee too and a spoonful of jam. Then we received our lunch which we had to take with us. It consisted of a piece of bread and some polony or cheese.

After breakfast we marched to that big square for the roll call and then work started. Some groups worked inside the camp doing odd jobs, others worked in the vegetable garden or in the neighbourhood of the camp building and improving roads, clearing woods etc. Those people were the lucky ones because they got seldom disturbed by Black Guards. They had to work very hard under strict supervision but it was not the work itself that made conditions so bad, because one got used to it, but the rude and cruel treatment by the S.S. These fellows came along and hit and kicked and chased us around without any reason or sense, just only to torment us. But, as I mentioned, it was not too bad near the camp. I state this as a fact, as I don't know the reason.

But about 3,000 of us were not so fortunate and I was one of these. Our working place was about two miles away where a huge brick and cement factory was under construction. We marched to that place every morning, closely guarded. Underway we were constantly beaten and kicked by the guards and had to run most of the way. This march was dreadful but it was even worse in the evening after work. Many collapsed and had to be carried by their comrades, under more beatings from the guards.

Work at this building place was partly very hard, partly very senseless. And on top it was made hell by the unceasing torment we received by the S.S. I shall give you a few examples.

Sand dug from a place where a canal was going to be constructed had to be carried to a remote place. This was done the following way: a chain of prisoners was formed with a distance of about five yards between two men. Each man was given a shovel and the sand had to be thrown from one to the next one until it reached that corner about a quarter of a mile away. Quite harmless is seems to be but when an S.S. man stands next to you and counts your shovel strokes and counts faster and faster and one has to follow his counter and certainly can't and gets therefore hidings and kicks etc, till he falls down, then you know what this sort of work means. Or, we had to put on our jackets reversed in order to form a pocket, got two shovels of sand into it and to carry it to that corner. Looks quite harmless but we had to run both ways, watched and driven by S.S. men beating us with sticks. After four to five runs one dropped to the ground being nearly unconscious. People with a weak heart could not stand it long and I have seen within four days three people carried away from that place. This section of that working place was the worst of all. Only when there were no S.S. around it was quite alright there because then nobody hardly moved and the work itself was no work at all.

Carrying cement bags of 100 lbs weight each is already no easy job when one does it quietly and undisturbed. But to have such a bag put on one's back and to walk half a mile without rest and then to run, not to walk back to the ship to get at once another bag and so on until one has carried 12 to 15 bags, means a strain only very few ones could bear. Most were finished after five to six bags and after having received the usual beatings had to be sent to some easier kind of work.

We worked from dawn, about 8 a.m. till dusk, at 3.30 p.m. During summer working time, we were told, was from 6 a.m. till 6 p.m. Half an hour break for lunch was allowed. Our march back to camp was again hell as mentioned before.

There was again a roll call and, back in our barracks we had supper. Cabbage cooked together with potatoes or a thick fish soup were the only dishes we ever saw. Twice during my stay we got boiled potatoes and meat – whale meat, treated in a special way. It looked and tasted exactly like beef, just a bit drier. It was not bad after all and it was a welcome change in our rather uniform diet. After supper when we had cleaned our dishes we were off duty. We could walk on the roads between our barracks and could meet our comrades from the other blocks. I personally could have a talk with my brother and father-in-law, who were in the same camp but in different blocks. Smoking was allowed outside the barracks provided we had cigarettes. There was a canteen in the camp but for the first fortnight we had no money to buy goods. After that period the money that had been taken from us in the registration office was returned to us. So we could buy bread, butter, cake, smoked meat, polony, sweets, chocolate, tobacco, cigarettes etc., as well as pipes, handkerchiefs, shaving outfits, braces and similar stuff, at the usual prices. But supplies were limited and we were only allowed to spend about ten shillings per week. Anyway, the canteen helped us a lot to pull through.

It was a bad punishment to be forbidden to buy in the canteen. There were several kinds and degrees in punishing prisoners, individual ones and collective ones. For individuals the most usual one was to stand at attention for three hours near the gate after the evening roll call, in the bitter cold, without cap or overcoat. It also meant loss of supper. A most severe punishment was to be tied up at trestle and to get ten or fifteen or twenty-five beatings with a leather strap over the bare back. Twenty-five meant almost certain death. It was always a big ceremony and the whole camp had to be present. It happened once during my stay to a chap who had slept in a barn during working time, had overslept and was missing at the roll call. After an hour's search they found him still sleeping, and the next day his fate was sealed. It was dreadful to hear that poor fellow scream, I don't know if he survived. These and others were official punishments by command by the commandant or officer in charge. Any S.S. man could, however, do with his block what he liked. Confinement to barracks, no supper, curfews, were just a few examples. At 8.30 p.m. we had to go to bed and the lights went out.

That was a day's course and all days were alike. There was no Sunday, we had to work seven days a week. The sole distinction was that there were less S.S. men about, most of them being on Sunday leave. So we could do our work more or less undisturbed. Christmas Day and Easter Sunday were the only official holidays in the camp.

We were allowed to write and also to receive two letters or postcards per month. I am showing you a postcard written by me to my wife on the official form. No parcels were allowed.

Medical treatment was insufficient. Old prisoners trained as orderlies did most of that job. Iodine, as-

Prisoners at work – Sachsenhausen Concentration Camp

pirin and castor oil were the usual medicines supplied. To see the doctor was dangerous because if he did not find one very ill, severe punishment followed for trying to
cheat. Pneumonia, kidney and similar sorts of serious illness were the only ones he
accepted and treated in hospital. The death rate was very high.

At the beginning of December release of the Jewish prisoners started little by little.
First people over 60, then youngsters, then the others. My lucky day was the 15th of
December, after my father-in-law had come home a week earlier - my brother
followed a week later. At the end of February 1939 nearly all the 12,000 Jews (in the
Sachsenhausen Concentration Camp) were home.

At home I had to report to Gestapo Headquarters and, at last, the worst period of
my life, so far, was over. After another two months my family and I left Germany for
Rhodesia.

And now, chaps, you may be allowed, too, to return to your country of lawfulness
and decency ...

1943

I was thrilled to receive a very special present on my eighth birthday – my first ever bicycle – a new black Phillips which sported a smart looking cycle pump clipped to its frame. All cycles in those days seemed to be black in colour – imitating Ford motorcars of an earlier vintage! Likewise, cycles were all very conventional in appearance and nobody I knew ever owned a fancy sports model of the type that were advertised in American magazines and comics of that era. Whether American cycles were ever imported into Rhodesia I cannot say, but none ever appeared in our town! Having one's own mode of transport now proved most practical and I made very good use of this bicycle until I outgrew it some years later – still with its bicycle pump attached to the frame in virtually mint condition! My cycle was eventually sold and a larger model purchased in its place.

Shortly after my birthday I joined the local Boy Cubs organization, a junior version of the Boy Scouts. Our group met once a week at the Scout Hall in Rhodes Street where we were taught the art of tying reef knots, learnt the rudimentary art of signalling with flags, basic first aid (with a definite emphasis on basic), we also somehow learnt to swim (difficult without a suitable swimming pool to practise in) and also learnt how to light fires without the aid of matches (which was useful as I had always used matches to light any of my previously set fires ...)!!

One of our assignments as Cubs was to pull an old cart around both the commercial and residential areas of the town for the purpose of collecting tin cans, old metal pots, pans, tins and items of similar nature from both shopkeepers and housewives – all in aid of the "war effort". Suitable material of this nature would be smelted down and the resulting metal content would subsequently be turned into bullets and weapons to help our troops smash the Axis powers.

These collections usually turned out to be great fun and once a month we spent an entire afternoon pulling the cart around the various areas of town, stopping to knock on doors and requesting any useful items. On one of these occasions the cart was particularly heavily laden, and whilst we were easing it down a lane which happened to be on an incline, the cart somehow or other managed to roll away from us, gathering momentum at a rate that astounded us. In fact it began to move so rapidly that we failed to catch up with it. Try as we might we could not stop the cart, for it appeared to us as if this vehicle had developed a mind of its own. The fact that the cart had never been fitted with brakes did not exactly help our quest either, and try as we might, it continued to outpace us. And, as luck would have it, it was heading straight for a fairly busy road on which cars were constantly travelling!

Although we continued to run after it the cart kept going, having now fully escaped from our clutches. It proceeded to shoot right across the busy road (a T-junction) − winding up in a ditch on the other side, with pots, pans and other items flying off in all directions. It was sheer providence that, for the few seconds it took the cart to cross Rhodes Street, no cars happened to be passing at that particular moment, thus preventing what could have resulted in a very nasty accident.

We proceeded to pick up its contents which had been strewn about and thanked our lucky stars that no passing motorists, cyclists or pedestrians had come to any harm. It was a very sobering experience for our group of eight and nine year olds, and not something we would ever want to experience again. Following this near catastrophe, future trips with the cart saw us accompanied by a number of older Boy Scouts so as to ensure that a potential disaster of this nature did not re-occur. And to make doubly sure, the cart was now fitted with a rudimentary hand brake of sorts!

From time to time the Scout Master, whose duties included instructing the Boy Cubs for a two-hour session one afternoon per week, failed to turn up, and we were left to fend for ourselves. Often no assistant scoutmaster was available to step into his shoes (it was of course war time and many of the men were in uniform serving out of the country − there was in fact a severe

manpower shortage in the country), we were thus left to our own
devices as to how to fill in the time designated for our weekly
session. Being dressed in our neat cub uniforms with nothing to
do appeared to be a complete waste of time as far as we were
concerned – so we decided to keep ourselves occupied at times
like these.

Adjoining the Scout Hall was a large and barren piece of
vacant property. Its terrain was covered by a multitude of stones
and rocks of various shapes and sizes. In addition the ground
was criss-crossed by several crevices, some deep enough to lie
in without being seen. The ground was not suitable on which to
play any form of sport, such as football, cricket or rounders, and
so we put on our "thinking caps".

This vacant section of ground, we decided unanimously, was
an ideal venue to play our own version of "war games". This
being 1943 – and most of the adults in the world appeared to
be involved in their own war. We devised a rudimentary set of
rules, stipulating that two opposing groups of equal numbers be
formed. Each group was to occupy a piece of "territory" at
opposite ends of this vacant piece of terrain. The centre section
was to be known as "no man's land". Each group, which consisted on average seven or eight "soldiers" per side, were then given
ten minutes in which to gather as many stones as they could
before the start of "hostilities" were announced. At the end of
these ten minutes a whistle was blown and the opposing sides
then attempted to invade each other's territory – the declared
winner would be the group that held most of the land at the
conclusion of the game.

Invading the opposition's territory in order to capture ground
meant hurling our supply of stones (or "hand grenades" as we
now dubbed them) onto the "enemy" positions – thus compelling
those who had ventured out into "no man's land" to beat a hasty
retreat back to their own lines before they had managed to
advance too far. With stones raining down all over the ground it
was indeed a miracle that no skulls were split open although
many "combatants" sustained skinned legs, knees and accumulated gravel rash after each skirmish! Counter-attacks were
launched and further stones and small rocks rained down upon
each participating side. The crevices in the ground were used as

convenient "fox holes" by those who needed to get out of the direct line of fire, and which also gave them a chance to replenish their stocks of "grenades"! A few of the participants who had anticipated possible "battle damage" had brought along some old tin helmets, no doubt filched from their grandfather's World War One souvenir box!

Eventually these "war games", which we played on a few occasions, were terminated by mutual consent, as matters had become somewhat out of hand. We had, surprisingly enough, drawn up a further list of loose rules after the conclusion of the second game), for a number of the "combatants" involved had begun taking these "games" fairly seriously, and attempted to introduce items like catapults ("Catties"/"Katties" in our jargon) into the game. These "gung-ho" types claimed that they had been elevated to the role of "sniper" ‐ and thus required more accurate weapons in order to secure victory for their respective side! It was indeed fortunate that no one had suffered a fractured skull up to that point, but we certainly did not require the now distinct possibility that eyes could well be taken out by "sharp-shooters" armed with catapults! Thus our "war games" were officially terminated and an honourable and permanent "cease-fire" was declared!

One or two afternoons a week we went to football practice and I normally played in the full-back position. Football was played in the second (winter) term of the year, the first and third terms being given over to cricket which, to be honest, was never my favourite sport, especially following the Partridge incident, of which more later ...

The Governor of Southern Rhodesia, Sir Evelyn Baring, officially opened our new school on 11 March 1943 and I recollect lining up with my fellow schoolmates and hundreds of local residents in a welcoming ceremony in the Gatooma municipal park. Sir Evelyn emerged from the rear compartment of his car, resplendent in a colonial governor's uniform, wearing a plumed hat. He looked most impressive ‐ but what impressed me most that day was the shiny 1942 Buick that he stepped out of on his arrival in the park ‐ it was by far the smartest looking car I had ever seen!

Bullying, thank goodness, did not appear to be a major factor at the school, at least as far as I was aware. But the fact that I had been born in Germany and that Southern Rhodesia was currently at war with Germany caused snide remarks and comments from several of the boys. Plus the fact that I happened to be Jewish caused further comments to be passed by some of those fools. Whether these remarks were made in crass ignorance, plain stupidity or both eluded me at the time, but these comments and insults caused me considerable hurt and anger. On the whole I learned to live with these disparaging remarks but there happened to be one boy in particular, of Afrikaans parentage, a known bully, who was both older and far bigger than I who took great delight in taunting me at every opportunity. This usually occurred during the mid-morning break period and continued for several months. One day I must have simply snapped, for when he started up again with his "bloody German Jew" remarks I slapped him right across his smirking face – putting every ounce of my eight year old body into this slap – and in fact did so right in front of his smirking hangers-on. Then, suddenly realizing what I had done, I stepped back, fully expecting him to retaliate. Instead, he stood stock still for what seemed to me to be an eternity, then turned and proceeded to walk away, followed by his now suddenly silent companions, none of whom could believe what they had just witnessed.

I must admit that I was somewhat taken by surprise at my reaction to his taunts, and even more so by his unexpected response in walking away. I was very relieved by his departure! But the best thing that came out of this was that he never passed any further remarks, to my relief.

Two of my closest friends at that time were brothers Peter and John Robinson, the two sons of the school's deputy headmaster. They lived in the very last house on Mornington Road, adjoining Orange Grove Farm. This was a small farm situated on the immediate outskirts of town. I often pedalled to their home on my new cycle and we spent a great deal of time in each others' company, either cycling or walking around town, visiting friends and often playing marbles, the latter being a most popular pastime. Many of our school friends possessed reasonable collections of marbles and we often challenged each other to a game, usually in the afternoons but often during the half hour school break period between 10.30 and 11.00 a.m. We soon discovered who the better players were and who were not so good. I was a "middle of the road" player and when we challenged each other on a "winner take all" basis I soon realized that in my case you win some and you lose some! The marbles we played with were made of plain glass, infused with various colours, blue, green, yellow, red, etc. Marbles came in different sizes, and could be purchased new in certain shops. Then there were the steel marbles which we propelled towards the glass ones – and the players had to be careful not to damage and chip the lighter, fragile and delicate glass ones. Should this happen, arguments were known to break out! We had great fun and in our case, the marble season lasted throughout most of the year.

One hot summer's day during a school vacation Peter, John and I happened to be cycling around town and feeling rather thirsty when we found ourselves close to the premises of the Star Mineral Water Works situated in Cam Road. We were all in agreement that a cold lemonade, or for that matter any ice cold drink would be more than welcome but, as we had already spent all our week's allocation of pocket money, it would have been futile to cycle to the nearest café for that purpose, so, being close to the mineral water factory, we rode into their grounds and politely asked the owner of the concern, a Mr Chinn, whether he had the time to provide us with a guided tour around his factory so that we could see for ourselves how our "favourite lemonade and ginger beer" was being manufactured! He willingly obliged and at the end of the brief tour he asked us whether we would like something to drink! What a question – he must have seen the tongues virtually hanging out of our mouths by that stage ...!! What's more, instead of handing us a bottle from the production line which we would have been more than happy to gulp down, he led us to a refrigerator stocked with ice cold lemonades, ginger beers, sparkling orange and lemon drinks and simply said "help yourselves, boys" ... Absolute bliss!

Unfortunately Deputy Headmaster Robinson was transferred to Umtali and the family left Gatooma. After we exchanged a few letters I lost touch with both Peter and John. However, quite by chance, some sixty years later, Peter Robinson and I met up in

Harare (Salisbury) and we renewed our friendship. He was by then a retired headmaster and one of the leading cricket administrators in the country. Sadly, barely a year after we had met up again, he passed away from cancer.

During school holidays I often spent time visiting the Gatooma Railway Station, watching trains arrive and depart. The locomotives pulling these passenger or freight trains were various classes of Beyer Peacock Garrett steam locomotives, an articulated locomotive completely different in shape and size to the great majority of locomotives found in other countries. I would sometimes stay on and watch the local shunting locomotive in operation and the driver and I exchanged greetings a few times. More often than not I was the sole onlooker. Train spotters, not that I was one, were not a known species in our town! The railway line intersected the town, and we could hear locomotive whistles being blown both day and night — although this often depended on which direction the wind happened to be blowing! Many were the times I lay tucked up in bed at night listening to the shrill sound of a locomotive whistle as a train prepared to leave the station, also when a train approached the Edward Street crossing. This crossing virtually divided the town into two — the "below the line" and "above the line" areas. In my mind train whistles constituted comforting sounds. For when the sound of the passenger train pulling out of the station and heading for Salisbury around 4 a.m. each morning had finally faded, the reverberating "dumpeta, dumpeta, dumpeta, dumpeta" from the little gold mine could occasionally be heard in the still night air. Its sound was considerably muted in relationship to when we once lived in Brading Street, for we now resided some considerable distance from that mine. For me, these were the distant sounds of childhood, long gone!

One afternoon, while visiting the railway station, I plucked up enough courage and jumped off the platform, walked across a number of tracks and, taking the bull by the horns, asked the engine driver of the 14th Class Garratt locomotive whether there was a possibility of my being allowed onto the footplate of his locomotive during shunting operations. As I had expected, his response was to tell me that it was strictly against all rules and regulations to let little boys into his "office" and that the answer to my request was therefore "NO!" But then, having no doubt seen my look of disappointment, he obviously relented and told me I could climb up and take a brief look around his cab. Wow!!

Excitedly, I climbed up the locomotive's steps into the cab and the driver proceeded to point out some of the dials, levers and gauges and explain the functions they performed. He suggested I sit on one of the benches in the cab and this I did happily, savouring my view of the marshalling yard, but expected at any moment to be asked to climb down and make my way back to the platform. This particular 14th Class Garratt was in actual fact a current mainline goods locomotive and had recently replaced the 13th Class Garratt of an earlier vintage that had for years performed the shunting duties at the Gatooma station. Imagine my surprise when, instead of asking me to leave the cab prior to shunting operation commencing, and without a warning of any kind, heave a shrill blast on the whistle! A cloud of steam hissed loudly out of several pipes situated beneath the cab and the locomotive slowly edged forward! I was instructed to sit still and under no circumstances get into the crews' way, which instructions I more than happily complied with! We thereafter proceeded to shunt wagons around the marshalling yard for the next hour or so, and from time to time the firebox was opened by the fireman who shovelled coal into the blazing inferno. Each time this door was opened we were greeted by the sight of a roaring furnace and a blast of hot air shot out which enveloped the cab. Before long my clothing was completely soaked through with perspiration. It was one of the most exciting moments of my life and I will always be grateful to that extremely kind and understanding engine driver who may himself have undergone a similar experience in his youth! His kindness greatly impressed me and he definitely made my day!

After all these years I have long since forgotten the driver's name, but we became "buddies" and he permitted me a few additional rides in the cab of his steam locomotive over the next few months. The rides ceased when the driver was transferred to another town, which I suppose was bound to happen eventually. But I will always remember those exciting afternoons which provided me with a thrill that most small boys very seldom had the opportunity to experience.

And reminiscing about railways – one of our favourite past-times on Wednesday afternoons a little after 5 p.m. was a visit to the Railway Station in order to meet up with the passenger train from South Africa which halted for about fifteen minutes during the course of its journey all the way from Cape Town to Bula-wayo and then on to Salisbury, its final destination. These regular weekly "mail trains" as they were called, brought back the majority of Rhodesian holiday makers from their vacations in South Africa or, after the war, also from journeys abroad on ocean liners. The departures and arrivals of these passengers to and from South Africa were treated as quasi-social events in the national press, for the *Rhodesian Herald* newspaper once a week published the names of all first-class passengers travelling to and from these two countries on the Wednesday train, eg "Mr & Mrs Bob Smith of Salisbury and their daughter have just re-turned from a three week visit to Cape Town" (provided they travelled first class). Occasionally local residents disembarked at Gatooma station – people whom we actually knew, some having just returned from the seaside. A magical place to most land-locked Rhodesian children, the majority of whom had never experienced a longed for visit to the coast ... Many passengers on their way to Salisbury disembarked briefly en route, taking the opportunity to "stretch their legs", pacing up and down the platform a few times, sometimes stopping to glance at or pur-chase magazines or newspapers that the two local newsagents displayed on trolleys. These had been wheeled onto the platform, whilst the two hotels displayed billboards aimed at any passen-gers intending to stop over in the town and might therefore require overnight accommodation. Hotel porters were in attend-ance with their own little trolleys in order to wheel passengers' luggage to their respective hotels, for in those days Gatooma had yet to boast of a taxi service. In the 1940s, prior to air links between some of the smaller Rhodesian towns, and when the "highways" linking all towns still consisted largely of no more than strip roads, the railroad remained the chosen mode of travel for the great majority of the population.

At one point I became the unwilling victim of a health food fad, for certain well meaning friends of my mother must have con-vinced her to serve me a diet of ox brains (for guaranteed health and vitality!) This is what awaited me upon coming home from school one day! It was a dish that I had never heard of before, but I was informed that brains were "very nourishing" and would make children grow up to be big, strong and healthy. Obviously the nourishment in this touted "wonder food" benefited only youngsters, for I noted that my father was not proffered this dish, and I am quite sure would have refused point blank to touch it even if he had been asked! Naturally I objected strongly to having to eat this blob of greyish matter, lavishly surrounded by mashed potatoes and covered with gravy. It was only after much persuasion that I tentatively sliced off a piece of this rubbery mass. In fact, it tasted only vaguely like meat and if my recollections are correct it took me a long time before I finally finished the portion. Every morsel required the assistance of a liberal helping of potato and gravy to enable me to swallow a forkful at a time!

The following day I was presented with yet another helping of brains for lunch and again baulked at this weird food. Somehow I managed to consume the helping, assisted once again by liberal helpings of potatoes and thick gravy. But when brains once more appeared on day three, I decided to use my own brains this time and firmly put my foot down. Enough was enough! I pushed my plate away and began a sit down strike at the dinner table. I was certainly prepared to try new foods from time to time but definitely NO MORE BRAINS!! I suggested that my mother could finish off these brains herself, although as far as I recall, she rejected this magnanimous offer ... The remaining brains were, I think, fed to our pet cat but I don't recall whether the poor creature bothered to play ball in this respect. But I made quite sure that ox brains were well and truly kept out of my diet following this experience!

My father later told me that he had wondered how long I would be prepared to endure eating brains and that he himself would never dream of touching them, no matter how healthy and nutritious and full of vitamins they were touted to be. Thereafter I returned to a diet of beef, chicken and fish, and thank goodness boiled brains never appeared on our table again ...

What I do retain with fondness however were the number of times, especially during winter months, when, after having been tucked up in bed for the night, I was given a mug of warm milk and honey to drink whilst a story was read to me prior to falling asleep.

A favourite of mine was a raw egg, to which was added a tablespoon of sugar, whipped up in a mug and drunk. This became a treat during summer months and may well have contributed to my cholesterol level in later years ... Likewise kugel baked with prunes aplenty, another winter favourite. And as for mocha-schokoladen-crème torte (mocha chocolate cream cake) – a sponge cake layered and covered with rich mocha chocolate crème – this was my all time favourite and was habitually a special birthday treat year after year. Childhood memories are made of these!

Comics, mentioned earlier, both British and American, featured prominently in our lives. Although we may not have appreciated it at the time, the 1940s were in due course to be called "The Golden Age of Comics" and every week a fresh supply arrived on the counters and shelves of our local newsagents – The Gatooma Mail Co. in Baker Street and the Rhodesian News Agency situated in Rhodes Street. The former received a far wider selection to choose from and my friends and I normally spent up to an hour or more paging through copies of *The Beano, Dandy, Film Fun, Radio Fun* and *The Wizard* before I invariably purchased my weekly copy of the *Champion* comic.

Paging through these various comics in a limited span of time whilst also attempting to make sense of particular story lines was, I am sure, an excellent introduction to the art of "speed reading"! The staff of the Gatooma Mail bookshop were pretty understanding and let us comic fans browse endlessly through the selection of comics on display, realizing all too well that each of us would, before leaving, purchase no more than a single comic. And despite the war raging on at the time, these comics arrived safely week after week from far away Britain in ships which at times sailed in convoys in order to protect themselves from the submarine menace. I found it hard to get over the fact that there were sailors putting their lives at risk in order to ferry consignments of comics to Africa so that we children could continue to enjoy reading them throughout the war years. It seemed quite incredible! And as for the aforementioned *Champion* comic that I invariably purchased each week – I could not wait to read about the exciting exploits of three of my favourite characters featured in this comic, namely Colwyn Dane, the Ace Detective, who, without fail, always managed to solve the most baffling of crimes. Rockfist Rogan, a crack R.A.F. pilot and a champion boxer to boot, who shot down Luftwaffe aircraft and knocked out opponents in the ring on a weekly basis, and Sgt Bill Ross, the fearless leader of a weekly tale entitled "Leader of the Lost Commandos".

We had the best of both worlds, for an excellent selection of American comics were stocked in a small tearoom cum magazine shop situated in Union Street, and owned by a Mr and Mrs Parris. These premises were also visited by us on a regular basis and there we paged through the exploits of Batman, Captain America, Captain Marvel, Superman and all the other caped heroes who spent their waking hours pitting their wits against arch criminals and assisting the armed forces in overcoming America's wartime enemies. And then there were Planet Comics which featured some very weird and malevolent looking aliens from outer space who, with the aid of death rays and space ships, constantly threatened to enslave mankind and take over the world.

Mrs Parris, a short and squat woman – in later years I equated her to being an early prototype of the "Grandma" character in the "Giles" cartoon series – always appeared to be in a bad frame of mind! She warily watched us with her beady eyes as we paged through the comic books knowing full well that we would more than likely read several of them prior to deciding amongst ourselves which particular comic to purchase before we departed – if, as a group, we bought one at all!!

Dick Tracy comic books were a firm favourite of mine and I read as many as I could manage, relishing exciting exploits as the master detective matched his wits against such odd named and weird looking criminals as "The Mole", "Flat Top", "Pruneface", "B-B Eyes" and "The Brow". Dick Tracy and his amazing two-way wrist radio (a sort of granddaddy of today's mobile phones) always triumphed in the end but usually at great odds! American comics at the time cost double as much as the British ones, but as schoolboys we exchanged these comics with other readers so money spent on them went a long way.

And when the comic books in Mrs Parris's shop had been thoroughly perused we moved to the "pulp fiction" section where American magazines with the most lurid of covers were on prominent display, sporting such titles as *Amazing Stories, Fantastic Stories, Weird Tales, All Detective Magazine, True Detective* and *Spicy Detective Stories*, plus an endless selection of western yarns. We very seldom purchased any of these magazines as the contents seldom seemed to match the excitement and drama as portrayed on the covers. Today however, both wartime pulp fiction magazines and comics have become great collector items.

When Mrs Parris found that the customers in the shop exceeded four or five at any given time she used to holler down the passage leading from the shop to the living quarters situated in the rear of the building, requesting her husband to assist her in keeping an eye on these schoolboy "customers". She always addressed him as "Mishter Parris" – never by his first name – (which happened to be Simon), and the way she addressed him never varied!! He appeared to spend most of his time in the residential quarters and only turned up in the shop when specifically required.

In July 1943 my father's application to join the Internment Camp Corps – a section of the Rhodesian Army – was finally accepted. He had volunteered to join the regular army the previous year, but his request at the time had been turned down due to the fact that he was not a British subject. Regulations and needs change however and his re-application was now found acceptable, but with the stipulation that he would not be permitted to serve in any military capacity outside the borders of the country.

The Southern Rhodesia Internment Camp Corps had been formed during 1942 to initially house enemy nationals from Tanganyika and elsewhere. The number of internees however expanded rapidly when some 4,500 male Italian nationals from Abyssinia and Somaliland were also transported to Southern Rhodesia. Internment camps to house these Italian civilians (not prisoners-of-war) were constructed in Gatooma, Umvuma and

Fort Victoria. Many of the German Jewish males who had arrived in Southern Rhodesia in the late 1930s as refugees volunteered to serve in the S.R.I.C.C. and my father was attested into the Corps with the initial rank of Sergeant and appointed Accounting Officer at No. 3 Internment Camp, Gatooma. This position would normally have been filled by a commissioned officer, and after a few months he was promoted to the rank of Warrant Officer 2nd Class. Promotion to Warrant Officer 1st Class followed but he was prevented from attaining commissioned rank due to his still current "alien" status. During one period he was transferred to No. 4 Internment Camp in Umvuma for some months, then back to the Gatooma Camp, where he remained as Chief Accounting Officer until finally discharged from the army in 1946, after the Italian internees had been repatriated to Italy.

The Gatooma Internment Camp housed some 1,500 Italian internees. Many were expert craftsmen – carpenters, builders, electricians, stonemasons. There were also a goodly number of artists, singers and musicians amongst the internees. Plays and operas were performed from time to time in the camp recreational hall, and my parents attended a number of these performances. Between the years 1943 to 1945 I paid quite a number of visits to the camp which was situated some five miles from Gatooma just off the main road leading to Bulawayo. On one occasion I was thrilled to accompany them to see a performance of the opera *La Traviata* – sung of course in fluent Italian! I recollect that the singers' voices were most impressive and highly professional. The period costumes worn by the cast were magnificent, designed and sewn by some of the highly skilled tailors in their midst. It was probably the first and only time that this opera would be performed in the wide open spaces of the African bush!

Their artists held exhibitions of their paintings and craftsmen opened a woodworking shop. Beautiful wooden furniture and toys were produced – these and the paintings were offered for sale, and proved most popular with the buying public.

Some afternoons my mother would take my sister Judy and I to the park where I would clamber onto the swings and see how high I could propel myself. At that stage Judy was learning to walk and we would sit on the lawn and coax her to practise her steps. She progressed well – all too well as it turned out on one particular weekday afternoon! After having practised her steps she was placed back into her pushchair and left with a biscuit and some fruit juice whilst I returned to the swings. Somehow Judy managed to clamber out of her pushchair unassisted and tottered towards me. Out of the corner of my eye I saw her approach but before I could slow down the swing she walked right into it, the swing caught her on the side of her head and she was flung on to the ground. My mother and I rushed to her prone little body and I was sure she had been mortally injured. However, after a few minutes she regained consciousness despite sporting a somewhat dazed look in her eyes and the beginnings of a sizeable swelling soon began to appear on her head.

It was a most unpleasant and frightening experience at the time and one that I have never forgotten. However, my little sister seemed to recover quickly enough and the incident obviously retained no lasting effect, for some twenty years later she obtained a university degree!

During the year a fire broke out at the Cotton Ginnery factory (in later years known as David Whitehead Ltd), which the local volunteer firemen found unable to extinguish, such were the intensity of the flames. I recall an aircraft flying in from Salisbury with fire fighters who brought with them more up to date fire fighting equipment. Despite this, it still took some considerable time to bring the conflagration under control. This event became the talk of the town but thankfully fires did not occur too often in Gatooma − one of the last fires I recall occurred some fifty years later when the town's fire station itself was burnt to the ground, including its vintage fire tender, which had remained parked inside the building throughout the course of the blaze!

Despite the fact that we now resided in the centre of town, we were nevertheless still visited by snakes from time to time, especially during the rainy season. Therefore when the warning "Passop − nyoka hamba lapa kia" (be careful, a snake has entered the house) was issued by our domestic servant, who by sheer chance may have spotted one of these reptiles slithering indoors, we became particularly vigilant. The snakes in question very often lived in burrows in the large vacant piece of ground adjoining our house (the land on which the new post office was to be constructed many years later) and these snakes more often than not were on the lookout for food.

Should said snake have been spotted in time we tried by all means to prevent it from entering the house, for once inside it would usually head with utmost speed for a spot where it hoped to remain undetected. This could be under a bed, behind a wardrobe, under the refrigerator or behind the kitchen stove. In cases like that the reptile managed more often than not to disappear from sight. One was therefore never certain in which room the snake was currently holed up in, or for that matter whether it was even still in the house. Unless the snake had been identified, one was likewise never sure whether it was a poisonous species or not, and although most snakes were harmless, one could never really afford to take a chance in this respect. Therefore walking around barefoot was not recommended with a suspected snake in the house, for even the so called "harmless" snakes could inflict painful bites. Cobras were fairly common in our area and one certainly did not want to get involved with one of these, for they possessed a lethal bite and the spitting cobra had a very nasty habit of ejecting a jet of venom towards an intruder's eyes. Should the venom hit its target, blindness could well result, unless the eyes were treated immediately. The common saying that "the only good snake is a dead snake" was unfortunately a very common pronouncement at the time!

However, our pet cat often came to the rescue by eventually flushing out these intruders from their hiding places, and the reptile was often dispatched with repeated blows to its head with an iron bar. It was recommended that dead snakes be incinerated, for to simply drop their bodies into a dustbin was said to attract their mates, who it was claimed, had a tendency to come out in search of their missing partners. It was deemed wise to follow this advice. Whether their mates did in fact tend to track down the corpse was difficult to prove, but as a precaution, dead reptiles were usually burnt in order to remain on the safe side!

Some of the year's movies that I recall seeing were *Madame Curie* starring Greer Garson and Walter Pidgeon, *Tarzan's Desert Mystery* (who can ever forget Johnny Weissmuller being menaced by a horrific looking giant spider!), *Hit The Ice* and *It Ain't Hay* – both Abbott and Costello comedies and *Bell Bottom*

George starring George Formby. *Lassie Come Home* – the first of the Lassie films, tugged mightily at the audience's heart-strings – especially canine owners – most families in town kept a dog, except mine of course, as we only ever had cats. But despite never having owned a hound, even I must admit that my own heartstrings were pulled on this occasion! Two war films come to mind, *Bataan* starring Robert Taylor and the British film *San Demetrio, London* – the story of a torpedoed tanker which was left burning in the water and initially abandoned by its crew during World War Two – based on an actual event.

The Children's Holiday and Convalescent Society ran a home called "Vumba Heights" situated in the Vumba mountains some twenty miles south east of the town of Umtali and close to the borders of Rhodesia and neighbouring country Mozambique. This Home catered for children between the ages of seven and twelve. As I had never been on a vacation, my parents decided it would be a good idea for me to take a holiday up in this mountain resort in the Eastern highlands. They applied to the Society for my admittance and I was duly accepted. I was certainly excited at the news, but nevertheless a little apprehensive at having to set off on the initial part of the journey to Umtali by myself.

In December I caught the mail train to Salisbury one morning at 4 a.m. – under the supervision and watchful eye of the train conductor. I disembarked on Salisbury station to be met by committee members of the Rhodesian Children's Holiday Society, together with a number of other children, most of whom were from the Salisbury area. We were provided with breakfast at the station and were later placed onto the Umtali bound train under the supervision of a number of the committee members who would accompany us. The journey to Umtali proved rather a long one, and upon arrival we were met by some elderly ladies who also belonged to this organization. After being treated to some refreshments, we all boarded a bus and thereafter headed out in the direction of the Vumba mountain range. We now travelled through

lush green countryside, so very different to the scenery I was accustomed to in the Gatooma area. The Eastern Districts of Southern Rhodesia afforded not only vastly different scenery but an almost complete change of climate. Before long we were driving through forests, surrounded by tall trees on either side.

The bus driver kept changing gear every few moments whilst wending his way along and up a narrow twisting gravel road which seemed to become narrower as we travelled. To our left was a solid wall of rock and on our right, the side I was seated on, there appeared to be a sheer drop into a misty valley far below. Stones and small rocks dislodged by the wheels of the vehicle hurtled off the edge of the road and spun out of view down the cliff face into the deep valley. I sincerely hoped that the driver was an experienced one and that he knew his way up this narrow mountain road! Soon it began to get quite chilly and the road enveloped in mist which partially obscured the view ahead. For all I knew, we might well be heading into the Transylvanian Mountains, perhaps never to be seen or heard of again. I had possibly seen one "Dracula" movie "trailer" too many!

After what seemed like an eternity the bus turned left and onto a tree-lined gravel road – thank goodness we were finally off this treacherous looking mountain road! Before long a large building loomed out of the surrounding mist – this proved to be our home for the next few weeks to come.

Despite my initial apprehensions, homesickness never became an issue – the beds turned out to be comfortable, the food good,

Vumba Heights Hostel - Vumba Mountains

tasty and adequate. I soon made new friends and the small staff running the hostel were most kind and helpful. We played games, went for long walks in areas that swarmed with monkeys and we even swung on vines that overhung rushing mountain streams, most of us becoming "pretend Tarzan"s let loose in the jungle! In short, we all had a great time. The weeks seemed to fly by and we were quite disappointed when our vacation drew to a close.

On the return journey to Umtali I made sure that I sat once again on the right hand side of the bus – but on this occasion however it meant that I was not required to peer down the sides of the cliff that dizzyingly plunged into the valley far below. My first experience of that view had more than sufficed!

When I arrived home a Christmas gift from my friends Peter and John Robinson awaited me – a book by disabled Rhodesian artist/author C.J. Shirley entitled *Little Veld Folk* which contained short stories featuring indigenous Rhodesian animals. The stories were all illustrated by the author, who had been born minus

both arms and legs, yet managed to walk on artificial legs and manipulated his paint brush with the stumps of his arms – a truly remarkable man. For many years, and despite his severe disabilities, he had succeeded in living an active outdoor life. Mr Shirley became a true inspiration to Rhodesians of all age groups.

De Havilland Tiger Moth

1944

The school year commenced on 25 January 1944, a month short of my ninth birthday, and I now found myself in Standard Three. My school report from the previous year had proven fine. However, the average age of the class (9 years 9 months) left me, once again, the youngest in the classroom.

Our Standard Three class teacher for the year was a Miss Innis. The two of us failed to see eye to eye on numerous occasions, but nonetheless my school report at the end of the 1944 year was a reasonably good one, although her final comment on the annual report stated: "Peter is inclined to dream in class ..." I suppose I cannot really dispute her observations at times, but they were probably due to the fact that my attention was often diverted by the spine-tingling and ear-splitting din of numerous Harvard aircraft making their approach to Gatooma airfield! Given a choice of either listening to the low flying aircraft directly overhead or attempting (unsuccessfully) to concentrate on what Miss Innis was trying to impart to us, invariably resulted in the aircraft winning hands down! Neither teacher nor pupil would have been heard, never mind understood, at those particular moments. Thus the raucous Harvard inevitably captured our attention – for not only did they succeed in utterly drowning out our teacher's voice, but managed to produce an infinitely more exciting sound in the bargain! As Harvards flew over our classroom a number of times each week, perhaps her observations were not entirely misplaced! This noise factor only applied to Harvard aircraft, for Tiger Moths and twin engined Airspeed Oxfords and Ansons were all powered by quieter and lower powered engines. When these aircraft flew overhead, our lessons, surprisingly enough, continued uninterrupted. So blame her comments fairly and squarely on the trainee fighter pilots and their steeds – the exciting North American Harvard advanced trainers!

For my ninth birthday I was given a book entitled *Desert Magic* by Herbert Leviseur − the author had penned this book whilst serving in the South African army in the North African campaign a year or two earlier. The stories contained therein featured spiders, ants, nulla birds, desert dogs and other wild life that the author had encountered during his stay "up north" and the book was dedicated to his young daughter. I thoroughly enjoyed reading the stories, still have the book and for that matter have never come across another copy anywhere else.

My father awoke one morning with a pain in his abdomen but nevertheless insisted on going on duty, being collected as usual right after breakfast by the army driver in the Internment Camp Corp's beige Chevrolet vanette (light truck). However, when I came home after school a little after 1 p.m. and sat myself down at the dining room table for lunch, my mother informed me that Dad had been taken to the Gatooma Hospital during the course of the morning. The pain had intensified, which had since been diagnosed as appendicitis, and he was to be operated on shortly. The operation, which he underwent later that afternoon, thankfully proved successful.

We walked up to the hospital every afternoon and spent time with him during visiting hours (these hours were very strictly adhered to. When the bell rang visitors were very quickly ushered out of the wards). His bed had been placed in the general ward − in those days patients who had undergone operations were mostly kept in their hospital beds for up to a week − "strict bed rest" it was called − none of this twenty-four hour in and out of hospitals as is wont to happen in this current day and age! The Gatooma Government Hospital at that time was kept in spotless condition, crisp bed linen, polished and subsequently gleaming floors, friendly and helpful nurses and everything under the control of a strict matron who brooked no nonsense! And we had full faith and confidence in Dr Murray, the government physician who had been our family doctor since our arrival in the town.

In the bed next to my father lay an old and gnarled gold miner/prospector who was suffering from the latter stages of blackwater fever − a deadly malarial disease which was still prevalent in the country, especially in outlying areas with poor accessibility to the nearest towns and hospitals. Blackwater fever resulted when one's kidneys become damaged due to severe bouts of malaria, and every time I visited my father this old miner appeared to be either completely motionless and fast asleep or alternatively he lay twisting and turning in his bed whilst continuously wheezing and on the verge of coughing his lungs out. This was not a pretty sight to see and it was at times like these that the nurses usually pulled a screen around his bed to shield him from the gaze of both visitors and fellow patients. During the week that I visited the hospital there appeared to be no change in his condition and I also noticed that he never had any visitors. And then, a day or two prior to my father's discharge from hospital, and from the very moment that I walked through the doors of the ward, I saw that the miner's bed had been stripped and was now empty. I realised immediately what must have happened to him – I had seen enough movies to recognize what a stripped bed indicated ...

Mosquitoes and the dreaded malaria they were capable of infecting one with was still a major problem in the Rhodesia of the 1940s and Gatooma was no exception. During the rainy season (November to March) sleeping under a mosquito net was virtually compulsory if one expected to have a good night's sleep and stave off the possibility of being bitten. The mosquito nets, usually white in colour, were affixed to a hook in the ceiling above one's bed while the lower end of the net was required to be tucked securely under the mattress as mosquitos had a tendency to fly under the bed and then find their way into the net itself. And unless nets were checked carefully for holes, no matter how small the openings in the net might be, the mosquitos more often than not found their way through and the slumbering victim could well be bitten several times whilst completely unaware that a mosquito had joined him or her under the net. Thereafter, having had its fill of blood, the mosquito, usually too bloated to make its way out again, flew to the top of the net where it generally settled for the rest of the night. When the sleeper awoke the next morning it was often to the sensation of a very itchy arm, leg or face, followed by the sight of a mosquito or two perched above one's head, unable to exit the confines of the net. In this case it was simple to kill the mosquitoes – the blood that now splattered out was one's own and the hope that the mosquito that had bitten one was not an anopheles, malaria carrying species! At night one was often kept awake by the continuous whining of these insects trying to find their way into one's bed, and one needed to keep both arms and legs away from the sides of the net or one could easily be bitten.

In order to try and eradicate mosquitoes from one's bedroom at night the doors and windows were closed and the room thoroughly sprayed full of insect repellent, usually from a flit-pump, the predecessor of to-day's cans of insect spray. This needed to be done at least an hour or two before retiring to bed, as the room tended to retain the repellent's less than pleasant odour for some considerable time, and if inhaled could well produce a headache or even nausea. Once the smell had dissi-pated the windows could be opened wide in order to let in some fresh air provided of course that mosquito screens were fully in place to stop further mosquitoes flying into the room. Virtually all windows and also doors that led to the exterior of residential buildings, whether these buildings were situated in cities, towns or in the countryside were fitted with mosquito screens made of gauzed wire and these screens needed to be constantly checked to confirm that there were no holes or openings in the fine wire mesh which might enable the little predators to penetrate. It was an ongoing battle ...

During the 1940s, and for a number of decades to follow, the local municipalities regularly sent teams armed with mosquito repellent to spray various sections of their respective towns and cities, especially during the rainy season, in order to keep mosquitoes at bay. Gardens, fields and pathways were checked out for stagnant puddles and pools of water which possibly harboured mosquito larvae, for if those wet areas were left untreated they often bred further colonies of mosquitoes. Malar-ia and related diseases were of major concern in Rhodesia and claimed many thousands of victims over the years. The disease remained rife until well into the 1950s and even today there are certain sections of the country virtually designated as "no-go" areas, any visitors entering them risk their health and very life unless they take the strictest of anti-malarial precautions.

As previously mentioned, my grandfather from Northern Rhodesia visited us at this time. It was from him my mother and I
learned that my father, at great risk, had, throughout the entire
six week period of confinement, conducted communal evening
prayer services after nightfall in one of the concentration camp
barracks. Prayer gatherings were strictly forbidden – the prisoners had been warned that those found participating in this
practice would be summarily shot. Although the prisoners involved had placed lookouts to warn of any approaching guards,
the prayer sessions nevertheless remained a most dangerous
and risky undertaking.

No mention of these activities had ever been made by my
father, which made me respect and look up to him even further.

For the past couple of years I had spent a few afternoons each
week at the local airfield watching the yellow painted training
aircraft of the R.A.F. landing and later in the day taking off in
order to return to their various home bases. These aircraft
belonged to the Rhodesian Air Training Group, which formed
part of the Royal Air Force's worldwide training programme
known as the Empire Air Training Scheme. Four countries,
namely Southern Rhodesia, Australia, Canada and South Africa
were involved in this massive training exercise. Most of my fellow
classmates at school, certainly the boys, followed the exploits of
the respective Allied armed services, be they the army, navy or
air force. A minority enjoyed reading about and following the
achievements of the army whilst the majority followed the sea
battles that the Royal Navy were engaged in. I could never quite
fathom (no pun intended ...) as to why the navy appeared to be
by far the most popular service of all as I am quite sure that
ninety percent of the boys at Jameson School had never been
anywhere near the sea in their entire lives. However, what
surprised me most of all was the fact that hardly anyone showed
any interest in the air force, which to me made little sense,
especially as we had such a large air force presence in the
country and in the very skies right above our heads. I was not at
all concerned about this in the slightest as it meant that I
virtually had the airfield to myself in the afternoons (and also in
the mornings during vacation time) in order to view the aircraft

from close quarters and experience the thrill of their landings and subsequent take-offs.

The local aerodrome, perhaps better described as a largish and well maintained grass landing ground, was situated at the south western perimeter of the town's outskirts, some two miles from the town centre and easily accessible by a gravel road. The field was partially ringed by a low wire fence and its entrance was secured by a farm style metal gate which was left wide open at all times, as no one ever seemed to be around to close it. In fact, as far as I recall, there were seldom any guards on duty unless military aircraft were left parked overnight, which only happened on the odd occasion. One could therefore enter or depart the airfield at any time of the day, and presumably, night. A building, walled to waist level and constructed of rough stone, stood near the gate. This structure was roofed with thatch, and had probably been erected a few years earlier. Together with a small outhouse type toilet close by, they constituted the only two buildings on the airfield. A windsock, situated in fairly close proximity, usually fluttered limply in the breeze. No hangars were ever installed on the airfield at the time, but in the early 1950s, if I remember correctly, a hangar and clubhouse were erected by the newly established Gatooma Flying Club on another section of the airfield.

Gatooma was conveniently situated equidistant between Gwelo and Salisbury, both of these larger centres possessing a number of aerodromes which were used for the current training of pilots, navigators, wireless operators, air gunners and bomb aimers. Cranborne, Belvedere, Mount Hampden and Norton air bases were situated in the Salisbury area, whilst Thornhill, Guinea Fowl and Moffat lay close to Gwelo. Aircraft from these training bases landed in Gatooma during the course of their cross-country flights. Row upon row of de Havilland Tiger Moth elementary bi-plane trainers from Belvedere, Mount Hampden and Guinea Fowl, North American Harvard advanced trainers from the Cranborne and Thornhill air bases and Airspeed Oxford and Avro Anson twin engine bombing, navigational and gunnery trainers, many fitted with gun turrets, flew in from Moffat. It was all exciting stuff and during the period 1942–1945 I must have cycled to and from the airfield two or three times per week. These cross-country flights occurred on an almost daily basis, for the Rhodesian climate provided virtual all-year round blue skies and clear starry nights for this vital training programme.

Regarding my visits to the Gatooma aerodrome, my routine remained pretty constant during those years. Having first completed my homework at the dining room table, once the lunch dishes had been cleared, I proceeded to set off on my bicycle, or "pushbike" as we were apt to call our cycles. On arrival at the airfield I usually leaned my cycle against the wall of the building, then proceeded to wander off to view the rows of aircraft neatly lined up, wing tip to wing tip. Some time later the pupil pilots emerged from the building, where they had, since flying in some time earlier, been provided with cups of tea and undergone a (navigation) briefing by their accompanying instructors.

Maps were being studied for their return flights to various home bases. I knew the routine, having been allowed to sit in on a number of briefings when the instructors, from time to time, felt in a sufficiently good mood to let me in on the goings on! The pupil pilots then proceeded to walk to their respective aircraft, carrying their bulky parachutes by slinging them over their shoulders, unless they had left their chutes in their aircraft upon landing.

After having settled themselves into the aircraft (rear seats in the case of the Tiger Moth if they were flying solo) and after having securely strapped themselves in, the familiar ritual of starting the Gypsy Major powered biplane began. One airman swung the propeller after the word "contact" had been called out by the pilot. If it caught first time all good and well, if not, the propeller swinging procedure required a repeat, sometimes several times. However, once the propeller was whirling away, a few bursts on the throttle were given, the motor was then left to idle for a few further moments before the triangular wooden chocks in front of the wheels were pulled away. A further touch of the throttle and the aircraft slowly proceeded on its way, Askari Soldier on Guard tail skid dragging on the ground, heading for the far end of the runway. During the dry season aircraft threw up large clouds of dust and dry grass in their wake. Upon reaching the end of the runway, the aircraft, now completely out of sight, could be clearly heard from the commencement of their take-off run. They soon came into view, and after take off proceeded to head in either an easterly or westerly direction. Occasionally, an aircraft engine failed to start. In such cases the aircraft would be wheeled back in close proximity to the building and securely tied down and guarded overnight by men of the Rhodesian Air Askari Corps. Within a day or two an air-mechanic would be flown in from the aircraft's home base and once the fault had been rectified the aircraft would be flown out.

When Avro Anson and Airspeed Oxford twin engined aircraft had landed I sometimes found myself fortunate enough to be shown around their interiors, and up into the cockpit to have the controls explained.

Often I was also allowed to peer through the glazing of their gun turrets, but quite understandably received strict warnings not to touch the machine guns triggers! But, as far as I was concerned, the most interesting aircraft that landed in Gatooma at the time was my favourite, the Harvard trainer − a low wing retractable undercarriage two seat monoplane powered by a Pratt & Whitney engine giving it a top speed of a little over 200 m.p.h. The Harvard, I reasoned, could closely be compared to many World War Two combat aircraft in size, looks and sound! For that matter, a fair number of Harvards served in operational areas during the war years. A large number of World War Two feature films − and for that matter many post war movies, featured Harvards depicting the role of German and Japanese fighter aircraft. No wonder the Harvard was, during the post-war period, often referred to as the "Hollywood Zero"!

Quite often, after the Harvards had departed for their respective bases, the pilot of the last aircraft to depart took the opportunity to "beat up" the airfield at extremely low altitude. This would provide me − usually his only spectator − with a most thrilling display of low level flying. Often he would bid me a "thumbs up" farewell on his final pass (at virtual zero level) before he headed into the fading light of the late afternoon until his aircraft became a rapidly decreasing speck in the sky. After the ear-splitting sound of the departing Harvards, the now deserted airfield seemed strangely silent. Only the sound of the wind rustling through the stalks of grass could be heard. What great memories and moments those long gone afternoons still evoke.

One afternoon a pilot needed to collect something from his aircraft, which happened to be parked at the far end of the flight line. He approached me and asked whether he could possibly borrow my cycle to ride to his airplane, thus saving him the walk there and back, to which I happily agreed. Unfortunately though, whilst peddling back from the aircraft, his weight proved a little too much for the tyres of my small cycle, for I heard a distinctive bang as one of the tyres burst! He apologized profusely, whilst I in turn envisaged a rather long walk home, including the inconvenience of having to push my crippled bicycle all the way back. My cycle had, without a doubt, indeed been transformed into a genuine "pushbike"! Fortunately, a Royal Air Force truck happened to be at the airfield that particular day and instructions were issued to its driver to take me home. My immobile pushbike was loaded onto the back of the vehicle whilst I excitedly clambered up into the passenger seat. Off to town we headed!

My mother was pretty startled when she saw this dark blue truck with R.A.F. roundels on its doors pull up alongside our front gate. Her son's bicycle was then unloaded from the rear of the vehicle by the uniformed driver, who then proceeded to give her a smart salute! As I stepped out of the truck I felt as thrilled as could be to have been given a ride home in a military vehicle!

Arriving at the airfield one afternoon I noticed an aircraft type I had not come across before, several of these machines being parked alongside a row of Tiger Moths. On enquiring what type of aircraft these were, I was informed that they were Fairchild Cornell trainers. An American aircraft, the R.A.F. intended to replace the dated and somewhat weary Tiger Moth elementary trainers with this newer design. In my opinion the Tiger Moth biplanes certainly did look antiquated, almost resembling aircraft of the Great War. Replacing them may well have been a good idea – but nevertheless, the Tiger Moths soldiered on and I do not remember seeing too many of the Cornells flying into Gatooma again.

Some time later, during one of my usual afternoon visits to the airfield, I was unexpectedly presented with a packet of genuine English toffees by one of the pilots. These sweets had been handed to him in order to pass on to me by the pilot who had punctured my cycle tube! I had already long forgiven him – the ride in the air force truck had proved to be more than ample compensation for a mundane burst tyre – but this wholly unexpected gift of toffees was nevertheless greatly appreciated and very much enjoyed!

During the year, if I remember correctly, an incident occurred that greatly distressed both the R.A.F. and the public alike. However, it had far worse repercussions for two hapless and unfortunate airmen. Crashes, injuries and deaths were regrettably part of the price to pay during the course of this massive air training operation, but the following incident proved to be the most tragic and unnecessary of all the fatalities that occurred.

A Tiger Moth took off from its base in Bulawayo, in order to undertake a cross-country training flight. Possibly due to an unfortunate navigational error, the aircraft flew off course, eventually crossing the border into neighbouring Bechuanaland (now renamed Botswana). Running low on fuel, the crew managed to locate a suitable patch of ground, making a successful forced landing. Both the flyers and the aircraft were unscathed. They were found by local African tribesmen who took them to their village. That evening they were fed dinner which consisted of giraffe meat. The two crew members were then put up for the night in a hut.

Giraffe had been declared "Royal Game" by the authorities, and the tribesmen, who had illegally poached the animal, feared that they would now be reported by their guests to the police for breaching the law. To prevent this possibility, they murdered both airmen during the night so as to cover up their crime.

An aerial search was carried out, and the Tiger Moth was soon discovered. An Oxford aircraft from Bulawayo, carrying additional crew members, flew to the scene, and the stranded Tiger Moth, now refuelled, was flown back to base. A police search for the pilots was now instigated, and the heinous crime discovered. Police brought the culprits responsible for this gruesome murder to court, where suitable justice was meted out to the perpetrators.

Occasionally we saw R.A.F. trucks drive through Gatooma towing lengthy trailers on which damaged aircraft had been loaded. These trucks were on their way to the aircraft repair workshops in Bulawayo. By the end of 1944 aircrew training began to wind down and by mid-1945 ceased altogether when the war ended. Naturally we all rejoiced that this major conflict had finally come to an end. But I was nevertheless disappointed that all the military flying activities at the Gatooma airfield had virtually ceased, for I realized that a particularly thrilling and enjoyable period in my life had likewise ended.

My parents greatly enjoyed fresh fruit and here in Rhodesia we were most fortunate to be able to indulge in an almost unlimited variety. Apart from locally grown fruit such as mentioned earlier, other fruits available included bananas (from Mozambique) watermelons and delicious oranges, the latter grown on the giant Mazoe Estates, near Salisbury, reputed to be one of the world's largest orange growing orchards. All these fruits were readily available. In addition, boxes of fruit arrived on a regular weekly basis from the Cape Province of South Africa – and local fruit and grocery shops stocked a most delicious variety of imported fruit – green and black grapes, peaches, apples, apricots, plums, nectarines and pears. Many of these fruits arrived in flattish sized wooden boxes and in order to check on the condition of the fruit one needed to prise away one or two nails which held down part of the lid. The lid was pulled aside, the protective straw covering lifted, and if the fruit was found to be to one's satisfaction (no bruising, etc) then the lid would be replaced, the nails hammered back into place and the box taken to the till for payment. A box of fruit lasted us for about a week and we alternated the selection on a weekly basis. A number of shops in town stocked a large selection of Cape fruit, we would usually purchase our weekly supply from Kewada & Co. in Union Street or from Campbell's Departmental Store, the latter situated opposite the Standard Bank in Baker Street and was at the time the largest grocery shop in Gatooma. My father loved grapes and I was thankful that he could now literally enjoy the "fruits of his labour" – especially after having been compelled to act so frugally when turning down the opportunity to purchase that box of grapes in Cape Town several years earlier! Thank goodness those financial concerns appeared to be over.

We continued to support the Saturday afternoon film shows at the Royalty Cinema and thoroughly enjoyed the Tarzan films which starred Johnny Weissmuller in the title role and Johnny Sheffield as his son "Boy". Whenever Tarzan movies were screened Joe Burke could be guaranteed a full house, be they evening performances or matinees. War films likewise proved very popular, as were the Lassie series of movies. But the films we as children looked forward to most of all were the Abbott and Costello comedies. They averaged two or three films each year throughout the 1940s, and we tried not to miss any of them! Bud Abbott and Lou Costello were two very funny American comedians who had come up through the burlesque theatre and scored a tremendous hit in *Buck Privates* (1941). Very soon they became Hollywood box office hits and remained so for much of the Forties. Looking back – with hindsight – their style of humour appealed to youngsters between the ages of eight and twelve – no wonder we found them so entertaining. The cinema was always packed to capacity on Saturday afternoons whenever their movies were being screened and they starred in many – *Ride 'Em Cowboy, Rio Rita, It Ain't Hay, Hit the Ice, In Society, Keep 'Em Flying, Buck Privates Come Home* and *Mexican Hayride* come to mind. The concluding scenes in their movies very often brought the house down – who can ever forget the hilarious sight of a rotund Lou Costello perched precariously on the end of a fire truck's extension ladder whilst the vehicle, recklessly chased a getaway car (being driven by a bunch of escaping convicts) in and out of heavy traffic! The finale of *Buck Privates Come Home* had Lou navigating a midget race car (with its throttle jammed) at breakneck speed along a crowded highway, miraculously missing oncoming cars with only inches to spare. Somehow he managed to veer off the highway and onto the runway of a busy airfield, narrowly missing decapitation by various aircraft landing and taking off directly overhead! After each of their movies we streamed out of the cinema still laughing our heads off, and we could hardly wait for their next movie to be screened!

One morning my mother requested our African domestic servant to wheel Judy (aged two) around the enclosed garden in her pushchair. Some time later she came out of the house to check on whether my sister had possibly fallen asleep, as everything appeared to be very quiet. However, there was no sign of

Judy, her pushchair or the employee. She walked out of the front gate, thinking that Judy was being wheeled up and down the sidewalk but there was no sign of them. Deciding that he was probably wheeling her around the residential block and that they would be home shortly, she went back into the house. But when a further half hour had elapsed and they had still not put in an appearance, she began to get worried and phoned my father, who returned from work, and together they searched the surrounding neighbourhood, with but with no success.

They were on the point of contacting the police to send out a search party when Judy and the domestic finally turned up. Almost two hours had elapsed since he had taken her for a "short walk around the garden". His explanation for having being away for such a lengthy period was that he had become somewhat bored whilst wheeling her around the confines of the small garden and had therefore decided to go for a worthwhile walk around town, but unfortunately had not thought of mentioning his intentions to my mother prior to setting off for a couple of hours!

Had the police indeed been notified and subsequently sent out a search party, this man could well have been charged with child abduction. Of course, in the light of what transpired, no charges were laid against him, but, taking his sense of responsibility into consideration, or rather his complete lack of it, his employment was terminated without further ado.

At some stage during the year I became friendly with a senior pupil at the school whose name was Dennis Stead. Dennis was several years older than I and had a very bad stutter, it took endless patience to listen to him attempting to complete a sentence. He also, I discovered many years later, suffered from epilepsy. He did not participate in sport and, because of his stutter, rarely engaged in conversation with fellow pupils. He cycled around town a great deal, usually wearing a distinctive pith helmet, and used to visit the two automobile showrooms in town, Duly & Co. (Ford) and Wilson's Garage (General Motors) very often. This is how I discovered his great passion for cars. I had finally met someone who shared an interest similar to mine.

Dennis invited me to visit his home, he lived with his parents and siblings near the park. There he showed me his collection of motorcar catalogues and brochures which he had accumulated since the 1930s. I was absolutely fascinated with what I was shown. For not only did he possess catalogues of most makes that had been sold in Rhodesia since the 1930s but he had written to overseas auto manufacturers who had mailed him catalogues of their various makes and models. Thereafter I spent many afternoons in his company and was thrilled when he presented me with a 1938 Chevrolet catalogue plus a Rolls Royce brochure of similar vintage that I now added to my own modest collection of catalogues.

Joseph Titus Partridge, known as Joe, turned out to be one of Rhodesia's all time cricket greats, playing in no less than fifty-six test matches for his country and taking almost three hundred wickets. He became a Springbok and played eleven test matches for South Africa against the likes of Australia, New Zealand and England during the years 1963–1965.

And why do I mention him? Because in the mid-1940s Joe attended Jameson School in Gatooma and at that stage was already recognized as an outstanding cricket protégé. He was by far the school's most outstanding cricketer, despite his tender age. Joe had been chosen to captain the Jameson School team to a very much expected win over the school's arch rivals – the Eiffel Flats Junior School. Their forthcoming annual encounter, a real needle affair, was eagerly awaited. In a sense the match was to be played for the local version of the Ashes.

The day of the match finally arrived but quite frankly I was little interested in going to watch this event, and had already made other plans for my afternoon's entertainment. I had (reluctantly) attended a few cricket practices during the term (semester) but my prowess as a batsman was pretty poor and when it came to fielding – that was, in my opinion, "the pits"! Even in the role of spectator the game left me unmoved. So my mind had already been made up – I was not going to go along to the school that afternoon and spend my time watching a game that simply did not interest me ...

On the day of the match I was called out of the classroom and asked to present myself at the school office. No reason for this request was given. On arrival I found a few of other boys already standing around and we were then ushered into the headmaster's office, where he cordially greeted us. Then his mood seemed to change, and in a rather sombre voice, informed us that a number of the school's First X1 cricket team had most unfortunately been compelled to drop out of the squad at the very last minute, due to injury and illness. In the circumstances therefore a number of "reserves" were now being called upon to replace these regular team members. I do recall passionately attempting to talk my way out of this totally unwarranted selection, as I felt that whoever had nominated me could surely have never seen me "play" cricket! Unfortunately, my pleas were firmly over-ruled. "There is no need to get nervous", we were told, "simply block the ball, don't attempt anything rash, and let Joe Partridge score the runs needed to take our school to victory". We were earnestly assured that, provided we stuck to this game plan, Jameson would win. I had the distinct impression that we had suddenly become unwilling participants in a real life version of some war movie scenario, in which an officer attempts to install a measure of confidence into his squad of doomed men prior to their undertaking of a near suicidal mission. All that was lacking at that moment were the background strains of Elgar's "Land of Hope and Glory" to uplift our sagging spirits!

I very much doubt that I managed to eat lunch that day, for my nervous system felt as if it had been shot to pieces. After a few hurried visits to the toilet, the world's most nervous "cricketer" presented himself at the school cricket pavilion that fateful afternoon. So much for my plans of not attending this match! And as this annual "derby" always drew a goodly number of additional spectators which included parents, teaching staff and pupils from both of the schools, all available seats surrounding the cricket field were pretty much filled. I do not recall which team won the toss and which one chose to bat – all I remember is sitting up on the steps of the pavilion and contemplating my forthcoming fate in front of so many onlookers.

Joe Partridge lived up to everyone's expectations – his batting proved superb and although the other Jameson batsmen played valiantly, Joe proved, as anticipated, to be the dominant player – a real pillar of strength. One by one members of the Jameson team were bowled, caught or stumped by the opposition, but the general feeling remained that as long as Joe remained at the crease he would carry the school to certain victory. Then another batsman was dismissed and suddenly it was my turn to bat and assist Joe in his brave one man quest to take our school to victory. That was my duty, nothing else mattered ...

A few words about Joe Partridge, on whose ability the whole of Jameson School's hopes rested. Joe was recognized as possessing great cricketing talent and in adulthood he went on to represent Rhodesia in no less than 56 first class matches in the late 1950s and early 1960s. He was a brilliant pace bowler, in a match against Eastern Province he ended with figures of 6-30 which included bowling out the brilliant Graeme Pollock with his first ball. Joe went on to become a Springbok cricketer, playing some ten test matches for South Africa.

So I began my walk from the cricket pavilion, down the steps and onto the field, en route meeting up with the unfortunate batsman who had just been dismissed and who was now on his way back to the pavilion after having had the unfortunate experience of being clean bowled – wickets flying in all directions! This, I convinced myself, is all that I now needed to have happen to me in front of all these spectators ...

I wish I could state that I faced the first ball with even an ounce of confidence but that would be telling a lie. My heart was pounding and I told myself that if I scored no runs at all, thus making a "duck", that would turn out to be only a temporary embarrassment. I felt I could live with that. I would in fact not have been the only player who had failed to score any runs that day, this having happened to a few of the others already. But only please, please, please and please again – do not let me be dismissed by the very first ball that I was now about to face, for that would simply be too humiliating to happen right in front of all these spectators.

So there I stood, facing a most determined looking bowler and his first delivery headed straight for my wickets, but it had been drilled into me to block the ball which, much to my amazement, I actually managed to do. Phew! The second and third deliveries were likewise blocked much to my relief but the following ball turned out to be somewhat wide and I reached out and managed to give it a whack with my tightly held bat. To my great surprise the nearest fielder, who could not have been overly concentrating on his allotted task, missed the ball in a clumsy effort to stop it. Here was an actual chance to score a run! And so I took the opportunity, ran to the other side of the pitch and felt a great sense of relief in having scored at least one run!

Joe went on to score run after run as was his aim and I continued to block as many balls as I was capable of. Slowly I began to feel a little more confident and somehow even managed to score another few runs along the way. With this newly found trust in myself I decided to hit out a little more which unfortunately prompted me to disregard my instructions – block the balls and leave the scoring to Joe Partridge. And so in the third or fourth innings of this now profitable little partnership with Joe I struck out yet again. The ball took off all right, but this time another fielder, somewhat more alert than the others, managed to scoop up the ball and threw it back to the wicket keeper. But by this stage I was already in full flight and half-way down the pitch hoping to score yet another run whilst Joe, not expecting me to run at all, had remained at his wicket, only commencing his run when I unexpectedly turned up in his territory. He simply had no choice but to keep running despite having virtually no hope of reaching the other end of the pitch in time.

The result of this little fiasco? Joe Partridge was run out by a member of his own team and the Eiffel Flats players were more than delighted with my unexpected assistance in their prime objective of the afternoon. In turn I felt like a fifth columnist! To this day I have no recollection of whether Jameson or Eiffel Flats eventually won the match – what I definitely do remember was that I was not voted "Man of the Match" – at least not by the Jameson team!

Malaria, as mentioned previously, was one of the major scourges of the African continent and in the 1940s it was still very rampant. Having fallen ill and been put to bed with a fever, our doctor, after examining me, felt I may well be showing the first signs of this disease and prescribed a course of quinine tablets.

Unfortunately I have never been able to swallow pills or tablets successfully and usually gagged when attempting to do so, a problem which unfortunately persists to this day. So the pills were crunched up into smaller pieces, mixed with either a small quantity of food or liquid to cushion the taste, and fed to me on a spoon. However, I found the taste practically unchanged, and simply spat everything out. Quinine is an alkaloid and has an extremely bitter taste. Considered a dangerous drug, it could only be prescribed under medical direction. People had even been known to die of quinine poisoning. I figured out that it was probably the taste that killed them, more than the actual medicine itself! But in my own case, worse was to follow. The doctor, accepting the fact that I was unable to swallow the pills, now prescribed quinine in liquid form – a substitute for the tablets.

Liquid quinine, as far as I was concerned, should have been banned under the Geneva Convention! It put even the taste of the crushed tablets to shame! The taste of this extremely bitter and vile liquid remained in one's throat for hours, obliterating the taste of any food or liquid consumed thereafter. Thus, when my daily dose became due I tried to escape the confines of our home and hide rather than be confronted with a spoon full of this poisonous tasting liquid. Eventually my mother had to lock all exterior doors and manoeuvre me into a corner like a caged animal (she never used a whip – I must give her credit for this – although I would not have blamed her if she had ...) whilst I desperately searched for an escape route. And the outcome of all this after having undergone several days of torture? The doctor decided that I was not suffering from malaria after all and thus my experience of being stalked by a tablespoon of quinine day after day came to an abrupt and most welcome halt. My health and sanity had been saved and my mother no longer had to corner her quinine hating son into taking his daily medicine.

My father had long felt that the town's Jewish community, which by now numbered several dozen men, women and children living in Gatooma and the surrounding district, was ready to form an official Hebrew Congregation and therefore arranged for the Reverend Dr Levin, Minister to the Bulawayo Hebrew congregation, to travel to Gatooma and address the local Jewish community with a view to getting this project off the ground. Thus on Wednesday 16 August 1944 a meeting was held in the Women's Institute Hall in Newton Street and a resolution passed that a congregation be officially formed. An interim committee

of six persons was appointed with octogenarian Mr MP Vallen-
tine elected chairman and my father elected secretary.

My parents never gave up attempting to keep in touch with
relatives who had been left behind in Germany after the outbreak of the war, and it was through the efforts of the International Red Cross that they managed to do so, but only at
prolonged intervals.

This was a laborious method of contacting people, and Red
Cross offices in Salisbury, Geneva and Berlin were involved.
Messages had to be short and to the point, and were obviously
censored all along the way. News from either source was terse,
and perhaps not always factual. Messages out of Germany stated
that relatives were healthy and that everything was "fine" – even
if some folk who were mentioned by name had not been heard
of lately ... Messages at times took several months to be delivered, and no doubt news out of Germany was well out of date
upon arrival.

On Sunday 3 September 1944 the fifth anniversary of the
outbreak of World War Two an intercession service was held at
the Royalty Cinema which was conducted by my father – he was
thereafter appointed to be the religious leader of the community.
His next objective was to raise enough funds to build a synagogue in the town but this project would take several years to
accomplish until sufficient funds were raised. The synagogue
was finally consecrated in 1953.

Despite living in a small town like Gatooma our school vacations never turned out to be boring for we visited friends and
when we were not challenging one another to games of marbles
we would play board games such as Snakes and Ladders, Ludo,
Draughts or Monopoly. I especially enjoyed playing Monopoly
and finally managed to talk my parents into purchasing this
game. We played it a few times but on the third or fourth
occasion my father hinted that we should change its name to
'Monotony' – for that is how he felt about it!! I took the hint and
thereafter he was happy to be left out of this game ... He did
however excel at chess but unfortunately there were few players
in town capable of challenging him.

A few fortunate friends possessed Meccano sets and we spent
hours constructing ships, cranes, aircraft and models of a similar

nature. I also enjoyed modelling with plasticine and made dozens of toy soldiers which I lined up on parade in conjunction with tanks, armoured cars and field guns courtesy of Dinky Toys ... My plasticine soldiers all sported colourful ribbons and medals on their tunics which they had "won" for bravery in the field – these awards were fashioned from discarded Black Magic chocolate wrappers! Nothing went to waste! I also possessed a small collection of pre-war motorcars – also manufactured by Dinky Toys.

The clockwork Märklin train set which we had brought with from Germany in the 'lift' was taken out its box every now and then and my father and I had fun setting up the tracks and having all three clockwork locomotives operate at the same time. There was unfortunately no space to set up the train in the house so the tracks were laid outside in the garden which prompted our cat to drape itself over the railway tracks and wait for a locomotive to plough into its midriff which always resulted in the train being derailed and the cat then moving out of the way only to eventually lie on another section of the track with the same predictable result. It was only after the cat had had its share of fun that it moved away and let us play in peace!

Most of the smaller towns managed to produce their own weekly newspapers – viz. *The Umtali Post, The Gwelo Times,* and the *Midlands Observer* (Que Que). Our local newspaper was *The Gatooma Mail,* which kept us up to date with local happenings and events. This newspaper hit the newsstands on Friday mornings and cost all of 3d (three pence) at the time.

On Christmas Day 1944, I was asked by my father to take a bottle of wine as a gift to the home of Lieutenant Barry, one of the two officers under whom he served at the Italian Internment Camp, the other being Captain Stowe, the camp commander. Lieutenant Barry and his wife lived at Pamela Flats, an apartment house situated a few streets from where we lived.

After breakfast I set off, clutching the precious bottle under my arm. Having arrived at their apartment I knocked on the door. Rat-a-tat-tat. No response. Another few knocks followed. Still no response. After knocking on their door a few more times, I decided that there was obviously no one at home and was just in the process of transferring the bottle from one hand to the other prior to setting off for home when the door suddenly burst open. This startled me to such an extent that the bottle slipped out of my hands and shattered on the concrete floor right in front of a bleary eyed, tousle haired and dressing gown attired English Lieutenant's Woman, busy rubbing the sleep from her eyes!! I don't know which one of us received the bigger shock at seeing the bottle of wine shatter at our feet whilst its crimson contents flowed out to form a large puddle amongst the broken shards of glass. Muttering an apology I fled – leaving Mrs Barry to mop up the mess!

A few days later my father presented Lieut. Barry with a replacement bottle of wine – and this time he made sure that he delivered it personally ...

Low level pass by Harvard over Gatooma airfield.
The Kaduma range of hills in the background.

Fairchild Cornell over the Rhodesian countryside.

1945

In January 1945 our class moved up to Standard Four and the age gap which separated my class mates from my own age continued to widen – I was now no less than thirteen months younger than the average age of the other pupils. At this rate I might yet evolve into a local junior edition of Dorian Gray!

John and Doris Simpson arrived in Gatooma in early 1945, John Simpson being appointed the new headmaster of Jameson School whilst his wife Doris joined the staff as an English teacher. She took an extremely keen interest in both literature and the dramatic arts and this husband and wife combination were to generate a very positive impact and wield a great deal of cultural influence on not only the school but also on the town and surrounding district. Doris Simpson played a prominent role in the resuscitation of the town's Amateur Dramatic Society, which had lain dormant during the recent war years, and she went on to produce a goodly number of drama and musical shows. The couple were extremely pro-active in many fields during their tenure at Jameson School (1945-1961) and were prominent in seeing the school develop into a fully fledged high school (1951).

Being an avid reader of the daily newspaper *The Rhodesia Herald* and with the conflict in Europe slowly but inevitably drawing to a close, I now followed the war reports with an even greater interest. I was distressed to read about new and completely foreign sounding name places – and what they represented – as they began to appear in the newspaper's war dispatch columns in the opening months of 1945. I had never previously heard or read of such places as Bergen-Belsen, Buchenwald, Auschwitz, Birkenau ... Further names such as these followed and as the ghastly realization of what the Nazis had done to European Jewry and to the citizens of occupied countries, those people that they had wished to eradicate from the face of the earth, the terrible truth sunk in. Soon photographs and magazine articles followed and the world learnt for the first time what the word "holocaust" stood for. Newsreels at the cinemas showed the harrowing and macabre scenes which made the reality of these crimes committed by the Nazis and their collaborators hit home even harder. I began to truly realize how extremely fortunate and blessed we were to have escaped these horrors by having been allowed entry into this haven called Southern Rhodesia, thus not suffering the cruel fate which befell so many others not able to escape from Germany or from any of the other countries in occupied Europe that had found themselves under the Nazi jackboot.

My heart bled for my parents, who had lost so many of their nearest and dearest relatives and friends to this horror which had dragged on for six long and terrifying years, a horror finally exposed for the whole world to see, or at least to those who wished to see and believe.

The newsreels screened at the cinemas were in due course followed by an extended and even more graphic documentary film that depicted scenes taken in these concentration and extermination camps – the piles of emaciated bodies, the gas chambers, the skeletal like survivors, many barely alive, all skin and bone and of course the camp guards, some even having the temerity to smile smugly at the cameras despite the cruelties that they had recently inflicted and the murders that they had committed. We children were quite rightly not permitted to view these films at the time but they were described to us in some detail and in later years we took the opportunity to see these films for ourselves, many of them having now been transferred onto video and thus becoming readily available to the public.

Having screened the first of these full length films depicting these atrocities, the Royalty Theatre in due course screened a further film showing scenes from other camps more recently liberated. But I could not believe my eyes when I read the *Gatooma Mail*'s newspaper advertisement appertaining to this documentary which showed further horrors and atrocities. For there, printed boldly with the title of this film were the following six words – "Even Better Than The First Film" – This advertisement must surely rank as a contender for the most tactless and insensitive advertising blurb of all time!!

During the school vacation I decided to cycle to the Umsweswe River, a distance of some twelve miles from Gatooma and situated on the main road to Bulawayo. It was my intention to picnic next to the river bank, and I therefore prepared an ample supply of sandwiches plus a large water bottle filled with Mazoe orange juice, placing them into the refrigerator overnight. The following morning I strapped these items onto the cycle's carrier situated behind the seat. I had prepared myself for an early morning departure in order to provide ample time in which to view the river and surrounds and also to cycle over the low level bridge and pay a visit to the Umsweswe Hotel situated on the other side. The following morning, shortly after sunrise, I departed and proceeded to pedal along the Gatooma to Bulawayo road leading towards the direction of the river. Traffic was sparse at that time of day and the early morning air proved most invigorating. I decided that I felt fit enough to even pedal all the way to Que Que should the mood so take me – some 45 miles distant!!

Before long I had reached the five mile peg situated near the entrance of the Italian internment camp, which signified that seven miles of pedalling still lay ahead. Everything was going to plan, and I dismounted a few times in order to quench my thirst, enjoying the taste of the cold Mazoe orange juice, a favourite drink of mine. It could be said that Mazoe Crush was considered the country's national drink, for virtually every household kept a bottle or two in stock. As often as not, when visiting friends, one was simply offered a "Mazoe" to drink – there was no need to elaborate any further. I continued to pedal along – from here on it was new territory for me, as I had never before been beyond the five mile limit on the Bulawayo road.

The strip roads were in good condition and every five minutes or so a vehicle either overtook me or headed towards me, compelling me to leave the tarmac strip and move onto the gravel surrounds. After some time I calculated that I must be fairly close to the Umsweswe River, perhaps less than half a mile or so. And suddenly, when rounding a curve in the road, and without any warning whatsoever, I came across the largest lizard I had ever seen in my life, scampering along on one of the strips and seemingly heading straight in my direction! I yelled, thinking that it was a small crocodile. At the very last second this enormous creature deviated from its course, veered off into the surrounding bush, and thankfully disappearing from sight, leaving the sound of rustling grass and a few swirling brown leaves in its wake. My heart was pounding as I hurriedly dismounted and stood on the road, wondering whether it would re-appear. Thankfully it did not!

By coincidence I had recently read the book *The Lost World* and here I was, alone in "uncharted territory" (as far as I was personally concerned) and meeting up with an unknown creature charging at me – a creature that I had never heard of nor seen before! Who knows what I may run into next??!! And where there was one "creature" there might very well be more! In the circumstances I decided that I had now cycled quite far enough, so turned around and made my way home. I even finished off my sandwiches once I had felt that I had placed a safe distance between myself and this unknown lizard that had very possibly emerged from the depths of the Umsweswe River!

That afternoon I visited the library and after a little research discovered that the giant lizard I had almost ridden into would more than likely have been a Nile water monitor, the largest of all African lizards. Found near rivers and commonly known in Southern Africa as a leguaan fully grown adults tended to reach well over six feet (two metres) in length. Judging from its size, this one had been a fully grown specimen! I also learnt that they were voracious carnivores, with powerful claws and tails. One sometimes learns – the hard way! And large ones are in fact mistaken for crocodiles!

World War Two newsreels always held my attention and when footage appeared of Japanese "kamikaze" aircraft attacking American warships off various Pacific islands such as Iwo Jima and Okinawa, I sat glued to the edge of my cinema seat and tried to imagine what it must feel like to have an enemy aircraft heading straight in one's direction, the pilot's suicidal mission being to blow up the ship and its crew, never mind himself, into fragments!! The expression "terrifying" would quite likely be an understatement.

I sat equally enthralled when footage depicting battle damaged United States Navy and Marine Corps aircraft now returning from combat missions came in to land on the heaving decks of aircraft carriers. Some of their pilots, who may well themselves have been wounded, attempted to land their crippled Hellcat and Corsair fighters and Avenger, Helldiver and Dauntless torpedo and dive bombers while often having to wrestle with damaged controls – often coming to grief when the aircraft's shot up landing gear collapsed, damaged arrestor hooks snapped and the aircraft's external fuel tanks ruptured. When events like these occurred the aircraft often slid along the deck and their external fuel tanks tended to rupture, spilling burning fuel around the wreckage. In these circumstances the pilot and crew needed to be rapidly extricated from their cockpits. Should brakes and arrestor wires fail, the stricken aircraft sometimes tended to slide over the side of the carrier and plunge into the ocean, taking trapped and injured crew members with them to a deep and watery grave.

My imagination must have literally been "carried away" after watching all those events on screen, for I thereafter devised a game based on those carrier landings – a game that, if played on weekdays, could only commence well after 5 p.m. when all shops and offices had closed their doors for the day, so as to ensure that there were very few pedestrians, or more importantly still cars, in the streets. It was important that there were only a minimal number of motor vehicles still parked in and around the town centre, especially in the vicinity of Barclay's Bank and its immediate surrounds, for this was the area that I had selected to play this newly conceived game of mine that I had dubbed "Carrier Landings". The basic requirements for playing "Carrier Landings" consisted of a pair of roller skates and a pair of look-alike aviator's goggles – the latter representing the type of goggles worn by the intrepid United States naval aviators – these were required in order to create an authentic look to the game's sole participant – myself! As all naval aviators appeared to wear flying goggles when landing their aircraft on flight decks, at least according to the newsreels that I had witnessed – these goggles were therefore necessary to set the correct tone! And as Phelps Chemist had just placed on sale similar looking goggles to those that I required, I used up a chunk of my accumulated pocket money to purchase a pair. The area chosen to play this game was along a section of pavement (sidewalk) in Edward Street which had a sloping gradient, this incline running from Phelps Chemist down to the main entrance of Barclay's Bank, the bank entrance being situated at the intersection of Edward Street and Rhodes Street, commonly known as Barclay's Bank corner.

By 5.30 p.m., with traffic pretty much thinned out, I was usually ready to embark on my game, which commenced on the pavement adjoining Phelps Chemist. Strapping on the roller skates and donning the goggles I was ready to bring my "Avenger" or whatever aircraft I had chosen to "fly" that day down to a "safe landing" on the "deck" of the "aircraft carrier", whose dimensions I had chalked out earlier on the Rhodes Street pavement running parallel with the bank building. One tended to pick up a fair amount of speed skating down the Edward Street incline and on reaching the Barclays Bank corner the game required the roller skating "pilot" to veer off sharply to the left in order to remain on the sidewalk which now ran parallel with Rhodes Street. One needed to come to a halt within a few seconds of having hit the Rhodes Street sidewalk, for the concrete terminated and was transformed into a gravel one. Coming to a halt on the remaining section of concrete pavement would complete a successful "carrier landing". But if one skated down the incline too fast, it became somewhat difficult to negotiate the corner successfully and remain on the sidewalk so the tendency on those occasions, after running out of paving, was to either overshoot and land up in some gravel at the end of the pavement or else to fly off the edge of the sidewalk and land up in the middle of Rhodes Street, sometimes on one's backside, if control of the situation was lost. Such mishaps would then constitute a "crash landing" and were deemed to be the equivalent of an aircraft skidding over the side of an aircraft carrier and into the ocean. I set myself a target of some dozen or so landings during each session of the game and gradually gained experience after a few spills and tumbles, which usually resulted in grazed hands, arms or knees. Eventually I learned to negotiate the corner successfully, thus bringing the majority of my "landings" to a safe conclusion. However, unexpected "crashes" could and did happen from time to time as they are wont to do.

This game had been played by me for several weeks until a "crash landing" just happened to coincide with the sudden and completely unseen and unexpected arrival of a motor vehicle. A loud and torturous squeal of brakes signalled the appearance of an automobile travelling along Rhodes Street whose very startled driver fortunately managed to avoid running right over me in an area that was (during working hours) the busiest intersection in town, but in the late afternoon was usually deserted. Well, that had been my assumption, but as I discovered that afternoon, assumptions can go horribly wrong ...

Having picked up a little more speed than usual whilst skating down the Edward Street incline I realized it was vital to slow down and veer sharp left in order to remain on the pavement, but quite likely I underestimated the rapidity that I was travelling at and on turning the corner I may possibly have also tripped, because I failed to negotiate the corner, toppled off the curb and careened into Rhodes Street, landing up in a heap in the centre of the road and almost into the path of an approaching car! Not a very smart manoeuvre at that particular moment of time!

A fair amount of verbal abuse (and not unwarranted either) was flung in my direction by a very shaken and annoyed driver who had only just managed to bring his car to an abrupt halt. In my dazed state the squeal of the car brakes kept reverberating in my ears. For if he would have failed to pull up in time he might very well have driven right over me, for I was lying spread-eagled in his path. I therefore endured his angry words which he flung in my direction from behind his steering wheel, for I knew only too well that he was totally in the right, and that this crazy game could very well have ended up with me under the wheels of a passing motor vehicle, which had in fact almost just been the case. Finally, still shaking his fist at me, he continued on his way. I decided there and then to abandon my carrier landing game – one consolation arising from this near mishap had been that my goggles had remained in place during the entire incident and the chances were that the driver had not recognized me, so could not notify my parents of their son's mad escapades. And the other consolation was that I was still, thankfully, alive! Although

I had tried to incorporate as much excitement into this game as I could manage, I now came to the reluctant conclusion that this so-called "game" had almost become as dangerous as the real thing that I had been trying to imitate! It was definitely time to call a halt to any further carrier deck landings ...

Singing lessons were introduced at school by Doris Simpson and once a week we sang stirring and inspirational songs such as "Hearts of Oak", "There'll Always be an England", "The Grand Old Duke of York" and "Rose of England". We partook in physical training exercises a few times a week on the school sports field, prior to the commencement of daily lessons, and once a year the Ministry of Health sent down a team of nurses from Salisbury to give all the pupils a thorough physical checkup. Jameson School's General Purpose Fees, which included all educational expenses, textbooks and exercise books, sports equipment and other related items cost our parents just two shillings and sixpence (twenty five cents) per term (semester) which meant that the annual cost of school fees amounted to the princely sum of seven shillings and sixpence per annum (the approximate equivalent of one United States dollar in 1945 terms). This must surely equate to the bargain of all time!

The Woodrow family had in the meantime left Gatooma and the adjoining residence was now occupied by Mr and Mrs Collins and their two children Patricia and Michael. They had arrived in Rhodesia after having been evacuated from the British Colony of Ceylon (now Sri Lanka) a year or so earlier, the island having been subjected to threats of a Japanese invasion on a number of occasions. Patricia was placed into my class at school and Michael, who was a few years younger, was placed a few classes below. We often walked to school together and Patricia later proceeded to Girls High School in Salisbury to complete her education, the same year that I set off for Prince Edward School.

World War Two came to an end amongst much rejoicing. Firstly the war in Europe ended and V-E Day was declared on 8 May 1945 and the war in the Pacific ended three months later when on 14 August 1945 V-J Day was declared after Japan surrendered, following the dropping of the two atomic bombs.

At the time I could hardly have imagined that, thirty-six years later, we were to personally host, at our home in Gatooma, the official RAF observer (Group Captain Leonard Cheshire, VC) who was flying high in the sky above Nagasaki that fateful day when Boeing B-29 Superfortress "Bockscar" dropped the atom bomb over that city, thus convincing the Japanese government that surrender was the only sensible option.

Joy reigned supreme now that the war was finally over. Union Jack flags and bunting were raised on all available flagpoles countrywide. Religious services, Victory Parades and various celebrations were held nationwide, and hotels staged Victory Dances which were well patronised despite the acute shortage of younger men available as dance partners! It was indeed a time for great jubilation.

To celebrate the end of the war an air display was staged by the Royal Air Force at the Gatooma airfield and that was when I saw my first genuine WW II fighter – a Hawker Hurricane, which flew down from its base at Thornhill (Gwelo). This machine turned out to be the first and only WW II fighter aircraft ever to land at the Gatooma airfield. We clustered around the aircraft and viewed it with great awe – a real live fighter aircraft! The Hurricane gave a marvellous display of aerobatics and low level fly pasts and the highlight of its all too brief visit was a mock dog-fight between this veteran fighter and a Harvard trainer. The Hurricane, hero of the Battle of Britain, although largely rendered obsolete at war's end by a newer generation of fighter aircraft, nevertheless outclassed the much slower Harvard in an exciting display. A large crowd witnessed the air show which also featured a number of other military aircraft but no one I have spoken to in later years seemed to recall that this special event had ever taken place ...!

Following the end of hostilities a number of surplus RAF Tiger Moths were advertised for sale in the national press. If my memory serves me correctly the Rhodesian Air Training Group invited the public to submit tenders for airworthy aircraft but I also recall that war weary Tiger Moths, with most of their instruments removed, were advertised for sale at £25 apiece – a real bargain by any standards.

I begged my father to purchase one of these aircraft for me but even I could see his point when he explained that there was insufficient space in our cramped little backyard to store a Tiger Moth, as small as the aircraft might be! It was also difficult to envisage my mother giving her approval to have three fruit bearing paw-paw trees, in addition to a couple of mango trees, demolished to make space available for an old biplane that would never fly again! I also appreciated that without providing adequate shelter, a fabric covered aircraft would not have survived if left out in the open to face the elements. I therefore wisely dropped my request without any further ado ...

Flying training had virtually ceased by this stage and so my visits to the airfield became somewhat fewer. The last few years had been some of the most exhilarating ones of my young life, but all good things eventually come to an end ... there were now other pursuits to follow.

Despite the war now being over – in Europe at least, and with the atrocities committed by the Nazis against the Jews out in the open for all to see, pockets of anti-Semitism nevertheless still continued to rear its ugly head in Rhodesia. The following letter, dated 8 June 1945 was written by my father on behalf of the Jewish soldiers serving at No. 3 Internment Camp, Gatooma in response to a letter printed in the *Rhodesia Herald* of the same date:

The Commandant,
8 June 1945
No. 3 Internment Camp, Gatooma
Sir,

We, the undersigned members of The Southern Rhodesian Internment Camp Corps stationed at No. 3 Internment Camp, Gatooma, beg to draw your attention to attached letter to The Editor of the *Rhodesia Herald,* dated 8 June 1945, by Mr Chas. Olley.

The undersigned consider themselves to be refugees which Mr Olley is styling as "runaways" who "slipped" into this country for "fear of their lives". We, like all refugees, and which action gives that word its true meaning, left Germany and Austria on account of Hitler's persecution of Jews and non-Nazis. Everybody who had the chance to get away from persecution and the well known atrocities would have acted in the same way.

At the outbreak of the war the great majority of the refugees volunteered for Active Service inside and outside the Colony. They were not accepted on account of their

nationality. Repeated offers were rejected for the same reason. Not until the Internment Corps was established were they approached to volunteer again. A great number
did so and were accepted. Mr Olley is alleging that all those who did join, did only so as
a means to a livelihood. The record of all those concerned shows clearly that Mr
Olley's allegation is completely untrue.

We, the undersigned members of the Internment Camp Corps, who have sworn
allegiance to his Majesty the King, and are members of the Armed Forces of the Colony,
consider Mr Olley's statement as an utter insult against which we protest.

We, therefore, beg to ask you, Sir to draw the attention of the authorities to this
state of affairs with the aim of having our honour restored.

We have the honour to be, Sir,

Your obedient Servants,

We, the undersigned members of the S.R.I.C.C. stationed at No. 3 Internment Camp,
Gatooma, express our full agreement with the above statement and join in the protest
against Mr Olley's insult to our comrades.

The above letter was in turn forwarded by Camp Commandant
Major Bowles to Colonel Hamilton, Director of Internment
Camps, who replied that he had referred the matter to the
Minister of Justice of Southern Rhodesia and that the text of the
Minister's reply amounted to the following comments:

The Minister is of the opinion that unique importance is being attached by Friendly
Aliens to the statement of Mr Olley.

Further, it is thought that no useful purpose would be served by combating the
views of Mr Olley in the press, and that to do so would merely give Mr Olley added
opportunity to air his views, which are not shared by the Government; the Minister has
already said so and has paid tribute to the services rendered by aliens in the
Internment Camp Corps. The Minister will probably see the signatories to the protests
forwarded to you during his forthcoming visits to the Camps.

As far as I know that is where the above matter ended but what
is known is that the notorious Chas Olley continued to spew out
his vitriolic anti-Semitic comments. In the end one learned to live
with that type of garbage.

I remember asking my parents what sort of stories and news
items would be published by newspapers in the future, seeing
that the war was now over. For war news had seemingly dominated the majority of pages of every newspaper that I had ever read
(except of course the *Gatooma Mail*) and I simply could not
envisage page after page of "non-war" news from now on. "Don't

be concerned", I was reassured, "there will be plenty of other news that will appear and will hopefully be worth reading". And so it proved!

Having become quite friendly with cinema proprietor Joe Burke through being in his company during evening film shows, he invited me to accompany him and his eldest son, Roland, a few years older than I, for a Sunday's fishing at the nearby Pasi Dam. This dam was the source of the town's water supply, some ten miles distant. I readily accepted, having never fished before, and my parents raised no objection in letting me accompany them for the morning's outing.

The Sunday in question arrived as did Joe Burke – I was collected as arranged and we set off in his grey 1941 Mercury, fishing rods poking out of the rear windows of the sedan. We travelled along the familiar strip road to Eiffel Flats, then turned right and followed the narrow gravel road that led to the dam, trailing clouds of dust behind us in the process. In my mind I had somehow expected to find a sleek cabin cruiser moored along- side a jetty waiting for us, but upon arrival discovered that there was neither jetty nor cabin cruiser – all that I found was a very small and weathered looking rowing boat tethered to a tree stump at the water's edge.

Not exactly what I had expected – and as I had been warned that the dam was inhabited by crocodiles – virtually all of Rhodesia's waterways were – I wondered whether this fishing expedition was really such a good idea after all. But I reckoned it was a little late at that stage to show my reservations, and, as I waded through the muddy water leading to the boat, I kept a sharp eye open for a protruding snout or two!

After clambering aboard and settling myself on the hard wooden plank that served as a seat, we cast off and rowed slowly and laboriously to the far side of the dam where the fishing was reputed to be good. Well, that might have been the case on some days but on this particular Sunday morning the fish must have decided to take the day off ...

After an hour or so had gone by in the hot sun and without anyone registering even a single nibble, let alone bite, I began to feel thoroughly bored when suddenly Roland, without any warn- ing, leapt up and cried out that he had hooked something.

Unfortunately he appeared completely oblivious of the fact that he happened to be in a small and vulnerable rowing boat and upon jumping up and reeling in whatever he thought that he might have caught he almost lost his balance. Lunging forward, his father only just managed to stop Roland from falling overboard. The boat rocked alarmingly, we wore no life jackets (did anyone wear life jackets in Rhodesia in those days?)! Thankfully however, apart from shipping a fair amount of water, the boat remained afloat. We then discovered that the packets of sandwiches which we had taken along for our lunch were now floating, completely sodden, in a pool of scummy water at the bottom of the boat. So these were tossed overboard to be consumed by the fish. We must have been the only crew on a boat that morning feeding fish instead of catching them! Losing our sandwiches put paid to any idea of "lunch aboard ship"! Half an hour later we had still caught nothing so agreed to call it a day and disconcertedly rowed back to shore. Following this introduction to fishing it took me a very long time, in fact no less than fifty years, until I ever went fishing again!

Sadly, Roland Burke drowned a few years later when, trapped on one side of a river by rising floodwaters and, much against the advice of his companions, he nevertheless attempted to cross a swollen river on his own. His body was recovered some days later.

One weekday evening, returning after my jaunt on the pavement outside the cinema in Joe Burke's company, having watched the usual newsreels and supporting programme, I crossed the road, closing the garden gate behind me. Whilst walking up the short concrete path that led from the gate to our front steps, I experienced the odd sensation of treading on a distinctly slippery surface. Every time I placed my foot on the ground a sort of squelching and crunching sound could be heard. I looked down in the semi-dark and could not quite believe what I was seeing – the pathway appeared alive with what looked like thousands of spiders, all busy crossing from one side of the garden to the other! I ran into the house, collected a torch and shone the beam onto the scene in the garden. The place was alive with spiders, there appeared to be hundreds of thousands of them! The next morning, upon examining the scene in daylight, I noticed a few crushed limbs and bodies which I must have stepped on, otherwise there was not a spider to be seen. This confirmed my experience had not been a figment of my imagination – the crushed spiders proved I had indeed stepped on something! I found out later that what I had seen were in most probability migrating rain spiders – said to be an extremely rare sight and one that I never encountered again.

During one school vacation my friend Jimmy Clarke and I were walking through town when we spotted a handbag lying on the side of the road. On opening it we found that it contained a fair sum of money in addition to a bunch of keys and other items, so off we set off to the police station to hand the bag in. The desk sergeant was fairly busy and kept us waiting a considerable time before finally giving us his attention. He went through the contents of the handbag and we were informed that the handbag belonged to a Mrs Green, the elderly wife of a well to do local miner. Her husband owned a prosperous gold mine in the vicinity of Golden Valley, a rich mining area situated some 12 miles north of our town.

The sergeant commended us for showing honesty in bringing the bag along to the police charge office when, at that very moment, in walked Mrs Green to report her missing handbag. The relief on her face was obvious when the sergeant handed her the handbag, but she simply grunted when he informed her that Jimmy and I had found her bag. He then recommended, in no uncertain terms, that in his opinion we both deserved a nice little reward for our honesty. She muttered something under her breath, delved into her handbag and eventually pulled out her purse, spending a considerable time fiddling around in it. Jimmy and I had visions of a reward which would, with luck, enable us to purchase a month's supply of comics and perhaps even have enough left over to buy a cinema ticket or two ...

Eventually Mrs Green produced two tiny "tickey" coins worth, in today's currency, approximately two and a half cents per coin, which she then very "graciously" handed over to us! We stood there flabbergasted, as Jimmy, the police sergeant and I simply could not believe a person could be so mean to two youngsters who had taken the effort to walk all the way to the police station to hand in her lost bag, contents intact. And whilst we all stood there not quite believing our eyes, she turned around, walked down the steps to her car parked outside the charge office and drove off! Not even a word of thanks from her! She was thereafter dubbed "Tickey" Green by my family! I realized there and then that honesty may very well be the best policy, but that it may not always prove to be particularly rewarding from the financial point of view ...

Night Must Fall, playwright Emlyn Williams' suspenseful and somewhat sinister thriller, was produced by the newly resuscitated Gatooma Musical & Dramatic Society in 1945. This was the first stage production I had attended, discounting the opera performed by the Italians in the internment camp. This nerve-tingling play about a psychotic killer was performed on stage at the Women's Institute Hall and Doris Simpson, our English class teacher, encouraged her pupils to attend.

In today's world, this production may well have been given an age restriction and would not have been recommended for 10 year old children to cut their teeth on, what with a crazed axe wielding killer on stage, carrying his victim's (thankfully unseen) severed head around with him in a hat box! *Night Must Fall* nevertheless left a lasting impression on me and in later years I became an avid theatre goer.

From the time we moved into the Newton Street house we always kept a pet — and it always turned out to be a cat, and no more than one at a time. My father loved cats and when they eventually died of natural causes — in the process usually surviving to a pampered old age, they were replaced almost immediately with a new kitten. Most cats seemed to be named "Moolly" (pronounced as in "woolly") and they came in all colours — white, black, grey, ginger or combinations thereof. All of these cats were loved by our family and all slept well, ate well and very seldom went AWOL, as many cats often do. All reported to the dining room at meal times on a regular basis and were usually well rewarded for their efforts! None of these cats were ever allowed to sit or lie on the furniture or beds, although a few tried their luck but never got very far, at least not when my mother spotted them!

To say that the Sternberg cats lived long, contented and stress-free lives could well be termed an understatement ...

That year cap guns were all the rage and those lucky enough to own one often played endless games of "cops and robbers" or "cowboys and Indians" – spurred on no doubt by the odd cowboy movie seen at Saturday afternoon matinees! These cap guns were in fact very realistically modelled on the genuine article and could almost pass for a revolver, although they were all somewhat reduced in size to fit 10 to 12 year old hand sizes. They even sounded like real guns when the little dot of gunpowder contained in the cap detonated, producing a loud enough bang to be heard some distance away.

We must have driven a number of adults crazy by our protracted "gun battles" whether on the street or in our gardens and these gun fights were great fun while they lasted. Eventually we outgrew them and peace once more descended on our neighbourhood! Replacing my cap gun in due course was a B.S.A. pellet gun which fired smallish pellets and made far less noise in the process. This gun was purchased from a local gun shop – and neither licence nor gun permit were required! I rigged up cardboard targets which I pinned to trees and went on to have shooting competitions with friends from time to time.

Most churches throughout the country staged annual fundraising fetes at their respective church grounds and the various denominations located in Gatooma proved to be no exception. These fetes were prominently advertised several weeks ahead in the local newspaper, in shop windows and on posters nailed to or tied to trees. They always attracted a sizeable attendance. Members of various denominations attended each others' fetes and many bargains could be secured at the second hand stalls. For a number of years I regularly visited the Anglican (Church of England) fete staged in the grounds directly behind our house and joined in the fun – lining up for donkey and pony rides and rummaging through the used books and magazine stands to pick up bargains. My spending was of course limited by the pocket money I had available but most items were very reasonably priced and I usually landed up with something to take home and read! One year the thought crossed my mind of purchasing a pony – yes, there were ponies for sale on one occasion at the Anglican Church fete. However, stabling one in our back yard would have been even more of a problem than storing a Tiger

Moth, so I never even bothered to bring up the subject with my parents, for I knew exactly what their answer would be ...

The Anglican Church fete however seemed a very genteel event in comparison to the fetes organized by the Dutch Reformed Kerk (Church), for these always turned out to be far more entertaining. Their fetes were exceptionally well supported, as there was a large Afrikaans farming community within our district – whose wives never failed to bring in mountains of food to sell, including carcasses of recently slaughtered oxen and sheep. Fires were lit and by mid-afternoon the aroma of roast meat pervaded the entire area as these animals were barbecued to perfection under the expert guidance of several "chefs". By this time smoke billowed from various braaivleis (barbecue) pits from where large cuts of roast meat were sold, together with generous helpings of sadza (cooked maize meal). Meat and sadza were heaped onto a large plate, followed by a delicious tomato flavoured gravy which was then poured over the food. It was quite mouth watering!! There was also a choice of steaks, mutton, chicken, beef and boerewors (beef sausages) on offer. After having consumed a good size helping of expertly barbequed beef and a generous portion of sadza and gravy one had the feeling that no further meals need possibly be eaten for the next couple of days ahead!

But meat was not all that was available in the food chain – not by a long chalk! The wives had cooked delicious koeksusters (a platted doughnut-like dough dipped in syrup) and melktert (a variety of custard tart) both of which were scrumptious and quite irresistible. Packets of homemade boerebiskuit (rusks) were also available and these likewise proved extremely popular and together with the above items were soon sold out.

The place hummed with activity – the men and older boys played various games in competition with each other – Afrikaans games such as bokbok, jukskei and the ever popular tug of war, the latter always drawing crowds of supporters who cheered on their respective teams. And almost everyone joined in the "volkspele" – traditional folk dancing to the tune of lively boeremusiek – Afrikaans music generally played on accordions by a small band.

Many of the children from these Afrikaans families participated in these annual fetes and those who competed in the various sporting events and dancing displays were often fellow pupils from Jameson School. In several instances, especially in the case of the girls, it was difficult to recognize some of them at first glance. For from being dressed in a blue school uniform whilst attending school, most of them were now garbed in traditional long flowing skirts, long sleeved blouses and a bonnet.

It appeared that most of the Johanna-s, Jacoba-s, Katrina-s, Marie-s and Wilhelmina-s that I knew from daily contact at school had undergone a metamorphosis of sorts and had somehow, in their now unfamiliar garb, been transplanted back to the days of their parents and grandparents. Dressed in this way, some of these girls appeared to give the distinct appearance of belonging to a bygone era, so that instead of expecting them to be driven back to their farms in their parents' cars after the fete was over, one expected them to clamber up and on to old wagons headed by spans of oxen who, under the lash of a whip, would then proceed to pull the creaking wagons along a rutted path and back to their candle-lit homesteads out in the African bush ... And not at all surprisingly, by going back in time by even a scant thirty-five or so years, this is probably how the above scenario would have played itself out!

Dutch Reform Church fetes had a great rural atmosphere about them – certainly the ones I attended in those years. Bales of straw and hay were scattered around for people to sit on. Because most of the church members were farmers and miners, their mode of transport consisted largely of vanettes (light trucks) of various vintages – the most popular makes being Fords, Dodges and Chevrolets. These vehicles were parked in the grounds or on the road (appropriately named Kerk Street) outside the church grounds. There were also horses tethered under the shade of surrounding trees which likewise provided the feeling of being out in the countryside. Attending the Dutch Reformed Church fetes was always an experience for town based kids and an annual event that many of us supported year after year.

G.S. Fitt & Co. had for years been the town's sole travel agent. Situated in Rhodes Street, the business also consisted of a stationery shop and bookshop, but as they stocked only a small selection of comics, I tended to patronise this shop far less than I did the Gatooma Mail bookshop. However, my parents always purchased the *Rhodesian Annual* from Fitt & Co. in December of each year, a quality magazine that has since become a collector's item. But whenever I did enter the shop I always stopped to admire the professionally constructed and exquisitely built ultra large scale model of a Union Castle passenger liner on display. It was constructed in metal by a leading firm of model craftsmen in Britain and was one of a number of scale model passenger liners distributed to their leading agents by the Union Castle Steamship Company, in order to garner publicity. This intricate model was housed in a large glass cabinet and was admired by many. I no longer recall the name of the ship but the model appeared to have been of a Union Castle liner of the early 1930s or thereabouts — it might have been a scale model of the *Dunbar Castle* or the *Dunvegan Castle*, but I can no longer be sure. When the Union Castle Line later terminated its passenger services between South Africa and the United Kingdom, this outstanding model was taken away. I wonder where it is housed today?

At some stage during the year my parents asked me whether I would like to spend some time in the Vumba Mountains once again as there appeared to be little chance of a vacation for the family in the immediate future, due to my father's current military commitment. Having of course been there two years earlier and having enjoyed the experience, I readily agreed to their kind offer.

However, it was suggested that on this occasion I should spend a full school term (three months) in the Vumba mountains situated in the Eastern Districts and attend lessons at the Vumba Heights school, which was in close proximity to the hostel. Apart from running a holiday/convalescent home, this organization also administered a small school that catered for children who required a fairly lengthy vacation to recuperate after having suffered an illness or trauma. I happened to be in the process of recovering from a bout of chicken pox, so this may well have prompted my parents to come up with the idea that a change of climate and scenery would be an ideal opportunity for me to get over the effects of the illness.

And so, on Friday 21 September 1945 I found myself once again standing on the platform of the Umtali railway station. Together with other pupils I was driven up the mountain road in the same old bus to await a familiar and comfortable bed in the dormitory, and meet up with the same friendly members of staff who had been there on my previous visit.

School lessons were most relaxed, and I was happy to be informed that there would be no homework involved during the entire term! In its place we were expected to have an hour's rest on our beds after lunch, thereafter being taken on a walk through the forest surrounding the school grounds, breathing in the invigorating mountain air. On our return we were greeted with tea, cakes and scones in the dining room, followed thereafter by games on the lawn. I felt that it was indeed a shame that all schools did not adopt this attitude to education – what fun it would have been to attend schools of this nature throughout one's entire school career!

The school itself consisted of only two classrooms, to which a small office was attached. Staffed by two lady teachers, they were required to supervise and teach the entire complement of children, who were aged approximately from seven to twelve. The 7 to 9 age group were accommodated in one of the classrooms whilst the 10 to 12 year age group occupied the other. From time to time a few of the older pupils were called in to assist the teachers with the reading of stories and I thoroughly enjoyed reading to the younger children when called upon to do so. Academic pressure on pupils was almost non-existent and after three months of this very "laid-back" schooling I returned

Judy in swimming pool with Mum

home to Gatooma with the prospect of now having to face the end-of-year six-week school vacation which loomed up to greet me! Sheer bliss!! Virtual retirement before reaching the age of 11!

The six-week vacation sped by swiftly, the town's newly constructed municipal swimming pool no doubt contributing to that fact. Half of Gatooma's population flocked to the pool to try out their swimming skills and attempt to keep cool during the summer heat! Lawns, trees and flower beds had been planted and neatly laid out and in due course an open air tearoom was established in the grounds. This too was filled to capacity by eager patrons over most weekends. A small and separate "toddler's pool" had also been built and this is where Judy first learnt to swim, as did the majority of the town's other young children.

However, towards the end of 1945 and shortly before I was due to return home from Vumba Heights, my parents moved house from Newton Street to a larger residence situated in Smith Street, just south of the railway line. The grounds boasted a large garden which contained many well-established fruit trees. Although the move had been expected for some time, I was most upset to discover on my return that my mother had taken the opportunity, when moving house, to dispose of my entire collection of pre-war automobile brochures and catalogues and wartime American and British comic books, a collection which I had built up over the years, and which I treasured. In later years I realized that many mothers tend to go into a "spring-clean" mode when moving house, and often cannot resist taking the opportunity of disposing of, what in their eyes, consisted of nothing more than accumulated "junk" ‒ especially such items as well read comics, magazines and car brochures. However, it is a mode that I totally disagree with, especially if one's much loved possessions are "binned" in this process ... What may well amount to "junk" in a mother's eyes may amount to a "valuable" and much loved collection in the eyes of the collector ‒ usually her own child!! I have since discovered that I am but one of many children who have undergone experiences of this nature and am well aware that my own particular case is far from being unique!

Having now moved house from Newton Street to Smith Street, it meant that my evening visits to the Royalty Theatre were terminated, for our new home was situated quite some distance away from the old "bioscope". As the saying goes, "all good things eventually come to an end". I certainly could not complain, for I had managed to amass almost five years of complimentary cinema viewing. As a now ten year old, I had been on a very good wicket indeed!! And to this day I am still grateful for the freedom that was granted to me by my parents to one so young.

1946

The year 1946 arrived and with it the realization that this year was scheduled to be my final year at junior school and also at Jameson. Our class had now moved up to Standard 5 and once more I was trailing way behind in age ...

Refreshed after my three-month stay in the Vumba Mountains plus the additional benefit of the six-week school vacation, I was happy to be back studying at a "real" school once again. This time, with the added knowledge that I required a decent pass rate in my final junior school year in order to be accepted at the high school of my choice, namely Prince Edward Boys High School, the largest boys high school in Salisbury and, for that matter, the largest in the entire country.

In 1946, the Rhodesian Education Department, instead of increasing Jameson School's academic standard to that of a fully fledged high school, had created what was then known as an "upper top" education level system. This meant that those pupils intending to further their education in order to attain university entrance level, were now compelled to transfer from schools such as Jameson on completion of the Standard 5 year. They transferred to high schools situated in the four larger cities and towns, namely Salisbury, Bulawayo, Gwelo and Umtali, in addition to Plumtree Boys High School, near the small town of Plumtree, close to the Bechuanaland (now Botswana) border. Pupils who chose to remain at Jameson and similar schools would be expected to write the Rhodesian School Leaving Certificate examination at the completion of Form 3 (the equivalent of which would have been Standard 8) and then would be expected to leave school. Jameson School was finally elevated to the full status of high school in 1951, in which year official figures confirmed that Jameson was by then the fastest growing school in the entire country.

My last year at Jameson proved to be an enjoyable and busy one but for the football incident, of which more later. Our class teacher was a Miss Spark, who, rumour had it, had once been a nun. She turned out to be an excellent teacher who got on well with her pupils. Mrs Simpson continued to take us for English lessons and she also taught us the rudiments of dramatic art, which she was passionate about. During the last term of the year she produced a one act play at the school, the title of which I have long since forgotten, and I was chosen to take the lead role. We performed on a very small stage erected on the concourse in front of the school office. The production went off well but all I recollect was that the cast were warned to remain on centre stage in order not to fall off the edge, for there was an acute shortage of available timber to construct a large enough stage area! Thank goodness we all managed to avoid falling off but it would not have surprised me if many in the audience were secretly hoping that some cast members would have done just that!

During an English class one morning Doris Simpson read us a ghost story. It was the tale of two men who were sitting in a small hut perched on stilts in some Asian paddy field. It was a moonless night, and they saw a horrific ghost-like creature crawling towards them with evil intent! This story sent shivers down our spines – but to this day I have not been able to trace either the title of this chilling tale nor the name of its author.

I was given a Kodak Box Brownie camera on my eleventh birthday, together with several rolls of black and white film. Thrilled, I spent the next few weeks photographing locomotives at the railway station, aircraft at the airfield and eventually even got around to taking photographs of my family! One day I was told that a serious car accident had occurred a few miles from Gatooma on the road to Bulawayo, so I leapt on to my bicycle and headed out in that direction. I located the damaged car, a 1939 Mercury, on the side of the road. It was owned by an employee of the Mines Office in Gatooma. Apparently no other vehicle had been involved.

The driver of the car had been killed behind the wheel and the police and ambulance had already been to collect the body. All that remained was a large bloodstain on the front seat so I whipped out my Brownie and took a photograph of the blood soaked seat through the open door! Shortly thereafter a tow truck came and towed the damaged car away. Events such as these turned out to be, thank goodness, a rare occurrence in our neck of the woods!

Mr David Livingstone now joined the staff as deputy headmaster and his wife, Gwen, likewise joined the teaching staff. They made a most conspicuous couple – he was at least six feet tall and thin as a reed whilst his wife was somewhat plumpish and barely reached five feet – and then probably only in high heels! When the two stood next to each other their height discrepancy proved very noticeable! They were parents to two small daughters – twins, both of whom were blessed with bright carrot red hair and when out walking together, this was one family one could not fail to notice!

Besides his teaching duties, David Livingstone also coached the school's senior football (soccer) teams and one day, during the mid-morning "tea break" a few of us happened to be kicking a ball around on the football pitch. I was standing in goal and warding off balls kicked in my direction. It so happened that David Livingstone was crossing the field at that particular moment and I suppose, on a whim, decided to join in the fun. He managed to intercept a pass between two of the boys and then, very much in control of the situation, he dribbled the ball closer to the goal posts. I was convinced that he intended to kick the ball right past me and straight into the net, thus easily outwitting his 11 year old "adversary" in goal, for he was by now close enough to score with impunity. Instead, David Livingstone kicked the ball with all his might and it rocketed straight towards my head!

Instead of using common sense and leaping out of the way of this leather missile flying in my direction and looking to take my head off, I foolishly reacted by putting out my hands in an attempt to intercept the ball. This was a dumb decision to take, although I must admit everything seemed to happen in a split second and there was simply no time to think logically. For at no stage had I expected him to kick the ball at me from such a short distance, and certainly not with the force that he put into it. The ball struck my left hand and CRACK – my wrist bent backwards with the full impact!! A searing pain shot through from the wrist right up into my shoulder and all I could do was stand there and clutch my arm in agony!

I was immediately walked by friends to the local hospital, conveniently situated just across the road from the school playing fields. The doctor on duty took an immediate X-ray and confirmed that some bones in my wrist had been splintered but fortunately not broken. My wrist and arm were thereafter placed in a Plaster of Paris cast. And that for me was the end of any further sporting activities for some months to come.

Fully concentrating on schoolwork without any sporting or other distractions obviously paid off, and in a class of thirty-one pupils I managed to come first in class in the second (middle) term mid-year examinations.

We had been subscribing to *LIFE* magazine for a number of years and my parents decided to also subscribe to another American publication, namely the *Aufbau* fortnightly newspaper. Although published in New York, the paper was printed in the German language, having been founded in 1934 by refugees from Nazi Germany who had been fortunate enough to find refuge in America. The object of this newspaper was to publish articles that would be of assistance to fellow refugees, in a language which they could readily read and understand, in order to help them find employment. Also to find their bearings in the "New World" of America that they had escaped to and which was both environmentally and culturally different to the one that they had recently left behind in difficult circumstances.

The German word "aufbau" literally means "to build", "to construct" and "to assemble" and this newspaper no doubt well fulfilled its purpose. And never more so than in those traumatic post-war years following World War Two when countless Holocaust survivors, plus those fortunate enough to have been able to exit the shores of Europe prior to the outbreak of the war were all now desperately trying to locate each other again after six years of war. Millions of people were trying to garner information on missing relatives and friends, not knowing whether these folk were dead or alive. Very few Jewish families could claim that they had not been affected by the immense havoc the war had caused, and tracing missing people now became a major priority in the lives of most families.

The pages of *Aufbau* were filled with "Missing Persons" and "Seeking Relatives and Friends" columns, all attempting to trace information on missing men, women and children. Not only had individual families been exterminated but whole communities, villages and in some cases even towns had been wiped off the map by the Nazis. Any scraps of information appertaining to family members and friends, whether they might be dead or alive, were now being desperately sought by people from all around the globe. My parents inserted a number of advertisements over several months and spent countless hours scanning the pages, month after month for a year or more but to no avail, and as time went by their hopes of ever finding traces of missing family members gradually diminished.

Time allowing, we listened to the daily radio broadcasts from the Salisbury studios of the Southern Rhodesia Broadcasting Corporation − to the news, the radio plays and to some of the musical programmes which were on offer. Although transmission times consisted of only a few hours during the day (10.00 a.m. to 2.00 p.m.) these were followed by a further transmission. Those listeners who had hoped to tune in until late would have been disappointed, for by 10.00 p.m. the station shut down for the night!

A very popular institution was the Rhodesian State Lottery and for 10/- (ten shillings) one could purchase a ticket to one's dreams. The draw was held on average four times a year in the State Lotteries Hall in Salisbury and on these occasions the public filled the hall to capacity in order to observe six revolving metal drums spill out the winning digits. The winning ticket numbers were then announced, together with the ticket holder's nom-de-plume (I.e. "Beginner's Luck", "Lucky Fred", "New Car" etc.) − names having been chosen by the ticket holder, followed in turn by the name of the town where the ticket holder resided (all information gleaned from the ticket stubs). This information would be published the following day in the two major newspapers (*The Rhodesia Herald* and the *Bulawayo Chronicle*) and newspaper sales were invariably brisk the day following the draw! In later years the lottery draw was broadcast on the wireless (radio) and whilst the draw was in the process of being conducted many people throughout the country stopped any activity that they were engaged in at that particular moment in order to gather around the nearest radio, all no doubt fervently hoping that good fortune was finally about to head their way! As a rule of luck it did nothing of the kind but that never deterred punters from purchasing further tickets for the very next draw!

Founded in 1935, the cost of a Rhodesian State Lottery ticket remained at a very reasonable ten shillings for very many years, as did the magnificent first prize of £10,000 (ten thousand pounds). Although it was naturally everyone's dream to win first prize, there were however another 42 monetary prizes to be won plus another 153 consolation prizes in each draw. Lotteries were banned in South Africa (and would continue to be for very many years to come). This ruling therefore prompted many residents of that country to purchase tickets in the Rhodesian State Lottery. Judging from the number of prizes drawn that went "Down South", as South Africa was referred to at the time, an awful lot of South African money must have found its way into the coffers of the Rhodesian State Lottery year after year! I personally knew two Rhodesian couples who had won the coveted first prize, and my parents once won a thousand pounds in the early 1950s which somewhat helped to boost our individual Post Office Savings Bank balances – the winnings being earmarked for a future overseas vacation! A high percentage of funds generated by ticket sales went towards good causes and the State Lotteries supported many worthwhile charities over many years.

My little sister Judy was growing up fast and she kept on bombarding us with an incessant number of questions – why this, why that, what is this, what is that?? We fielded all her questions as best we could and her keen and enquiring mind never seemed to let up. This was great – but when she tried to tag along with me to the cinema, whenever she found out I was going to meet my friends there, I felt the line had to be drawn somewhere! After all, what eleven year old boy would want his four year old sister to accompany him on these occasions?! Likewise, having heard me make arrangements to go cycling with a friend Judy would plead with me to take her along for the ride. This was just not on for if I gave in to her pleas my social life would soon be in ruins ... Something simply had to be done ... whether by fair means or by foul!

It really turned out to be quite simple. Judy was by nature a good little girl and listened to what she was told to do or told not to do – well, most of the time, anyway! And that being the case, the next time she requested me to include her in plans which did not suit me, I informed her that the request that she had come up with was quite simply "against the law". Of course her immediate reply was to ask "why is it against the law?" To which I replied that the law being the law, there was nothing that we could do to change it or even to question it, because the law quite simply stated that little girls could not come along! And, being a law abiding child she accepted the explanation. For the next few weeks I managed to get away with this answer but I could see that this approach was starting to wear a little thin when she started questioning this law business and I realised my reasons would not wash much longer! So this "legal" matter was finally dropped – but I had, in the interim, managed to gain a few weeks' respite!

In due course we were notified that my application to attend Prince Edward School had been accepted. Some of my class-mates had also been accepted for places at various boys' and girls' high schools of their choice in various parts of the country. My mother and I travelled to Salisbury one weekday during the third term in order to have me "kitted out" with a new school uniform. We purchased the various items of clothing and acces-sories from the outfitting firm of McCullagh & Bothwell, situated in Stanley Avenue, one of the official stockists of Prince Edward school uniforms. On arrival we were confronted with a vast selection of boys' wear and a member of their staff assisted us in choosing the items of clothing required – one felt he had performed this duty for countless mothers and their sons over the years and knew exactly what was needed and what was not. Items required included shirts, khaki shorts, long grey trousers, school stockings, a school tie, a grey hat with a green and maroon hatband plus other items. And, no doubt, like the majority of parents, my mother made sure that the maroon coloured school blazer (jacket) fitted me comfortably yet with

enough "leeway" so that it could hopefully be worn for at least a
further year or two so not have to be replaced every year – for
a school blazer turned out to be by far the most expensive item
on the list of required clothing!

Shopping completed, and clutching a number of large parcels,
we walked into the conveniently situated Pockets Bakery & Tea
Room right next door to the outfitters.

There we settled ourselves at a table and scanned the comprehensive menu, the variety of ice cream desserts and the choices
thereof were mind boggling. I finally settled on a Knickerbocker
Glory – a sundae consisting of various layers of vanilla ice
cream interspersed with sliced banana, layers of red jelly, canned
peaches and topped off with a cherry perched on a dollop of
fresh cream! Served in a tall parfait glass and consumed with a
long dessertspoon – this delicious concoction, which cost the
princely sum of two shillings and sixpence (twenty-five cents) at
the time, turned out to be worth every penny of the price! I
decided a Knickerbocker Glory was a special treat for a special
occasion – and to me the day was indeed a special one and
brought home the fact that high school was now imminent.

My final examination results at Jameson School turned out
well, and I was presented with the Rhodes Trustees prize for
English in the form of a certificate, together with a book, *The
Phantom Fleet*, which proved an enjoyable read.

The end of the school year finally arrived and those pupils who
were leaving Jameson School for other institutes of learning bid
their farewells to friends and fellow classmates who would
continue their schooling at Jameson – amongst those whom I
recall bidding farewell to were Willie Jamieson, Cynthia Edwards
and twins Tony and Ann Gerber. Friends leaving for other
schools included John Davis – off to Technical College (High
School) in Bulawayo and Patricia Collins – heading for Girls
High School in Salisbury.

Life in small towns such as Gatooma livened up considerably
over the Christmas period, even more so now that the austere
war years were finally over. The latter half of the nineteen forties
and virtually the whole of the nineteen fifties would reflect both
peace and prosperity in the country and a feeling of great

optimism for the future – and never was this mood so prevalent than during the month of December.

Christmas lights and decorations reappeared in local shop windows in 1946 after years of austerity, and quite a number of businesses entered the "Best Window Display" competition sponsored by the local branch of the Chamber of Commerce. Devised in order to brighten up the overall appearance of the town's commercial centre, this competition was invariably won, year after year, by the firm of Kidias Departmental Store, erstwhile known as the Eastern Silk Bazaar. Owned by the Kidia family, this business was founded by a Mr Bhana Kidia, one of the town's pioneers, who had emigrated from India in the early part of the century. He had started off his career as a street vendor, pulling his fruit and vegetable laden cart around the then dusty unpaved streets of the town.

We often took a stroll around the town centre in the evenings during the period leading up to Christmas, comparing the various window displays of firms who had entered this competition. Noticeable was the fact that the two garages in town, namely Duly's Garage and Wilson's Garage, were once again displaying a range of new cars in their showrooms – showrooms that had stood empty or else only displayed pre-owned (second hand) vehicles since war broke out. Although the "new" cars now on display were in reality only warmed over models of pre-war or early 1940's design, it was good to see that passenger vehicles were once again in production and back on the show room floors.

Sports clubs, the police force, the Municipality and various other organizations held private Christmas parties for their employees' younger children and these parties were usually held on the Saturday afternoon preceding Christmas Day. A jovial Father Christmas fully dressed up for the part (despite the sweltering December heat) arrived at these outdoor venues riding either a horse or driving a motor vehicle or farm tractor and carrying a large sack of gifts (usually chosen and prepaid for by the parents) which were handed out to the excited children. Once the children had sated their appetites from trestle tables laden with cakes, buns, sweets, ice cream and lemonades the games began – everyone joining in playing hopscotch, rounders, running races, musical chairs and suchlike. Donkey rides were often provided and the children had a marvellous time.

The Mayor's Christmas Cheer Fund was instituted and appealed for monetary contributions to assist the town's poor and needy. This fund raised a goodly amount of money each year – those who donated to the fund had their names mentioned in a special column of the weekly *Gatooma Mail*, which also reflected the sum donated. In those years it was customary to donate money in guineas so that if two guineas were donated then this amounted to two pounds and two shillings. And likewise, it was the custom that most monetary gifts presented in the event of weddings, birthdays etc. were also made out in guineas, a habit that died out once decimalization came into effect many years later.

The majority of adults let their hair down on 24 and 31 December when Christmas Eve and New Year's Eve dances were held throughout the country. These two nights were particularly popular and well patronized, especially if one considers the relatively small white population at the time. In the Gatooma district alone dances were held at venues such as Specks Hotel, Grand Hotel, Gatooma Sports Club, Eiffel Flats Mine Club, Golden Valley Mine Club, Chakari Sports Club, the Umsweswe Hotel, Hartley Hotel and the Hartley Sports Club. These venues were all within a radius of 25 miles of Gatooma and these events were filled to capacity – in most instances early table bookings were essential! Beef, turkey, chicken, duck, together with all the usual trimmings, Christmas pudding and brandy sauce, mince pies, champagne, wine, beer and spirits all appeared to be in plentiful supply. Some of the hotels made a point of advertising their menus in the *Gatooma Mail* and these always looked most mouth watering! And as for the men who had recently returned from war service, whose lives had often been on the line, how could anyone begrudge them and their families all the enjoyment they could derive over this festive season.

It was also the time of the year for the eagerly awaited Christmas bonus that all employees, both commercial and domestic, were awarded. Domestic staff (ours) were often given new shirts or trousers together with other items of clothing, a Christmas cake, sweets and biscuits and, most important of all, money.

An event witnessed for the first time occurred on the morning of Boxing Day (26 December – the day following Christmas Day) – a public holiday throughout the country. The beating of tom-toms (small African "talking drums") heralded the approach of a number of African dancers garbed in various animal skins. Some dancers wore outlandish looking masks and had daubed their arms and legs with paint, others had plastered their limbs with chicken feathers. They all sang and gyrated to the rhythmic beat of the hypnotic sounding drums.

Groups of Black African's walked from house to house, up one street and down the next, stopping in front of each house to perform their dances. They remained in the relative safety of the street, making quite sure that the front gate leading to each house was securely closed – for the dogs in the neighbourhood went into an absolute frenzy caused by the incessant drumming and singing. The sound was enough to drive residents crazy – never mind the canines with their far more sensitive hearing!!

After each impromptu performance the householder or his children would come to their gates and place coins into the outstretched hands of the performers, who thereafter moved to the next house to repeat the process. Although relative calm returned to the area as the group moved on and eventually out of sight, and finally out of earshot, the dogs nevertheless continued their howling and barking for some considerable time. And even the household cats in the neighbourhood were conspicuous by their absence on occasions such as these!

Soon other groups arrived upon the scene. They turned out to be the local postman, milkman, garbage collector, members of the municipal malaria eradication team etc. Each group being followed in short order by the next. Their mission – to collect their "Christmas Box" (gift) for services rendered during the previous twelve months. They too received a monetary gift for services provided on a regular basis come rain or shine. However when they arrived the majority of dogs either barked a welcome or simply ignored them altogether – for these people were well known to the pets on a daily basis!!

Thus, although the town's business centre may have been very quiet over Christmas and Boxing Day periods, the residential areas hummed with noise, song and dance, especially over this uniquely celebrated Boxing Day!

During the month of December we celebrated the Jewish festival of Chanukah which is also known as the "Festival of Lights". This festival lasts a total of eight days and each evening candles are lit on an eight branched candlestick, known as a menorah. A single candle is lit on the first night, two on the second and so on until on the last night of Chanukah all eight candles are aglow. Each evening, immediately the lights had been lit, we sang a Chanukah song with a beautiful and lilting melody entitled "Ma'oz Zur" – this song dates back many centuries and in my view personified the spirit of Chanukah. First my father lit the candles on his menorah and then my sister and I lit the candles on our own slightly scaled down "children's menorahs". The room radiated a warm and cosy glow as we sat down on the sofa and sang this lovely song, watching the brightly burning candles placed on the mantle-piece.

Chanukah was also a time of giving and receiving gifts and Judy and I always looked forward to that time of year! We took our time in choosing to buy presents for our parents each year – a box of Black Magic chocolates, or possibly some handker-chiefs, perfumed bath soap or bath salts, sometimes a book, or a bottle of imported Devon cider – these were examples of gifts we purchased to give them from one year to the next. Shops in Gatooma seldom stocked a great variety of goods of this nature so it always took us a few weeks of shopping around until we managed to find suitable gifts falling within the range of our pocket money.

I had been fortunate enough to have seen quite a few good movies during the past year, including Rex Harrison in *Blithe Spirit*, Gregory Peck in *Duel In The Sun*, Michael Redgrave in *The Way To The Stars* and David Niven in *A Matter of Life and Death*. I sincerely hoped that I would not miss out on too many movies by setting off for school in Salisbury, for I suspected that our freedom of movement in a hostel would be considerably restricted as compared to the freedom that I had enjoyed to date.

We continued to tune into the radio broadcasts regularly and such bright and breezy songs as *South America, Take It Away, Five Minutes More, The Girl That I Marry, Old Buttermilk Sky* and *Zip-A-Dee-Do-Dah* were among the "hit songs" of 1946 which brightened the musical scene. Likewise I hoped that there would be a radio in the hostel at Prince Edward School so that we would not miss out too much in the world of song and radio entertainment over the next five or so years ahead!

Gatooma Railway Station

Strip roads and highways

1947

I awoke early on New Year's Day 1947 to the stark realization that not only were there now five long years of high school looming ahead for me but that, for good measure, I was to spend most of this rather lengthy period residing in a government school hostel a hundred miles away from home ... Not the greatest of thoughts to be waking up with on the first day of 1947, but as this was the choice I had made, there was no one else to blame but myself ...

The next few weeks sped by and suddenly school holidays came to an end. New boarders like myself had already been advised by "friends in the know" of what to expect, and we were briefed on boarding school "do-s and don'ts". These tips included regulations regarding the taking with to boarding school of "tuck" – foodstuffs such as biscuits, chocolates, sweets, dried fruit etc. for one's own personal consumption and what's more, it was recommended that they be kept in a securely locked container. Local carpenter Mr Francisco Serino, a former Italian internee in the Gatooma camp, constructed a small wooden chest for that very purpose, onto which a solid hasp and padlock was affixed. I am sure that it would have required someone with an axe to have broken into this box and its solid appearance likewise gave that impression – for no one ever attempted to open it! This box served me well for my entire sojourn at boarding school and for that matter is still in use to this very day, although no longer used for its original purpose!

My personal "D-Day" (departure day) for boarding school arrived soon enough and it was with somewhat mixed feelings and not a little trepidation that my parents, sister and I found ourselves, around noon on Monday 27 January 1947, on the platform of the Gatooma railway station to see me off on the Salisbury bound "school train". However, do not misunderstand me in this respect, for I am positive that the trepidation felt on this particular morning in question was entirely mine, not theirs!

The "school train", consisted of three or four passenger coaches hitched onto a dozen or two goods/freight wagons and pulled by a Garrett locomotive. This train was laid on by Rhodesia Railways in order to convey pupils residing in the smaller towns and surrounding farms and mines along the line of rail between Bulawayo and Salisbury to travel from their places of abode to boarding schools at the beginning and at the end of each of the three annual school terms. These composite trains of both passenger coaches and goods wagons were known as "mixed trains" in local parlance. Boys and girls of all ages joined the train at the various stations en route, and the large variety of school blazers worn by the pupils signified the numerous schools attended by pupils who lived in smaller towns and in the countryside. Prince Edward School, Girls High School, Dominican Convent, St George's College, Queen Elizabeth Girls High, Alan Wilson High and even Umtali High School blazers were to be seen and amongst the junior schools represented were such Salisbury schools as Avondale, Blakiston and Selborne. The majority of these school names were entirely foreign to me – we must surely have lived an isolated life in Gatooma during those years!

I boarded one of the crowded passenger coaches and, making my way down the corridor, eventually located a compartment which had one vacant seat – and a window one at that, for the train appeared to be pretty full. My tin trunk containing clothing plus Mr Serino's wooden chest had already been consigned direct to the guards van at the rear of the train by the railway staff. Having settled myself into the seat, it was now time to bid farewell to my family – with everyone trying to retain a brave and cheerful countenance, whilst pretending (mistakenly) that I could not wait to be heading off to boarding school! If this impression was given by me it proves how wrong one can be!

As the minutes prior to departure time ticked by I no doubt promised to study hard, try my best not to become homesick (whilst already feeling the first pangs thereof ...) and to "enjoy" high school ... I tried to work out how one could "enjoy" high school – I knew how to enjoy a school vacation but to "enjoy high school"?? Who were my well meaning parents trying to fool??

Farewells having now been repeated a number of times and further topics of small talk having been exhausted, I was quite relieved when the Garrett locomotive finally emitted a loud blast on its whistle, signalling departure time. Belching vast quantities of black smoke from its smoke stack whilst hissing copious amounts of white steam from various pipes, the train slowly eased out of Gatooma station, rumbled over the Edward Street rail crossing and began to gather speed, whilst now transporting me into an entirely new chapter in my life. A month short of my twelfth birthday, this was the moment that I had been looking forward to for several months, and now that moment had finally arrived. But somehow, my previously held enthusiasm suddenly appeared to have evaporated. But only too well I realized that I had better make the most of this opportunity that I had been presented with, and so decided to firmly combat any thoughts of homesickness which at times might threaten to overwhelm me. I am pleased to note that, apart from a few instances during the first year, I managed to overcome these negative feelings.

My fellow passengers in the compartment turned out to be pupils from various Salisbury schools, none of them however from Prince Edward School. Meanwhile the train seemed to grind to a halt at every little siding along the line, and in the process allowed trains travelling in the opposite direction – from Salisbury to Bulawayo – to pass by without stopping. Rhodesia had but a single railway line linking towns and cities, these trains were known as the "up train" and the "down train" between these two cities. Having only a single track naturally slowed down rail travel considerably, and resulted in many stops and often unnecessary delays, especially if trains were running late. In 1947 the "main roads" linking towns and cities still consisted of the ubiquitous strip roads – a method of road construction found in only two countries of the world, namely Rhodesia and New Zealand. The strip roads in Rhodesia were largely constructed in the early 1930s by white labour. Many whites found themselves unemployed in those austere Depression days and, in order to put food on the table, they volunteered as labourers to work on the construction of this new road system. For the first time in the country's history white men wielded picks and shovels on a large scale.

However, strip roads, constructed initially of concrete and later of tarmacadam, were not exactly conducive to fast motoring and speeds in excess of sixty miles an hour (one hundred kilometres an hour) on these roads was considered by many to be foolhardy, especially more so during the rainy season. It was a toss up as to whether a car journey was any quicker than a rail journey, especially for those passengers who needed to arrive at their destination within a specified time frame.

Our train pulled to a halt at Martin Spur for a brief stop, then again at Chigwell siding and a little while later we arrived at Hartley railway station some 21 miles from Gatooma, where a goodly number of pupils boarded. I noticed that a number of them wore Prince Edward School blazers, but none entered my compartment. The train steamed out of Hartley station and a few minutes later we crossed the Umfuli River bridge, the Umfuli being one of the country's major waterways. Virtually all road and rail bridges throughout the country were separate entities and road bridges were of "low level" type construction. This meant that vehicles travelling across a bridge were barely a yard or two (one or two metres) above the river itself. During winter months the road bridge may span what looked like a river of sand, with an odd shallow pool of water dotted here and there. But during the November to March rainy season, depending to a large extent on how much rain had fallen in the river's catchment area, which often lay very many miles upstream, a river, within a short space of time, could suddenly be transformed from a tranquil and slow flowing stream into a raging torrent. Unsuspecting or foolhardy motorists were occasionally swept off bridges, over the low guard rails and into the foaming and swirling waters, which often carried the unfortunate vehicles and their occupants hundreds of yards downstream, often to their deaths. Motorists could also be left stranded by suddenly rising floodwaters and left marooned, sometimes for days on end, between two swollen rivers that had burst their banks, thus rendering both road bridges impassable until the waters had subsided. Motorists at times took a definite chance when travelling long distances during the Rhodesian rainy season.

Rail bridges more or less guaranteed the safe arrival of trains at their destination, as these bridges were generally constructed sufficiently high enough over the river to keep floodwaters well below the level of the railway track. However, exceptionally heavy rainfalls occasionally could and did cause washaways in certain areas of the country and both locomotives and rolling stock were known to have been derailed after the track they were travelling on had been washed away. So even rail travel was no guarantee, but it was certainly safer to let Rhodesia Railways take care of one's travel needs during an exceptionally wet rainy season.

Thereafter our train stopped at a further three sidings, namely Gadzema, Selous and Makwiro and then we pulled into the station at Norton, a small town serving a fertile farming area situated some twenty-five miles from Salisbury. More pupils boarded the train here and shortly thereafter we crossed the Hunyani River, another major waterway. Our journey was finally drawing to a close.

In due course we approached the outskirts of Salisbury, steaming parallel to a busy road filled with cyclists, cars, trucks and buses before gliding through the marshalling yards where large Garretts and smaller shunting locomotives huffed and puffed on alongside our now slow moving train. We were approaching the main platform which, further ahead, featured a sign which stated quite clearly SALISBURY – altitude 4,825 feet. The train finally drew to a halt and my first journey on a "school train" had ended. It might have been the first journey but it was far from being the last!

The moment the train stopped a mad scramble to disembark ensued in order to make our way to the guards van (baggage car) at the rear of the train to collect our individual items of luggage. These were taken to the station entrance for collection by the various school buses or trucks. Both high schools and junior schools sent their vehicles to meet these trains in order to collect both pupils and their belongings as the distances to some schools were considerable. I added my trunk and wooden box to the pile of suitcases and trunks due for collection by the Prince Edward vehicle, which had not yet arrived. Whilst still waiting for this vehicle to arrive, a group of pupils elected to walk to the school rather than wait to be collected, and invited me to accompany them, which I was happy to do.

Off we set through downtown Salisbury, our route taking us into sections of the city that I had never set foot in before. After walking for about an hour we found ourselves approaching the gates of Prince Edward – or "P.E." as we soon learned to call the school! The anticipation was over – I had finally arrived at my new school! A few in our group were also first year juniors and we were shown to our individual hostels, the three boarding hostels being Jameson House, Rhodes House and Selous House. Each of the hostels consisted of four dormitories, two on the ground floor and two on the first floor, and each hostel accommodated approximately eighty pupils who ranged in age from 12 to 18 years. I was taken to the Jameson House junior dormitory situated on the first floor and told to choose a bed.

A short while later we were called to help unload our cases from the school bus which had now arrived and we assisted each other in carrying the luggage and placing it under our beds. Cupboard space was allocated to us in which to hang clothing but before we could commence unpacking we were all summoned to the communal dining hall, this building being in close proximity to the three hostels. The tables allocated to the Jameson House boarders were pointed out and I am sure we were all most grateful for the evening meal that was served – after the train journey followed by a long walk from the railway station, a plate of hot food was more than welcome!

The dining room superintendent cum cook matron, a Mrs Blunt, turned out to be a lady of ample proportions and she was known to all as "Ma Blunt". Her speciality appeared to be bananas and custard, a dessert which she served on average three or four times a week throughout my entire five year sojourn as a boarder! I calculated that I must have been served – and probably consumed – close up to six hundred helpings of bananas and custard during that period!

After a good nights sleep we were woken up early the next morning by a reveille call on a bugle which signalled the first of many such wake up calls. A new dawn and a new awakening! What would this day – my very first day at high school, hold in store for me?

It was then that I discovered, much to my embarrassment, that I had difficulty in knotting my school tie correctly – having never ever been required to wear a tie before! But after struggling for a few moments I received some friendly guidance and soon mastered the art! School uniform worn on a daily basis consisted of a khaki shirt, a pair of khaki shorts, aforementioned tie, a grey hat sporting a Prince Edward School hatband, regulation school stockings and black shoes. Our hair was expected to be neatly combed and worn reasonably short. We made up our beds to the best of our abilities – and we were expected to clean and polish our own shoes. From time to time the house prefects checked on our proficiency in that respect – but not too frequently ...

Another bugle call and we all lined up in front of the hostel, roll call was taken and thereafter we trooped off to the dining hall for breakfast, occupying the same benches that we had occupied the night before. Breakfast normally consisted of either mealie meal (maize meal) porridge (which I enjoyed) or maltabella, a dark brown coloured smooth grain porridge which I disliked! This course was followed by a helping of bright yellow scrambled egg which had been placed on a slice of often soggy toast, and when on the odd occasion that bacon was served with the egg I made it quite clear to Mrs Blunt and her assistants that bacon was to be left off my plate completely. It took a little time for this request to sink in but after a few weeks the message had got through and no problem in that respect ever cropped up again. Tea and sometimes coffee was served, plus bread and jam or marmalade. Although I enjoyed marmalade on toast it has never appealed to me when spread on bread and as for the jam – this often consisted of a vile tasting tomato jam and I avoided it at all costs! After breakfast it was back to the hostel to clean up, brush our teeth and then we set off for school, a walk of approximately five minutes' duration.

The school day commenced with an assembly held in the Beit Hall, where prayers were conducted and attended by all pupils and teachers who belonged to the Anglican, Roman Catholic, Dutch Reformed, Methodist and Baptist faiths. Those pupils belonging to the Jewish, Seventh Day Adventist and Jehovah's Witness faiths were excluded from attending prayers and were expected to wait near the front steps of the Beit Hall. At the conclusion of prayers, we were then called into the (by now standing room only) hall in order to hear the newly appointed headmaster, Mr H.H. Cole, address the school for a few minutes. The assembly ended and we all trooped off to our respective classrooms. These assemblies were held every weekday.

Prince Edward School as an educational facility could claim a long tradition – certainly by Rhodesian standards. The year 1898 saw the opening of the Salisbury Undenominational Public School which catered for both boys and girls. By 1908 the number of public school pupils had increased to such an extent that it was decided to separate the sexes and the Salisbury Boys High School thus emerged. The girls in turn moved into their own school, appropriately named Girls High School and which too became a thriving institute of learning.

In July 1925 the Prince of Wales (later King Edward VIII) visited Rhodesia and the school was named Prince Edward School in his honour. The following year the school moved to its current 50 acre site in North Avenue. All three boarding houses and the dining hall were constructed during the years 1926/27. When I arrived in 1947 the enrolment stood in the vicinity of 600 pupils and the school was acknowledged to be the largest school in the country. It's motto read "*Tot Facienda Parum Factum*" ("So Much To Do – So Little Done") words attributed to the country's founder, Cecil John Rhodes.

I found myself assigned to Form 1B. There were four Form One grades ranging from 1A down to 1D and each class averaged some 25 to 30 pupils. We were now faced with several subjects that we had never studied before – Latin, algebra, geometry, plus a choice of two foreign languages – Afrikaans or French. The majority of boys plumped for Afrikaans (a goodly number stemmed from Afrikaans backgrounds and could speak the language fluently) so as far as they were concerned this "foreign language" now offered as a subject was not foreign to them at all! I chose to study French, doing so mainly because the pupils attending the French class were far less in number.

The experience of now having to share "two seater desks" with fellow pupils was also new to me. In junior school we had all been allocated single desks with individual chairs, the cramped desks we were now expected to share had certainly not been

constructed with comfort in mind and judging from their condition had probably been installed around the turn of the century!
Initials had been gouged into most of the wooden desk tops by
previous occupants, if judging the number of indentations that
scarred them was anything to go by! These desks were fitted with
small round bakelite inkwells filled with grainy government ink
of a dubious quality, for at times this ink was hardly legible after
having been transferred by scratchy pen nibs to paper, so we
usually purchased our own ink from shops. The inks of choice
were usually Stephens Ink, Watermans Royal Blue or Quink Ink
and teachers could now finally read our writing in our homework exercise books. We also purchased our own blotting
paper – does this product still exist in schools today?

And while on the subject of desks – a year later I shared one
of these double desks with a fellow pupil who quite literally
suffered from "the shakes". No, not caused by imbibing alcohol
but by some unfortunate physical condition from which he
suffered. His continuous twitching and jerking in close proximity
to me made a complete mess of my handwriting. When one of
the teachers passed a comment about my untidy handwriting I
offered to change places with her! After I had explained the
position she understood my problem. Thereafter my desk-mate
was moved to a single desk at the rear of the classroom and the
problem was solved. This pupil in later years graduated as a
chemist and it is just as well that he did not become a doctor, for
I am confident that no chemist would have been able to read any
of his handwritten prescriptions!

During the mid-morning break (10.30 to 11 a.m.) most boarders trooped back to the dining hall where hot sweet tea and
slices of brown bread spread with tomato jam were served. I
decided to rather visit the school library and reading room and
forgo the mid-morning tea session – and especially the vile
tasting tomato jam sandwiches that went with it – this turned out
to be a wise choice. For now I could spend this half hour
perusing the daily *Rhodesia Herald* (which also included reading
the "Fur & Featherland" Curly Wee comic strip from which I had
not yet been entirely weaned ...!) and to also page through the
magazines on the reading room table. The library stocked a
good selection of books on its shelves and one of the books that

I recall taking out and hugely enjoying was John Hersey's recent masterpiece *A Bell For Adano*.

Boarding school hostels at that time still put the first year students through an "initiation ceremony" shortly after their arrival, and we boarders were given a few weeks to prepare ourselves for this event. These initiations, we were told, had been toned down considerably over the past few years ever since a new boy had been compelled, much against his will, to walk along the parapet of the first floor balcony as part of his initiation ritual, and in doing so had lost his balance and toppled over the edge, crashing onto the pathway below, seriously injuring himself in the process. We did not really believe this horrific tale as the details provided were somewhat vague – the unfortunate victim's name was never divulged, the year this was alleged to have occurred was never disclosed and the hostel where it was meant to have occurred was never mentioned. We felt sure that this story was no more than an urban myth, but no one could be certain ...

The Jameson House prep room one Sunday evening a few weeks later was filled to capacity as some twenty or so nervous and embarrassed youngsters awaited their turn to perform in front of an audience of older boys. As usual there were always a number of extroverts amongst some of the newcomers, who could hardly wait to take their turn on stage, no matter how bad their individual acts might prove to be! Most of the presentations that evening turned out to be quavering versions of popular songs, the recitation of poetry, the dancing of a jig, the nervous playing of a musical instrument (mouth organs/harmonica's being the most popular) or the cracking of a few weak jokes. When my turn came I fortunately received more cheers than jeers at the conclusion of singing *You Are My Sunshine* – one of the few songs whose words I had truly memorised!

The boarding house prefects, numbering about half a dozen, were accorded the privilege of having the first year students "skivvie" for them – this meant the prefects each selected a number of juniors to perform "light duties" for them, duties which included polishing the prefect's shoes and cadet boots, making up their beds, running various minor errands on their behalf, conveying messages, carrying their school books to and from school and the like. This meant that first year juniors were literally at their beck and call, and although these duties were not particularly onerous as such, they could prove annoyingly time consuming. A sort of minor slave trade – but as "skivvying" (as it was known) only affected us during our first year at boarding school we soon learned to cope with these tasks!

Jameson House was fortunate in having the school's deputy headmaster, Mr E.J. Hougaard, known to both staff and pupils of the entire school as "Jeeves", as our housemaster. He was a strict but fair disciplinarian and had been a member of the school's teaching staff for over 20 years. A well known and colourful character he also coached school rugby. He was an exemplary housemaster and if anyone had problems and wished to discuss these in confidence, "Jeeves" Hougaard was there to lend a sympathetic ear and offer good and sensible advice.

I soon discovered that apart from the school's excellent teaching standards, Prince Edward was also well known for its extremely high sporting standards. It excelled at cricket, rugby and tennis and swimming, boxing and athletics (track) were of an extremely high standard.

The school possessed a well maintained swimming pool and a well trained swimming team, and the spectator stands at the annual galas and inter-school swimming competitions were always filled to capacity. In 1947 the Prince Edward swimming team won every team competition that they had entered for and proved to be the most successful team in the school's history. A fellow classmate, Mickey Flint, showed excellent promise and two years later would go on to represent Southern Rhodesia at the South African swimming championships where he won both the 100 and 200 yard events.

In the second term (semester) of the year I was introduced to the game of rugby and enjoyed this game from the outset. In later years I was selected to represent Jameson House in the senior inter-house competition, initially playing in the eighth-man position and later on as a fullback. The school also ran a well stocked tuck shop situated in the area between the playing fields and the swimming pool and after we had finished playing afternoon sport we normally congregated at this well run and popular venue for an ice-cold Coca Cola and a packet of potato crisps or sugared peanuts. Other popular items included sherbet fountains – finely powdered sherbet in a packet supplied with a liquorice straw with which to suck up the contents. Then it was back to the hostels for a hot shower, supper in "Ma" Blunt's establishment which in turn was followed by a few hours of homework in the adjoining prep room. Then eventually we made our way to bed for an all too brief reading session and finally lights out was called. A number of boys had brought crystal sets with them – fiddling around with the wires produced the same result as did a radio and one could then listen to music from the local broadcasting studio, situated a few miles down the road. No one in our hostel possessed a bedside radio (or a wireless as we called them) – these would only appear on the scene a few years later. When it was time for lights out, listening to crystal sets or gramophones (there were a few of them around too) was not permitted. So operators of crystal sets simply placed them under their blankets, attempting to listen to their now muffled tones, whilst at the same time trying to keep a vigilant eye on the windows and main door of the dormitory, in case a passing prefect appeared and confiscated the crystal set.

Latin was a subject I particularly disliked and the rhyme:
"Latin, Latin, Latin,
As dead as dead can be,
It killed the ancient Romans,
And now it's killing me"
perfectly conveyed my feelings on the subject. During one lesson our Latin master, Duncan Whaley, almost broke a ruler over my head in frustration to an incorrect answer. It was there and then that I decided to drop the subject, much to the relief of both master and pupil! Many years later Duncan Whaley was appointed headmaster of Jameson High School in Gatooma and we became quite friendly – but any mention of Latin was studiously avoided! I doubt that he remembered that particular incident – but I most certainly did!

In April 1947 the greatly anticipated Royal Visit took place – King George VI, Queen Elizabeth and their two daughters, Princess Elizabeth and Princess Margaret Rose, visiting Rhodesia as part of their South African tour. All school pupils in Salisbury had been given the day off from lessons and several of the schools were allocated places on North Avenue to line up on the side of the road to cheer "Their Majesties" as they drove past. We had also been handed small "Union Jack" flags and were instructed to wave them in unison, accompanied by some hearty cheering!

The great day finally arrived and we patiently stood for hours in the sun waiting for the cavalcade to appear. Our enthusiasm perked up considerably when we finally heard the B.S.A.P. (British South African Police) outriders approaching on their motorcycles, followed shortly thereafter by the King and Queen in their open Humber limousine, waving graciously both to left and right. I clicked away furiously on my little Brownie camera and managed to come out with a few reasonable photographs of the cars, but both King and Queen turned out a little blurred! A few moments after they had passed the two princesses arrived in their limousine and both of them, sitting in their "Royal Humber" were also photographed for posterity by my faithful Box Brownie!

The first "long week-end" of the year fell on the Easter weekend (Good Friday to Easter Monday) and boarders were permitted to travel to their homes. After school was over on Thursday we dressed in our "Number One" uniform consisting of white shirt, school tie, long grey flannel trousers and school blazer. Then, clutching a small suitcase holding sufficient clothes for the weekend, I set off to walk along North Avenue – both Jameson House and Rhodes House faced North Avenue. Several hundred yards further along North Avenue became known as the Gatooma Road. Once we were fairly clear of local traffic we placed our cases down on the ground and attempted to thumb a ride to our various points of destination. As school trains were not laid on for exit-weekends, and many parents of boarders were not in a position to collect their children personally, we boys were permitted to hitch-hike to our homes on occasions such as these.

In those days, prior to the era of muggings, car hijacking and road rage, motorists tended to stop and offer rides to hitchhikers, more so if the person at the side of the road was neatly dressed in a school uniform. This is why we always wore school blazers, even during the hottest of days, when attempting to "thumb a ride" – it more often than not paid dividends to do so! But being offered a ride in someone's car did not automatically guarantee a direct journey to one's destination, and I recall once accepting no less than four individual rides before finally arriving in Gatooma. Likewise, one never knew until the vehicle stopped as to who one's travelling companions would turn out to be. Once I found myself wedged into the back seat next to two immature schoolgirls who, between irritating giggles, whispered endlessly into each other's ears for mile after mile after mile. On another occasion I found myself perched atop some sacks of foul smelling fertilizer on the back of a bouncing pickup truck, closely surrounded by half a dozen farm labourers, most attempting to light their "stompies" (cigarette butts) in a howling wind that threatened to whip off my jacket. I would never have taken this particular ride if it had not been for the fact that it was already getting fairly late in the afternoon and offers of better, or for that matter any further rides, were fast becoming doubtful, as dusk was rapidly approaching. Besides, it was already my third or fourth ride of that particular afternoon. It was a case of "I will see you in due course" to our parents which meant in effect "don't worry, I will eventually arrive home"! Likewise, one was expected to be back in the hostel by 6 p.m. on Easter Monday and, if late, one needed a very convincing excuse to escape punishment!

The long exeat weekend for the second term fell over the Rhodes & Founders weekend in early July of each year. We were allowed off from lunchtime on Friday and were required to be back in the school hostel by 6 p.m. Tuesday. Once again we thumbed our way home and relished every minute of being with our families, enjoying a warm and comfortable bed and savouring home cooked meals. However, these weekends literally flew by and before we knew it we were back on the road, thumbing our way back to Salisbury in order to once again embrace the joys of hostel life ...

The third and final term's exeat weekend occurred during the month of October but consisted of just a Saturday and Sunday (a weekend on which no homework was set). However, as the end of year examinations were approaching, most boarders (myself included) tended to remain in their respective hostels in order to devote that weekend to revision.

Prince Edward School was well noted for its prowess on the sporting field and I now began to take a greater interest in sport than I had done in the past. The school boasted a strong boxing team which included a number of Rhodesian national and provincial champions and this team was matched against various other high schools on a fairly regular basis. In addition, amateur boxing tournaments, both at senior and junior levels took place in the Drill Hall in Moffat Street and we boarders were often permitted to attend these events, usually held on a Saturday night.

As the months went by I began to take a greater interest in boxing which prompted me to follow the blossoming career of the extremely popular and newly crowned South African heavyweight champion Johnny Ralph. The newspapers were filled with his exploits, and this took me to the next stage. It was not long before I could name the top professional boxing champion in many countries around the world. I borrowed a few copies of the monthly American boxing magazine *Ring* from a friend and avidly read these from cover to cover – I became hooked on the sport!

I must have discussed boxing incessantly with my friends, most of whom probably had only a passing interest in the game. I was soon nicknamed "Joe" – after Joe Louis, the then world heavyweight champion. This nickname stuck with me throughout the remainder of my schooldays, most boys were under the impression that this was my given name! In fact, until the day I left Prince Edward School the majority of my school friends addressed me as "Joe" rather than Peter!!

The eagerly anticipated three week April/May 1947 school vacation arrived and I caught the train back to Gatooma. It was great being back with my family again and not being awoken at 6 a.m. each weekday morning by a bugle – I could sleep late. A highlight of school holidays! During this particular vacation Clyde, the Scottish football team, happened to be touring Rhodesia and they played one game in Gatooma. I was given to understand this was the first time an international football game had been staged in our town and it also turned out to be the first international sporting event that I ever attended.

I was also given the news by a friend "in the strictest of confidence" that a former classmate of mine at Jameson School, aged all of thirteen, had fallen pregnant and my friend had it on good advice that she would shortly be expelled from school. Although this information was totally unexpected, on reflection it did not come as a complete surprise as the girl in question looked far more mature than her age belied – she could easily have passed for a seventeen or eighteen year old. I felt very sorry for her as we had been good friends at school and assisted each other with our homework in Standard 5 on many occasions. However in the 1940s unmarried motherhood was severely frowned upon and especially so when schoolgirls aged thirteen were involved. My former classmate was indeed expelled and seemed to vanish off the radar screen and I never saw or heard of her again.

The vacation was all too soon over and I found myself back in Salisbury. Invitations for Sunday lunches were gladly accepted from good friends of our family, namely Herbert and Margot Stiefel, who lived in an apartment in Ottawa House in Angwa Street. Originally from Germany, their hospitality proved more than welcome and they helped me to "keep in touch" with the comforts of home life. Spending a Sunday with them always gave me that "home from home" feeling. Margot, a trained photographer, was employed by the well known Salisbury firm of photographers Atelier Ltd, situated in First Street. In the early 1940s, whilst on a visit to the city with my parents, I had called in at her place of work to say hello. She was busy in the darkroom developing photographs. Instead of asking me to wait until she had completed her work, she kindly invited me into the darkroom and explained the development process. I was fascinated by what she was doing, and appreciated her kindness.

These Sunday visits to the Stiefel's took on a familiar routine. After a somewhat leisurely breakfast in the school dining room (fried egg and fried tomato – our treat on Sunday mornings), I set off for my walk to their Ottawa House apartment. En route I stopped over at the Queen Victoria Library in Moffat Street where the public reading room was kept open seven days a week, and here it was that I spent up to an hour or more catching up with the many magazines and newspapers available. I had at last found a substitute for my much missed Gatooma library! This library stocked a comprehensive selection of international newspapers including the informative *Christian Science Monitor* which, although always a little out of date, nevertheless provided good reading. The Queen Victoria Library, one of the earliest buildings in the city, also housed a very interesting museum that was unfortunately closed on Sundays.

In early 1947 Herbert Stiefel's younger brother Norbert, likewise a close family friend of ours and who, in the early 1940s had briefly found employment in Gatooma, was awaiting his bride-to-be to fly out from the United Kingdom to join him in Salisbury, where they planned to marry shortly after her arrival.

Herta Sichel, Norbert's fiancee, joined a charter flight from England to Rhodesia but en route, somewhere over the jungles of the then Belgian Congo, the Douglas DC-3 Dakota developed problems in mid-air and the pilot was compelled to make an emergency landing in an inhospitable and fairly inaccessible part of the country. Fortunately whilst descending he spotted a small clearing in the jungle and managed to land the plane relatively unscathed. In due course radio contact was established with the outside world and supplies of food were parachuted into the clearing. Herta, being strictly kosher, persuaded the Dakota's radio operator to advise base of this fact and subsequent food drops included parcels of kosher food very clearly marked "For Miss Herta Sichel"!!

Some days later passengers and crew were evacuated from the jungle and it was a very relieved Norbert who greeted his wife-to-be when she finally arrived at her destination after a long and extremely taxing journey. They married in March 1947 and I attended their wedding. In the years to follow I spent many an enjoyable Sunday in their company at their apartment in the Salisbury suburb of Eastlea and Herta's excellent cooking always proved a treat to look forward to!

All pupils were expected to attend scripture lessons which were provided once a week at the school by local ministers of religion. Separate classrooms at school were set aside for each religious group and lessons for the Jewish boys were provided by Rabbi Maurice Konvisor, rabbi to the Harare Hebrew Congregation. He knew my father well and had been notified that I would be attending Prince Edward School, so the Rabbi made a point of looking out for me.

As anticipated, I was asked as to when he could expect to see me at afternoon chader classes (Hebrew lessons) at the synagogue, for it was imperative that I attend at least two of these classes per week. My barmitzvah was due the following year, and a fair amount of preparation lay ahead of me. Having expected this question, I enquired from him as to what particular afternoon these classes were held, and was told four afternoons a week, Mondays to Thursdays. I informed him that I would let him have my answer the following week. I checked on the sports practice time tables and carefully noted that cricket practices for the Under-13 age group took place on Tuesday and Thursday afternoons. Without any hesitation I selected these two afternoons for my Hebrew classes and in so doing, managed to avoid virtually all cricket practices for the remainder of the year! Initially special permission had to be obtained in order to leave the school grounds but once this had been granted by the housemaster, further afternoon exeats became routine and I could choose to come and go as I pleased.

Hebrew lessons lasted an hour and were conducted by the Reverend Clapper, the class consisted of six or seven boys. Afterwards I took a stroll into the city centre, some ten minutes walk from the synagogue, and usually headed straight for the bookshops. I felt it pointless to return to school as it was still relatively early in the afternoon and if I had done so I would probably have arrived half way through cricket practice, which I felt would not have been a smart move on my part!

I browsed through the shelves and magazine racks of the city's many leading bookstores, including the Rhodesia Herald Bookstore, E.B. Shepherd, Ness & Archibald and others, after which my next port of call would usually be to some of the various motor show rooms dotted around the city. These included Puzey & Payne (agents for Dodge, Packard and also the popular Morris, M.G., Riley and Wolseley cars), Duly & Co. (agents for both the British and American Fords, plus Mercury and Lincoln Zephyr automobiles), Cairns Ltd (the General Motors franchise, with a good display of Vauxhalls, Chevrolets, Pontiacs, Buicks and Oldsmobiles, but with only an odd Cadillac on display from time to time). Kimpton Motors (the Rootes group of cars – displayed Hillmans, Sunbeam Talbots and Humbers, plus Chrysler products) on the showroom floor, and S.&S. Cars (Studebaker, Standard, Jaguar and Triumph) always had an interesting variety of cars on display. These firms mentioned were just a selection of the new cars being sold in Salisbury at the time – there were further dealers with even more makes of cars available to the motorist!

At other times I paid visits to some of the major sports shops in town, notably Bain Brothers and Fulton & Evans. The latter shop stocked many current sports magazines which were left on a table for the benefit of customers to page through whilst waiting to be served, and there I discovered the weekly British trade paper *Boxing News.* I began visiting this shop on a more regular basis in order to catch up with the latest results in the world of boxing. The owner of this business was the redoubtable Willie Fulton who had won no less than FIVE South African senior amateur boxing and two Empire (now Commonwealth) Games bronze medals (1934 and 1938) – a truly impressive record in the annals of local and international boxing. And to crown these feats he went on to captain the Rhodesian national football (soccer) team and in later years represented his country at golf. Quite some feat. From time to time I purchased a few table tennis balls and always waited around so that this sporting icon would serve me personally! And for the record, I also had him sign my autograph book!

Approximately once a week I dropped in at the Popular Cafe in First Street, situated next door to the Palace Theatre. "The Palace", as it was referred to, was the city's largest cinema and a venue where local and international stage productions and musical shows were still performed on its commodious stage situated directly in front of the big screen. The Popular Cafe was indeed popular and often filled to capacity. Apart from purchasing an ice cream cone which I consumed on my way back to the hostel, I first stopped to listen to a few of the 78 rpm records played on the very glitzy jukebox which appeared to be in constant use. This jukebox, an importation from America, was the first I had come across and was one of the few that had been imported into Rhodesia at the time. In 1947 popular songs such as *The Woody Woodpecker Song, Put Another Nickel In* and *Civilization* – (the latter sung by Danny Kaye and the Andrews Sisters) topped the charts in an era that was noted for its catchy tunes.

Salisbury's leading departmental store, Barbour's, situated on the corner of First Street and Stanley Avenue was likewise paid a visit on the odd occasion. I remember once purchasing a pair of socks and paying for them at the cash desk. Now Barbour's employed a very unique system in their acceptance of money, they did not use the conventional cash register which other businesses seemed to do. Instead, they placed the money handed in for one's purchase into a small cylinder, this cylinder was then inserted into a pneumatic tube attached to their cash register. The money was then somewhat noisily fired up through a system of tubes to an office situated somewhere upstairs in the Barbour's building. In due course the cylinder was returned via the tube to the cash desk, and opened up by the assistant. Your invoice and receipt, together with any change due to you was then handed over, together with the purchased article.

My frequent visits to the shops, motor showrooms and streets of Salisbury during my first year of high school gave me the belief that I was conquering the sense of isolation that I may possibly have developed through having grown up in a small town. Perhaps I had "missed out" all these years on what "city life" actually had to offer. Yet, was this really the case? I continued to feel very much at ease and at home in Gatooma, and had not developed similar feelings for Salisbury, certainly not at that stage in my life.

Most of us were now reaching an age that we began to take an interest in the opposite sex, girls were beginning to be seen in a different light! Numerous "mini-romances" (usually very short lived) began to develop between the boarders of Prince Edward School and the lasses of Girls High, the latter school being situated "just down the road". "Crushes" developed which often lasted a few short weeks, and then other girls were discovered and new friendships developed. Competition was rife between the boys for some of the prettier girls but the majority of those fleeting "romances" were brief in the extreme, as both boys and girls usually met socially for no more than thirty minutes once a week after the church services that they attended on Sunday mornings.

Many of the boys professed to "discover religion" for the first time in their lives, for this revelation enabled them to meet current and future girlfriends regularly on Sundays. This was often their sole motivation for attending church, in the process no doubt boosting church attendances to the benefit of all concerned! Many of the starry-eyed young suitors spent Sunday evenings discussing their latest "conquests" but one was never quite sure which particular girl was being talked about as on most occasions the girl's names were different to the one that they had raved about the week before!

I received an invitation to come to Sunday lunch from the Marks family – Willie Marks and his wife were likewise friends of my parents. He was, as far as I recall, manager of the OK Bazaars supermarket and departmental store in First Street. They had also emigrated from Germany in the late 1930s and had a young daughter, Eva, several months younger than I, who attended Convent School for Girls (also know as the Dominican Convent – my old school!). Eva and I hit it off from the start and formed a very good friendship. This friendship continued throughout my entire sojourn at Prince Edward School, which saw me pay visits to her home a few times each week, sporting or other commitments allowing. Her parents worked and were out all day ... Sunday lunches were always enjoyable – the Mark's family resided at No. 41, Harvey Brown Avenue, Milton Park, just a short walk from Prince Edward. I was fortunate indeed to have had such a constant and steady girlfriend for my entire five year stint at high school – fairly unusual I guess at that age. I sympathized with my fellow boarders regarding their brief romances and regular break-ups that they experienced with their girlfriends. Very few fellow boarders could believe or understand that I had but one single girlfriend for the entire period that I spent at high school – this concept seemed almost unheard of amongst schoolboys!

When volunteers were called upon to audition for roles in the Gilbert & Sullivan operetta *H.M.S. Pinafore* I decided to step forward. This popular operetta was to be produced by Mr C.A. Wootton, commonly known to all as "Fussy". He had taught at the school since 1930 and in his younger and somewhat leaner days had been a tennis player of no mean ability. A bachelor, he was deputy housemaster of Rhodes House, where he resided. "Fussy" was known to be a character

In fact, I also discovered him to be an eccentric of the first degree! During a rehearsal, should a cast member happen to sing off-key, or happen to fluff a line, that unfortunate member was as a rule given only a single admonition by "Fussy", and told in no uncertain terms that should such error be repeated then he (the cast member) would simply be given his marching orders without any further ado and, what's more, be dismissed from the production. FOR GOOD. No further warnings or a second chance would be given! And "Fussy" turned out to be as good as his word!

His ruling initially seemed to apply to members of the chorus line only, but as rehearsals continued a number of leading members of the cast also experienced his ire. A rehearsal seldom went by without one or two unfortunates being given the boot and at the conclusion of some rehearsals the stage looked somewhat depleted of cast! Although our producer apparently showed no concern, the remaining members of the cast became most uneasy with the situation and wondered whether this production would ever see the light of day.

Likewise, he showed little or no concern when members of the cast who had been churlishly fired a few nights earlier mysteriously reappeared at subsequent rehearsals and resumed their roles as if nothing had happened! And, with about two or three weeks to go before opening night I too, a lowly member of the chorus, received my marching orders! Despite having studiously avoided putting a foot wrong and singing to the best of my limited ability the dreaded "Go, get out of here and be gone" or words to that effect were yelled in my direction by our esteemed producer, and thus it became my turn to exit the stage. Was this to be the end of my budding thespian career ...?!!

I thought the matter over for a few days and decided to simply take my chances and reappear on stage as if nothing at all had happened, thus following the route taken by others. What had I to lose, except having wasted four weeks of rehearsals? And a few dozen mugs of delicious hot cocoa and buns which we all partook of after the conclusion of each night's rehearsal – a small but much appreciated bonus, certainly by the boarders taking part in the show. Besides, I was starting to quite enjoy attending rehearsals and was looking forward to opening night just a few weeks away. And so, after a short break I ventured out and rejoined the chorus line on the stage of the Beit Hall. No one passed any comments – least of all our valiant producer!

I had been cast as a young maiden in the chorus of "sisters, cousins and aunts" and I must confess, when looking back at the cast photograph, we made a pretty convincing group of "young ladies" – especially after sufficient makeup had been applied to our still youthful looking faces! The show was well received and played to full houses on the Beit Hall stage. One evening members of the audience included His Excellency the Governor of Southern Rhodesia, Major-General Sir John Noble Kennedy and Lady Kennedy and the Mayor and Mayoress of Salisbury – quite a gala evening. "Fussy" went on to produce many more school productions including his beloved Gilbert & Sullivan operettas but I decided that I would no longer volunteer for any further theatrical productions at Prince Edward School. Not whilst they were under the direction of Mr Clifford "Fussy" Wootton, anyway. Not even the prospect of unlimited mugs of hot cocoa and platters of sticky buns would have persuaded me to change my mind!!

On the 14 October 1947 Mr Hougaard wrote a letter to my parents informing them that their son has definitely contracted measles – "the spots showed this morning" – and that I had been taken to the school infirmary where I would be kept for a period of about nine or so days. He also recommended that, after being discharged from hospital, I should spend a few days at home to recuperate.

I must have recovered reasonably well for there seemed no need for me to travel home and I was soon back in the classroom attempting to catch up with any lessons I had missed out on. My parents' feelings were that the forthcoming six week school vacation would in itself provide ample time for their son to recover after a week spent in a hospital bed, and they were proved correct!

Following World War Two, Britain continued to experience severe shortages of food and, as a consequence, food rationing remained in place for a number of years. My father's relatives, Julius and Elsa Weinberg had likewise managed to flee from Nazi Germany and arrived in England in 1939. Their four children had arrived in England via the renowned Kindertransport earlier that year. Conditions in Britain prompted my parents to assist the Weinberg family food wise and so arrangements were made to send them food parcels whenever possible. Commencing in 1947, and continuing for some years, foodstuffs never off the market, consisting of cooking oil, rice and other items were dispatched to them. Most packages arrived safely but some did go "missing" – prompting one to speculate that these packages may well have landed up on the notorious British black market, which had developed into a thriving institution during those bleak years of food shortages.

Conversely, we considered ourselves extremely fortunate that food rationing was almost unknown in Southern Rhodesia during the war and post-war periods. A few items were rationed at one stage, but never off the market. For example, butter was restricted to a quarter of a pound per person per week, and sugar three quarters of a pound per week, but these restrictions caused no real hardship in any sense.

Despite my earlier apprehension that, being confined to boarding school for most of the year would deprive me of viewing new movies, I was happily proved wrong and managed to see several enjoyable films, if not during the school term then at least during the vacation periods. They included *The Secret Life Of Walter Mitty, Odd Man Out, Broken Journey, Captain Boycott* and *Buck Privates Come Home* – the latter one of Abbott & Costello's better films with a climactic chase that proved, as always, to be the highlight of the film!

1948

I had always possessed a good appetite and enjoyed my meals, but oddly enough, whenever the time arrived to catch the train at the commencement of a new school term, my appetite all but vanished. Departure day left me unenthusiastically pecking at the food set out in front of me, and more often than not unable to finish the contents of the plate – a sure sign of depression! I felt the way a condemned man must probably feel when offered his last meal – not a good sign! The prospect of another three months at boarding school, with its restricted way of life and monotonous school food was enough, I am sure, to put many boarders off their food!

My mother noticed this trend and no doubt comprehended my position, and decided to adopt a new strategy. On departure day the luncheon menu was amended to now include my favourite dish – a piece of sizzling grilled steak garnished with fried onions, a liberal helping of French fries plus a bowl of rich gravy, topped with a fried egg. Dessert consisted of a bowl of yellow canned peaches! Now who could possibly resist a meal such as this placed in front of one! Her strategy certainly worked, because after that meal, and realizing what could be expected on future departure dates, my imminent thoughts about school evaporated, and my dinner plate was left as clean as a whistle! I was ready once more to face another three months of boarding school – for better or for worse!

My sister Judy was growing up fast and in January 1948 she entered Kindergarten School (then housed in a section of the Jameson School complex). She was enrolled in the infants class and in her first school report (dated April 1948) her class teacher (May Horrocks) stated that Judy was obviously an academic pupil. A good and early perception of a child only aged six, because an academic student is exactly what my sister turned out to be throughout her entire school career.

In 1952 Gatooma's new junior school was officially opened by the Governor of Southern Rhodesia, Major General Sir John Noble Kennedy, the school unsurprisingly being named Sir John Kennedy School. Judy found herself, together with her fellow classmates, studying at desks set up in the school grounds in the shade of a copse of trees, whilst the painting of the classrooms was being completed. She also found herself in the same position as I had – throughout her entire school career she was on average well over a year younger than any of her fellow classmates.

By 1954 she was at Jameson High School and entering Form 1A, remaining at Jameson until the end of her school career in 1959, obtaining the Higher School Certificate and being elected Head Girl (Head Prefect) of the school in her final year. Besides her academic side she was also a regular member of the First Team Hockey and Tennis teams. During 1960/62 she studied at the University of Cape Town, graduating with a B.A. Degree in Languages.

If there was anyone who was unsuited to competing in athletic (field and track) events it was yours truly. After invariably coming last in preliminary heats during Jameson School's annual sports days, where I represented Martin Sports House, I was not at all keen on participating in athletic events at my new school. It was therefore my intention to keep an extremely low profile upon my arrival at Prince Edward School with regard to athletics and with it the annual sports day. Unfortunately, competing in the athletic championships turned out to be compulsory for first and second year pupils, much to my regret! I was therefore compelled to participate in the preliminary heats of the junior 100 yard hurdles. Having never jumped over a hurdle before, I was now expected to leap over several of these wooden contraptions in order to reach the finishing line ... When the starter pistol went I ran as fast as I could so as to build up enough speed to clear the hurdle. But I had not yet got out of first gear on reaching the hurdle and so simply bypassed it, then headed for the second one in my path. However, having only attained second gear (I think I only possessed two gears in my repertoire) I swerved past this one as well. I felt compelled to leap up and over the third hurdle at any cost and, when I calculated that the time was ripe to do so, I jumped. Whump-thud-bang-crash!! My feet collided with the top of the hurdle and the unfortunate hurdle and I both landed up in a tangled heap on the track − probably around about the time the winner of the event was about to breast the tape at the finishing line ...

Some friends of mine informed me afterwards that they had never laughed as much in their lives as they did that afternoon whilst watching my attempt to compete in the hurdles event and even the sports master, after hearing about my misadventures on the track, spared me the indignity of competing in any further events − a real blessing to everyone concerned!

But that had happened in 1947, my first year at high school, and here we were in the first term of 1948, and with the annual athletic championships once more due to be held! Would it be possible to avoid competing this year? I sincerely hoped so, but my hopes were soon dashed. A notice went up to state that all Form 1 and Form 2 juniors were to compete in the cross country event in our age group, and that no excuses would be brooked − only those pupils currently disabled with broken legs, ankles or similar disabilities would be considered for exemption!

And this is where I met up with the schools latest "wunderkind" − a lanky young athlete who was already making a name for himself in local running circles and showing outstanding promise. As all juniors was expected to compete in the cross-country event there must have been close on one hundred and twenty competitors at the starting line when we set off on our "mini-marathon". Terry Sullivan was the name of the athlete in question and he probably became the best known runner in the annuls of the school. Terry was widely tipped to win this race − which he in fact easily did. I managed to run/stagger/walk approximately a third of the distance before coming to a halt with a severe stitch in my left side, and that after trailing way back in the field together with a couple of friends who kept each other company, so we certainly proved to be no danger to Terry's extremely promising career! For that matter, the chances were that Terry had already crossed the finishing line long before I finally panted to a halt whilst clutching my side in agony!

Terry confirmed his extraordinary running potential and broke record after record as the years went on. And on the

25 September 1960, some 12 years after I had "competed" against him, Terry Sullivan became the first man from the African continent to run a sub-four minute mile in a time of 3 minutes 59.8 seconds. He did so at a stadium in Dublin whilst competing against world record holder Herb Elliott of Australia, Peter Snell (New Zealand), Laszlo Tabori (Hungary), Ron Delaney (Ireland), Albert Thomas (Australia) and Gordon Pirie (England). And in that truly illustrious field the slim Rhodesian came in no less than second, edged out only by the unbeaten Aussie whiz Herb Elliott. That year Sullivan was named, for the second time, Rhodesian Sportsman of the Year.

The year 1948 was to prove a somewhat special one as I was due to turn thirteen years of age which meant that I would be celebrating my barmitzvah. My father had provided the necessary tuition during the six week school vacation and these lessons were in turn followed up by a further tuition period by the Reverend Clapper. By tradition, a boy's barmitzvah is normally held a week or so after he attained the age of thirteen. However, in my case this would have meant holding the barmitzvah during the first or second week of March, whereas it was our intention to hold the barmitzvah in Gatooma during the course of the three week school vacation due to fall in April/May 1948. The date therefore chosen for my barmitzvah ceremony was Saturday May 1 and I began to concentrate on learning to read the portion of the law that was due to be read from the Torah on that particular day – (Acharon Shel Pesach) – which happened to be the eighth and last day of the festival of Pesach (Passover). My barmitzvah was to be the first to be held in the town for many years – for in previous years the young boys residing in Gatooma had undergone their barmitzvah ceremonies in either one or the other of the two synagogues in Salisbury.

The rite of passage from boyhood to manhood for a Jewish boy takes place in the form of the barmitzvah ceremony. His taking part in the normal Saturday (Shabbos) morning service on his barmitzvah day requires him to read a portion from the Torah scroll (the First Five Books of Moses) in Hebrew (as fluently and as clearly as possible) in front of the entire congregation. Attaining the age of thirteen entitles the young lad to now become part of the minyan (quorum) – for a minimum of ten men are required to be in attendance in order that a Jewish religious service may be held. At the age of thirteen he therefore qualifies to fully participate in the religious life of the community.

Over the next few years my father would go on to provide barmitzvah lessons to several other Gatooma youths, and their barmitzvahs were all held in our town. In these instances my father conducted both the religious service and performed the barmitzvah ceremony. Thus remaining in Gatooma for both their barmitzvah lessons and the eventual barmitzvah service, it saved their parents the inconvenience and expense of having to travel to Salisbury for lessons spread over several months. But first the barmitzvah boys had to learn to read Hebrew – and these lessons were in turn provided by my mother for the benefit of all the Jewish children in Gatooma, boys and girls, one afternoon per week being set aside at our house. There was neither a synagogue nor a rabbi situated within almost a hundred miles of our little town and visits by rabbis were very infrequent in our neck of the woods! In future years my father was also invited to provide lessons and conduct barmitzvah ceremonies in both Que Que and Gweru, and not for nothing was he referred to as the "Chief Rabbi of the Midlands"!!

Not possessing a synagogue (this would come about only in 1953), religious services in Gatooma were held at several venues – a special memorial service was held in the Royalty Theatre in 1942 when the terrible fate that had befallen European Jewry became apparent. On High Festivals – Rosh Hashonah (New Year) and Yom Kippur (Day of Atonement) the services were held in such diverse places as the Women's Institute Hall in Newton Street and the Dutch Reformed Church Hall in Godwin Road. Other services, including barmitzvah ceremonies and those on minor festivals were usually held at various private homes or at the abovementioned W.I. Hall, and virtually all services were conducted by my father.

Several weeks prior to my barmitzvah date, my parents received another terse letter from housemaster E.J. Hougaard, dated 17 March 1948: "Just to give you the cheerless news that Peter was admitted to the school hospital suffering from chicken pox. If there is any change in his condition of which you should know I'll write again."

It would appear that I recovered reasonably well and was discharged in time to make my way home for the Easter weekend. Now for the countdown to my barmitzvah!

Apart from the entire Jewish community of Gatooma and the surrounding district being invited to my barmitzvah, a goodly number of friends made the journey from both Salisbury and Que Que and stayed over for the sundowner party which was held the following evening, also in our garden at Smith Street. My uncle and aunt, Julius and Marta Philippson, and cousins, Enid and Elmer, motored from Bulawayo, where they were now living, in their 1934 Hudson Terraplane. Eva Marks arrived from Salisbury a week prior to the barmitzvah to lend a hand where asked and a number of the local ladies assisted my mother with the food preparations. It was great having Eva come and visit and we had a most enjoyable time during her all too brief stay. I read my barmitzvah portion from the almost one hundred year old Torah which had travelled with us on the "Ussukuma" a scant nine years earlier, the Torah that my great grandfather Herz Sternberg had donated to his community in Erwitte. In his wildest dreams he surely could never have envisaged that one day this Torah would be utilized in Africa by his grandson and now by his great-grandson on his barmitzvah day. For, when this Torah had first been read, the country of Rhodesia was non-existent, being just a portion of land in "Darkest Africa"! However, I am pleased to say that both the barmitzvah ceremony and the party held the following day went off very well indeed and a good time was had by all! And years later that same Torah was used for the barmitzvahs of my own two sons.

The Jewish community living in Gatooma and the surrounding district in the late 1940s consisted of some sixty souls, more or less equally divided in number between Sephardi Jews (originating from the Middle East – in this case virtually all originated from Rhodes Island (Rodos) in the Dodecanes – situated in the Aegean Sea), and Ashkenasi Jews (Eastern Europe – many from Lithuania, and a few from Western Europe). Most were involved in retail trading in the town, the majority owning small to medium sized businesses, with the wives often assisting their husbands in their shops.

Families tended to socialize over the weekends by playing cards – rummy and poker being their games of choice. From Mondays through to mid-day Saturdays shop-keeping formed the basis of their lives, but Saturday afternoons after lunch they met at various homes to play cards and in the evening most attended Joe Burke's bioscope (their seats being permanently reserved for them). Whilst some followed the story line of the movie, others simply slept throughout the film! Saturday night attendance at the cinema appeared to be almost obligatory – many patrons attended regardless of what movie was being shown, who starred in the film, and for that matter what the story was about ... Films screened at the Royalty Theatre were advertised in Joe Burke's *Gatooma Mail* – films were usually classified as being either comedies, musicals, thrillers, horror, melodramas or dramas. The latter classification was widely used and should the story line/theme appear unclear the film was automatically tabbed a drama. Problem solved!

Sunday mornings after breakfast card games resumed and continued throughout the day, the poker school often going well into Sunday night. Routine conversation around the tables often centred on business matters – the cost of goods, the current availability of goods and about the competition posed by new shops opening up in the area. A number of these new shops were owned by Indian traders, who at times tended to undercut the competition's selling prices. The usual discussion around the poker tables one Sunday morning (on 1 February 1948, to be exact) was interrupted when news of Indian leader Mahatma Gandhi's assassination, which had occurred on the previous day, was announced on the radio.

"WHO died?" asked one of the players when the startling news was broken to the group seated around the poker table.

"Gandhi" was the answer.

"Who is Gandhi?"

"Gandhi the Indian – surely you know of him?"

"Gandhi the Indian? No, I don't know him. Where's his shop?"

And believe it or not the questioner was being perfectly serious! Obviously business, not politics, was his forte!

Husband and wife Sam and Tilly Cohen owned a small retail business in Cam Road selling clothing, the shop going under the name of Railway Cash Store. Tilly was a well spoken and very voluble person, whereas her husband appeared to have great difficulty in not only recalling the names of other people, but also in completing sentences which he had started. Sam was nick-named "Watchchemacallit" for good reason. When talking about someone Sam stated that he had recently spoken to "Ahem, I was speaking to (pause) ahem, you know what I mean, I mean to say – I was speaking to Whatchemacallit, who told me (pause) ... Tilly then took over the conversation by supplying the person's name that Sam could not recall and valiantly tried to carry on with Sam's long winded story, but usually by that stage the listener had lost interest in the conversation ...!

I do not recall ever having had a full length conversation with Sam Cohen without his wife taking over and finishing off Sam's story. And when mentioning Sam to others one only needed to say "Whatchemacallit" and everyone knew exactly to whom one was referring!

Several of the Sephardi members of the community tended to have extremely short fuses and took offence easily, frequently getting into arguments, more often than not with fellow Sephardis. When this happened they tended to cold shoulder each other, and news soon spread around town that so-and-so was no longer speaking to so-and-so. When invitations were issued to play cards these currently "feuding" couples were always placed at separate card tables! During the course of the spat they often treated the other party as being virtually "non-existent". This could last from several days to several months, until some sort of "truce" was brokered and the art of the spoken word was once again resumed.

One weekend afternoon Sam Hasson, reputed to be the wealth-iest man in town (he owned the largest wholesale business in the entire district) met up with one of his friends (let us call him Joe) whilst out on an afternoon walk. But Joe was accompanied by the very person whom Sam was (currently) not on speaking terms with! This did not upset Sam in the slightest. Without batting an eyelid and cutting dead his former friend, Sam greeted Joe with a loud "Hello Joe, what are you doing here ALL BY YOURSELF?"

Now that's what I would call the perfect snub!!

Sam's younger brother Jack was a confirmed bachelor, and when he tragically died at the age of 64 in 1970, his nephew Reuben, when sorting through the contents of the stock in Jack's shop in Gatooma (which catered for the Black African market) in order to stock-take for estate purposes, had great difficulty in costing the goods. For Jack, it would appear, had placed orders with seemingly every commercial traveller who had ever called on him. Consequently his shop was crammed full of men's, women's and children's clothing, shoes, cycle spares, items of hardware including long out of date paraffin stoves, all stock-piled literally from floor to ceiling. This left scant space for customers to enter the premises! Reuben discovered to his complete amazement that hundreds of bundles and cardboard boxes of completely out of date clothing and perished cycle tubes lay hidden at the rear of the shop, covered by piles of blankets and other items. These articles were still wrapped in the original newspapers of the day in which they had arrived from the manufacturers – and many of the newspapers were dated a few years prior to the outbreak of World War Two!

Following my barmitzvah, the rest of the vacation sped by and I soon found myself back at Jameson House to face the second term of 1948. This boarding hostel, which accommodated some 80 boys aged between 12 and 18, was home to only one other Jewish boy besides myself and he was a year or two older than me. Let us call him "Solly" (not his real name). He too came from a small Rhodesian town and my identification as a conforming Jew seemed to trouble him for some reason or other. All the other boys and teachers accepted my religious denomination – notwithstanding the occasional dumb anti-Semitic remarks uttered by a few fellow boarders from time to time.

Solly appeared to be almost permanently dissatisfied, and had been upset with me for quite some considerable time. For at homework sessions in the prep room on Friday nights following dinner, I refrained from undertaking any written homework, for I had been brought up not to write on our Sabbath. He informed me proudly that HE had no problem whatsoever in writing on the Jewish Sabbath. He became even more upset when I replied that what he did was entirely his decision and that, as far as I was concerned, he was welcome to do whatever suited him best.

I told him to stop criticizing me, for what I did or did not do should be of no concern of his.

For I had discovered that if you are true to your own beliefs, most reasonable people will respect those beliefs and I told him emphatically to back off.

Solly also became "cheesed off" (to use a parlance of the time) when I attended synagogue on various religious festivals throughout the year, in the process having to take days off from school. His criticism became even more intense as the months went by so I decided to have a chat with "Jeeves" Hougaard, our housemaster, and explained this somewhat unhealthy position to him, for it appeared to me that Solly appeared to be rapidly heading out of control. No doubt this prompted Jeeves to have a chat with Solly, who thereafter proceeded to ignore me for the next few weeks. The majority of these incidents with Solly took place during our first year of high school, but when it now became obvious that I was spending time in early 1948 studying for my forthcoming barmitzvah, all of Solly's resentments and frustrations appeared to resurface. He again began to criticize anything and everything pertaining to the Jewish religion but matters worsened (for him) when a number of fellow pupils began to question him as to why he (Solly) failed to attend synagogue on religious festivals and why he persisted in doing his written homework on Friday nights when clearly he should not be doing so! Was he not proud of his religion? It seemed obvious that he was rattled by these questions which he had clearly not anticipated.

During the second term of 1948, just a few short weeks following my barmitzvah, Solly let on to the fact that when he himself had turned thirteen the previous year, his parents had refused to allow him to have a barmitzvah. Thus, observing the preparations leading up to my barmitzvah seemed to have stirred up further resentment, and this is most probably why he decided to take his frustration and anger out on me rather than on his parents. His situation now began to make some sense, and in one of his more friendly moments (he could surprisingly enough be fairly amiable at times depending on his frame of mind) we discussed this matter. I put the proposition to him that I might be able to borrow some Hebrew books (and I knew I would be able to source some without any problem) and offered to teach him the basics of reading Hebrew. This would then enable him to proceed with his studies and, in due course, hopefully undergo a barmitzvah. He seemed amenable to the idea and so, for the few weeks that remained of the second school term, I taught him the Hebrew alphabet and some basic reading. It may almost have been a case of the blind leading the blind, but he appeared to enjoy the all too few lessons we managed to complete and his outlook on life seemed to improve, for his criticisms on religious matters and his other gripes came to an abrupt and welcome halt!

However, the following school term Solly failed to turn up at Jameson House and we never saw or heard of him again. I never learned the reason for his dropping out of Prince Edward School, and no one else seemed in a position to shed any light on the matter either. My recollections of Solly faded over the years until, some fifty years later, and quite by chance, I discovered that he had recently died in a ward of the Ingutsheni Mental Hospital in Bulawayo, in which institution he had been detained as a patient for very many years. A sad ending indeed to an obviously troubled individual ...

I continued to attend Sabbath morning services at the Salisbury Street synagogue and was astonished to find that quite frequently there were not enough men to form the necessary minyan (prayer quorum of ten males aged 13 and over) in order to hold a service. This in a city of several hundred Jewish men, the majority of whom could quite easily have devoted a few hours of their time to ensure that the regular Saturday morning service was held. When instances like these occurred, Rabbi Konviser simply halted the service at a given point and requested that one or two of the congregants in attendance visit a few of the men residing in close proximity to the synagogue and ask them to interrupt their mid-morning siesta or whatever else they happened to be doing and come over to the synagogue so as to make up a minyan in order to be able to continue with the service. This procedure never failed, and after a break of perhaps ten to fifteen minutes we managed to continue with the service!

A further letter from Mr Hougaard dated 27 July 1948 informed my parents that I had recently had my eyes tested by the visiting government doctor. This doctor had recommended that I consult an eye specialist for further check ups with a view to possibly having to wear spectacles. My eyesight had obviously deteriorated since I caught measles the previous year, and this in fact proved to be the case. In due course I went for a further examination and the outcome was that I became the not so proud owner of a pair of spectacles – or as we called them – "goggles"!

I wore these spectacles in the classroom so as to see the blackboard better and to read books more clearly – once I was out of the classroom the "goggles" came off!! How vain can one get??!! One afternoon I happened to be walking through Salisbury Gardens on my way to the city centre when a pretty young lady walked past. Her face seemed slightly familiar but, to be quite frank, I could not place her – especially as I was, as usual, not wearing my spectacles. We smiled at each other as we passed and a few seconds later she called out and asked whether I was on my way to going blind and if that was the case I should invest in a pair of spectacles! To my intense embarrassment this pretty young lady turned out to be Herta Stiefel (who was well aware that I should have been wearing my spectacles on a permanent basis) and whose voice of course I instantly recognized! I apologized profusely and promised to wear my spectacles henceforth! Which I promptly proceeded to do!

The first Olympic Games to be staged since 1936 – the first post World War Two Olympiad, took place in London during the months of July/August 1948 and I followed the events through the columns of the *Rhodesia Herald* and the *Sunday Mail.* Athletes such as McDonald Bailey, Fanny Blankers-Koen and Emile Zatopek become overnight heroes and many athletic records were broken but it was the progress of the richly talented South African boxing team that I was particularly interested in. Bantamweight representative Vic Toweel, who boasted a phenomenal amateur record and had been hotly tipped to win Olympic gold, was eliminated in the very first series, the victim of a most dubious decision. In contrast, near novice Johnny Arthur (S.A.) managed to win a bronze medal in the heavyweight division, while featherweight Dennis Shepherd (S.A.) won no less than a silver medal. But the glory went to two other South

African's - Gerald Dreyer (lightweight) and George Hunter (light-heavyweight) who both won their weight divisions and the gold medals that went with it. The Val Barker Cup, awarded to the most proficient boxer of the Games, was contested between Dreyer and Hunter with Hunter edging out his compatriot in the voting and thus receiving this prestigious trophy. It established South Africa as the top amateur boxing nation in the world at that point in time, and I would never have imagined that, many years later, I would personally interview George Hunter in his home near Johannesburg for a magazine article that I intended to write. He let me handle his Olympic gold medal - the first (and to date only) Olympic medal I had ever seen!

It was at the Palace Theatre in Salisbury that I saw one of the funniest and at the same time scariest movies that I have ever seen when *Abbott & Costello Meet Frankenstein* was screened. Introducing the Universal Studios monsters - Dracula (Bela Lugosi), the Wolfman (Lon Chaney Jnr) and the Frankenstein monster (Glenn Strange) into the Abbott and Costello comedy routine whilst playing their monster roles in true horror configuration made for exciting viewing and the film received rave reviews. Unfortunately it was also the last occasion that I can truly say that I enjoyed watching an Abbott and Costello movie, for I felt that their humour and the quality of their films no longer appealed to me. Perhaps I had outgrown my childhood heroes of the screen ...

Salisbury's other three cinemas which I also frequented on occasion were the Prince's Theatre, which was in actual fact a large dance cum banqueting hall which could seat some 800 people for official events. The building had started out as the venue for Rhodesia's first parliament in May 1924. It was later converted into a cinema but the seats remained removable, and it was occasionally used as a dance hall. Then there was the more modern Victory Cinema, situated at the corner of First Street and Jameson Avenue, which screened movies released by 20th Century Fox and a few other selected studios. And finally there was the infamous Little Palace which was to be found just around the corner from the Palace Theatre, with its entrance leading into Union Avenue. The Little Palace, as the name implies, was a very much smaller cinema that specialised in screening the then still popular cowboy movies churned out by Hollywood. Colourful posters bearing such titles as *Last Days of Boot Hill, West of the Pecos, Desperate Trails* and *Roll on Texas Moon* – often as not starring Gene Autry, Roy Rogers, John Wayne and Johnny Mack Brown were prominently displayed to lure in the patrons. Weekly serials, also popular at the time, were likewise screened at this cinema and some of the posters that I recall seeing were *Spy Smasher, Superman, King of the Rocket Men* and *New Adventures of Batman and Robin.* Despite this cinema being known as "the bug house" (and not without good reason), schoolchildren nevertheless gathered in large numbers for Saturday morning and afternoon matinees and traded comic books, consumed ice cream and popcorn. These items were usually purchased from the nearby Popular Cafe. Laden with confectionery, the young patrons lustily cheered on their heroes who either galloped or flew across the silver screen.

Feature films were screened most Saturday evenings in the Prince Edward School Beit Hall, on the school's 16mm projector, Rhodesian Regiment Drill Hall and, although the films shown were generally not of the very latest vintage, the shows were nevertheless well supported. After all, what else was there to do on a Saturday night in a boys' hostel? One of the first films I saw at the Beit Hall was *Green For Danger,* a thriller starring Alistair Sim and Trevor Howard, both at the time popular stars of the British screen.

As previously mentioned, amateur boxing tournaments, featuring local and provincial teams competing against each other were the norm but a number of times a year an all-Rhodesian team was pitted against various South African provinces and I well recall standing room only at the Drill Hall in Moffat Street one Saturday night when the Rhodesian and Natal boxing teams clashed in a real donnybrook of a fight bill. We seldom missed out on these all action and well supported events. The Drill Hall became my local version of Madison Square Garden for a couple of nights per year!

My interest in boxing kept growing and I now spent some considerable time in the school gymnasium watching the school boxing team train. Prince Edward boasted quite a number of good junior boxers during those years and eventually I began to train with them. This in due course led to a few tentative sparring sessions with boys of my age and weight. Inter-school boxing matches against schools and clubs such as Umtali Boys High, St George's College and St Joseph's Home for Boy's formed part of the regular school sports calendar and many of the school's top boxers regularly participated in provincial and national championships. The more skilful boxers were chosen to represent Southern Rhodesia in international competitions and were also selected to represent the country in the South African National Junior championships. Some of the Prince Edward boxers held Mashonaland (provincial) and Rhodesian titles and quite a few had boxed internationally. Amongst the top boxers at Prince Edward in those years were Brian Chappell, Raymond "Ray" Robinson, Robin Hein, Johnny Lewis, Donny Wallace, Clive Mandy, Roy Morris and last, but by no means least, "Telf" Juul, regarded by many as an almost "semi-professional" due to his prowess in the ring and the fact that he already sported a nose that any professional boxer would have been proud of!

I sparred a few times with fellow classmate Roy Morris, an exceptionally well-schooled, fast and hard punching boxer who was a regular representative on the boxing squad, being a top calibre exponent in the noble art of self-defence. Shortly after leaving school Roy joined the Southern Rhodesian Air Force in March 1952, eventually retiring with the rank of Wing Commander. At one stage he also joined the Royal Air Force and flew as a fighter pilot with No. 266 (Rhodesia Squadron) based in Germany. Later he went on to join the Sultan of Oman's Air Force in the Middle East, flying jets. He appears to have had a most exciting and satisfying career.

Schoolmaster Jim Wright was the school's head boxing coach and he encouraged me to continue training in the gym and later in the year suggested I enter for the 1948 Prince Edward School championships (novices division), which I was happy to do. And so, sometime in late October I found that I had been drawn against one Peter Alexander in the first series of the lightweight division. Alexander, although obviously in my weight class, proved to have a six inch height advantage with a corresponding reach to match, and would therefore quite literally prove to be a "tall order" for me to come up against in my very first amateur bout. I approached Mr Wright for advice on how to combat such a tall opponent and he passed on a number of valuable tips on to me in this respect.

His good advice paid off handsomely, for Peter Alexander hardly laid a glove on me and I won a fairly comfortable points decision over the scheduled three round distance.

With this win I now found myself in the quarter-finals, but my opponent pulled out at the last minute and I therefore received a direct bye into the semi-finals. My opponent turned out to be Rafael (Raffi) Cohen, a tough looking Jewish kid. Not only did he look tough but he was – and when the opening bell rang he charged out of his corner throwing punches from all quarters. His all action style forced me to trade punches in return in an effort to stay in the fight and my upper body and arms were aching all over when the bell rang to end the first round.

We both came out punching at the start of the second round, for I realised that I needed to attack if I was to stand any chance of winning. At that instance Raffi aimed a blow in the direction of my head – I managed to slip the punch whilst instinctively throwing an overhand right in the general direction of his jaw. My punch must have landed spot on, for Raffi suddenly found himself on the seat of his pants! The knockdown appeared to be far more spectacular than damaging, but I had scored some valuable points in the process and this no doubt helped influence the referee in awarding me what must have been a narrow points decision at the end of three action packed rounds. I was through to the finals!

The finals were due to be held on the night of Saturday 6 November 1948 in the Prince Edward School Beit Hall, but this particular choice of date upset me no end. For it coincided with the "big fight" that was being staged that very same night in Johannesburg between my hero Johnny Ralph, the heavyweight champion of South Africa, and Freddie Mills, Britain's reigning world light-heavyweight champion. They were scheduled to meet each other in a 12-round eliminator for the right to challenge Bruce Woodcock for the latter's British Empire heavyweight crown. Having tuned in on the radio to a number of Ralph's fights over the past two years, this was one fight broadcast I was not going to miss listening to if I could possibly help it! The fight was anticipated to break all South African box office records which indeed it did.

The night in question found me sitting hunched up over a small radio set in a corner of the dressing room, a dark and gloomy place situated under the stage of the Beit Hall, and lit by a few dim light bulbs. The commentary from South Africa was often interrupted by loud and prolonged static Johnny Ralph vs Freddie Mills hisses and it took a great deal of concentration on my part to fathom what was going on in the ring at Johannesburg's Wembley Stadium, several hundred miles to the south of us, where a delirious crowd roared out support for their hero. At the same time I was trying to blot out the local crowd's cheers and yells which filtered through from the Beit Hall just the other side of the dressing room wall. My mind was fully focused on the Ralph fight, round two had just ended, and Johnny seemed to be holding his own against the fearsome punching world champion. Provided Ralph stuck to his boxing and kept away from Mills' winging punches he would surely go on to win ... Having already donned the red vest of Jameson House, I found a hand suddenly placed on my shoulder which startled me – until I realized that it was time to glove up and make my way up the basement steps into the hall, and from there into the ring! And, with my mind still firmly attuned to the fight in Johannesburg, I ducked through the ropes to be greeted by a chorus of loud cheers from the Jameson House supporters.

My opponent was the lanky Trevor Ruile, a future Rhodesian and Springbok hockey international, who unfortunately used his trombone like left to keep me at bay throughout virtually every minute of the three rounder. Try as I might I could not get sufficiently close enough to punch effectively to his body, and there was no doubt in my mind at the final bell that he rightly deserved the decision. I was not at all upset in losing, and was only too thankful to leave the ring to make my way back to the dressing room. There I found the little radio still hissing away in the corner where I had left it. But alas, the big fight was over and brave Johnny Ralph had been defeated – knocked out in the eighth round. I was utterly devastated – my hero had just lost his first fight. The fact that I had just lost MY first fight did not trouble me in the least – it was Johnny Ralph's defeat that upset me! But I was not alone – I read later that most South African boxing fans had gone into mourning following their hero's first loss in the professional ring! And ironically, this fight had proved to be Freddie Mills' last win of his own professional career, which had been a lengthy one.

My sole consolation that night was the fact that the certificates awarded to all finalists at the conclusion of the evening's boxing were to be presented by no less a personality than Don McCorkindale, a former South African heavyweight boxing champion (1930-1933). He had once been rated fifth in the world rankings in the early 1930s and had fought many of the leading heavyweights of his day. I was thrilled to be able to shake his large hand as he handed me my certificate. To me this was indeed an honour. What was clearly obvious however was the fact that none of the other boxers being presented with certificates that evening seemed particularly impressed by his presence. I very much doubt that they had ever heard of him, his name obviously meant nothing to them. But what I did not know at the time – but only read about some years later, was that Don McCorkindale's former wife Chrissie had only recently married Freddie Mills, the fighter who earlier that evening had knocked out my hero Johnny Ralph!

For the past few years I had been nagging my father to purchase a motorcar, for it appeared to me that all my friends' parents owned cars – why therefore could we not have one as well? The standard answer I received was that although he had every intention of acquiring a car, he had decided to purchase a new vehicle and not a second-hand (pre-used) model, and that he was still in the process of saving up for one. As I could find no fault in his reasoning, I bottled up my disappointment and refrained from repeating the same question for at least another few months!

I purchased my first book on boxing, a recently published hardcover entitled *Ring Battles of the Century* by the noted British boxing historian and writer Gilbert E. Odd. I little realized at the time that this was to be the first of a fairly comprehensive library of boxing books that I would accumulate over the years that followed. This particular book, which cost all of 8/6 (eight shillings and sixpence) was purchased at Ness & Archibald, one of Salisbury's leading bookshops at that time. The book contained vivid descriptions of many exciting fights and even covered the epic 1932 contest between Larry Gains of Canada and Don McCorkindale of South Africa – yes, the very same McCorkindale whose hand I had recently shaken whilst being presented with my certificate! I realized there and then that I was well and truly hooked on boxing and have remained so to this day!

On Rhodes & Founders weekend (early July) I had hitch-hiked home for the four day vacation. To save me hiking back to school on Tuesday afternoon, my father had managed to secure a ride back to Salisbury for me with one of his clients, an Asian shop keeper. This person was quite happy to collect me from my home directly after lunch and, what was more, drop me off right outside the front steps of Jameson House, thus ensuring that I would arrive well in time to beat the 6 p.m. curfew.

I was duly collected in a very antiquated mid-1930's half tonne pick-up truck which sported an extremely narrow cab with a single bench seat just wide enough to accommodate the driver and one passenger. A long gear lever arose from the floorboards and ending up half way across the seat between driver and passenger, restricting passenger space even further. Climbing into the cab, I found that the passenger seat was already occupied by an elderly gentleman, likewise travelling to Salisbury. After he had moved up a little to provide space, I just managed to squeeze myself in. This person now found himself seated, or shall I say crushed, between the driver and myself, with the added inconvenience of having the top of the gear lever prodding into the lower regions of his stomach. With a driver and two passengers, for which the cab was never designed, it meant that I was hemmed in tightly between the left hand passenger door and this now semi-trapped individual in the centre. To make matters worse, the passenger door would not shut properly and required three or four hefty slams before it would stay closed. It rattled alarmingly throughout the entire journey. These were the days long before the introduction of seat belts – only racing drivers and aviators appeared to wear such devices at that time!

Although July was classified as a "winter" month it nevertheless became uncomfortably warm in the cab with three people practically sitting on top of each other. The perspiration soon began to flow. After we had travelled for about fifteen minutes the elderly gentleman began to nod off, no doubt having dined well prior to our departure and now ready for his afternoon nap. And so it proved to be, for he soon fell fast asleep and not only did he begin to snore loudly but also to belch and burp at an alarming rate, which soon caused the interior of the cab to fill up with a most rank and sour smell. Before long I began to feel distinctly nauseous.

The solution, I figured out, was to open the passenger door window and take in a breath of fresh air. But in this respect I was thwarted. The window would simply not roll down – the handle was tightly jammed! I tried a number of times – nothing budged. Upon asking the driver why the glass would not lower he laughingly replied that the handle had been broken for many years and that he intended to repair it "one day". However, he lowered the window on his side of the cab to its full extent and gradually the foul air was extricated. I began to feel a little less queasy and decided that the worst part of the journey was now hopefully behind me. But how wrong can one get!

Some time later the old man awoke, somehow managing to straighten himself upright on the cramped seat and proceeded to fumble around in his trouser pockets. Eventually he let out a grunt of satisfaction when obviously locating whatever he was looking for. He extricated something from his pocket and proceeded to pop it into his mouth. A short pause and then began a prolonged period of chewing. After some time I noticed that a reddish coloured fluid began to drool out of his mouth. This fluid slowly dribbled down and proceeded to mix with the stubble on his unshaven chin. The steady sound of chewing continued as I tried to keep myself occupied by looking out of the cab window, attempting to read the milestone markers which were placed at even intervals along the side of the road. I tried to calculate how long it would still take before we finally reached our destination. Never before had I been so keen to arrive back at school!

And then it happened! This old fellow, despite his continued chewing, appeared to have dozed off again but suddenly he manoeuvred himself up with a start. He turned his head in my direction and without any warning whatsoever, expelled a stream of reddish tinged liquid towards the tightly shut window on my left – expelling a seemingly endless stream of what turned out to be betel nut juice, liberally mixed with saliva. This delightful concoction barely missed my face and splattered onto the glass, just above the spot where my left shoulder was tightly wedged!

Within seconds the juices began to run down the window pane and onto my white shirt. Due to the cramped conditions in the vehicle there was absolutely nothing I could do to move myself out of harm's way. This left me no choice but to allow the vile liquid to seep onto and down the length of my left arm, turning my shirtsleeves into a distinct shade of red in the process. It was even impossible to reach into my trouser pocket to pull out my handkerchief to assist in wiping this mess off. No apology was tendered – not that it would have made any difference – and the driver appeared quite oblivious as to what had just taken place. Once again the old man began to drift off to sleep, completely unaware that the window pane had not been open and that the betel juice was liberally running down my arm and trouser leg instead of having targeted the roadside as had no doubt been his intention ...

At long last we arrived in Salisbury and I was deposited outside Jameson House as had been promised. I collected my small suitcase from the rear of the vehicle, bid farewell to the driver and made my way into the hostel as unobtrusively as I possibly could. My shirtsleeve would undoubtedly have given the impression that I had been shot in the shoulder and that at least half of my lifeblood had managed to drain out in the process! I caught a glimpse of myself in the mirror on my way to the showers and a Hollywood make-up artist could not have produced a more realistic portrayal of a "blood soaked" individual in distress! Thereafter I probably had the longest shower I had ever experienced before or since as I stood under the hot water trying to scrub away the betel juice which had permeated my skin over the past hour or so. And my white shirt required several washes and some bleach before it could be fully restored to its natural colour!

In due course I related this incident to my parents and strongly intimated that in future I would much prefer to hitch-hike back to school on my own, even taking my chances of arriving after the curfew hour had elapsed, rather than ever having to accept a ride of this nature again. I must say both agreed wholeheartedly with my sentiments on this matter!

A table tennis table was purchased during the year, and my mother and I enjoyed playing against each other. I also introduced the game to a number of friends, for there appeared to be very few tables in Gatooma. As there was no space to set up the table indoors, we played out in the garden, but the vagaries of wind and weather curtailed many a game. A table tennis table was likewise acquired by Jameson House and a number of us played in the prep room over weekends. This was one game I thoroughly enjoyed, and after leaving school played Mashonaland Province league table tennis, managed and captained the Gatooma team against teams from Salisbury, Que Que and Gwelo, whilst also competing in the Rhodesian table tennis championships which were held annually over the Rhodes and Founders weekend.

Tradition had it that Guy Fawkes night (5 November) was celebrated by all the Prince Edward School boarding houses individually. We boarders all had a few shillings deducted off our pocket money (kept in safekeeping by housemasters in each individual hostel) towards the purchase of suitable fireworks, in order to commemorate this old British custom. With starbursts exploding in the night sky all around us as far as the eye could see, we too joined in the fun and enjoyed an exciting fifteen minutes or so. During this time we set off our modest contribution of squibs, firecrackers, whizzers, flashbangs and rockets which all added to the light and noise reverberating around the night skies above the city of Salisbury.

Tradition also had it that on every Guy Fawkes night the hedge surrounding the Jameson housemaster's private garden was set alight by an "errant" firework that somehow managed to zoom off course, despite having been allegedly aimed into the sky! The tinder dry foliage of the hedge always seemed to lie directly in the path of this errant missile, causing the unfortunate hedge to burst into flames within a few seconds of being struck. By the time a bucket of water had been brought onto the scene by an unwilling junior, it was generally too late to douse what was left of the smouldering foliage ...

End of year examinations followed some weeks later, and soon it was time to head back home for the six week school holidays –

to many of us unquestionably the highlight of the entire year! And when I arrived home I was pleased to see that we had recently had a telephone installed in our house, our given phone number being Gatooma 187. In later years as the town expanded, an automatic telephone exchange was installed, and this number was upgraded to read 2187. However, until that time came about and automatic dialling became the norm, we were still compelled to place calls through the town's manually operated telephone exchange. The operator would then phone the number requested and provided it was answered, connect the two lines. Although the system then in use may have been a well dated one, at least the telephones always seemed to work without fail!

Other films I managed to see during the year included *Treasure of the Sierra Madre* (Humphrey Bogart), *Oliver Twist* (Alec Guinness), *Sleeping Car To Trieste* (Albert Lieven/Jean Kent), *The Red Shoes* (Moira Shearer), *Sorry Wrong Number* (Barbara Stanwyck), *Easter Parade* (Fred Astaire and Judy Garland) and *Words and Music* (with an all star cast). I was not missing out on movies after all!

1949

Having now reached the required age, I was duly attested into the school cadet corps programme. This brought home to me the fact that for the next few years, Friday afternoons would from now be devoted to donning uniform and partaking in military training of one kind or another. And so it turned out, for one Friday afternoon early in February we first year recruits found ourselves lined up outside the school armoury, where we were duly issued with a khaki shirt and a pair of knee length shorts, a pair of stockings, an army belt, puttees, a khaki hat, a pair of black boots and other necessary paraphernalia. Thereafter we were made to sign on the dotted line for all the items that had been handed to us, and were advised to spend the next seven days thoroughly cleaning and polishing our newly issued boots until they literally sparkled. This, so that our drill instructors would be able to recognize their own reflections in our highly polished boots during the course of our first parade, which was due to be held the following Friday afternoon!!

In the week that followed, in between all our other myriad duties and activities, we concentrated on polishing our boots as we had been advised to, and buffed up our dull and drab belt buckles until they too shone. Spit and polish was the order of the day, and the following Friday afternoon we lined up on one of the school sports fields which had been allocated as an assembly point for first year cadets. There we were instructed to sit on the ground and listen to a lecture by one of the Staff Corps sergeants. There being no sports practices and activities on Friday afternoons, a number of fields were utilized for cadet activities, for there were close to four hundred cadets at Prince Edward School at that time, probably the largest number from any of the high schools in the country. The lecture was provided by one of the many Southern Rhodesian Permanent Staff Corps instructors who were seconded to Prince Edward each Friday afternoon. However, not a single instructor bothered to come close enough to view their reflections in the toe caps of our boots – much to our combined relief!

Over the next few weeks we began to learn the rudiments of parade ground drill and this activity went on for months on end – Atten-shun! Forward march, right turn, left turn, about turn, left wheel, right wheel, halt! Mark time, halt! Stand at ease. Atten-shun! Forward march, halt! About turn! Quick march, halt! Were we ever going to be issued with actual weapons or would these endless drilling routines continue unabated?

Eventually our question was answered. One Friday afternoon we were ordered to line up outside the school armoury and were finally issued with weapons – fairly old and well worn rifles from some previous conflict – some joked that they may have well been relics left over from the legendary Allan Wilson Patrol which dated back to 1893! The rifles were certainly not in the best of condition. We were shown how to dismantle these weapons, oil and clean them thoroughly and then reassemble them, so that the mechanism once again worked the way that it had been intended to. Now that we had finally had some contact with a rifle most of us were under the impression that we would soon be taken off to the rifle range for some shooting practice. How naive can one get – the rifles had only been issued in order that we could now learn the rudiments of rifle drill. This meant that the terms "present arms, shoulder arms", "slope arms", etc. were added to the lexicon of instructions that were to be learnt by rote!

Most of our drill instructors were sergeants from the previously mentioned Southern Rhodesian Army Permanent Staff Corps, and with few exceptions they tended to bellow out their instructions at the very top of their voices, injecting the maximum number of decibels into their commands. This I felt somehow defeated their intended purpose – for instead of issuing an order that could clearly be heard and understood by all concerned, their commands often tended to culminate in a yell that virtually no one in the squad could meaningfully decipher! Their philosophy appeared to be that the louder they shouted the better, even if the orders given to the cadets often proved to be completely unintelligible!

We soon came to the conclusion that certain members of the Staff Corps could be termed competent instructors whilst others were judged to be barely qualified for the role. However, there was no doubt that we all looked up to one of them – John "Ox" Barritt who just happened to be a member of the Rhodesian rugby team (1947-1956) and a Springbok trialist to boot. He garnered respect both on the rugby field and on the parade ground and all the cadets in our squad valiantly tried to follow his commands and instructions to the very best of our abilities. To us "young squaddies" he was definitely regarded as being one of the "good guys"!

For those now having attained entry into Form 3, cricket thankfully no longer became a compulsory sport in the first and third terms. I happily dropped this sport, although I doubt that anyone had even noticed my absence these past two years at cricket practice! I commenced playing tennis a few times a month on the school courts, these being conveniently situated right next to the Jameson House hostel. Unfortunately at the time I never took the game seriously enough to bother registering for actual tennis coaching, an omission I very much came to regret in the years that followed. Many of the tennis coaches at the school were themselves either current or former national champions and were well versed in all rudiments of the game. The standard of tennis has always been very high at Prince Edward and a fellow boarder at Jameson House in my final year was Adrian Bey, a future Rhodesian champion. He would in due course go on to play top class international tennis, including appearances at Wimbledon, and he further distinguished himself as a regular member of the Rhodesian Davis Cup squad over a period of many years. He was just one of many top players produced by the school, in later years the list would include Colin Dowdeswell, a doubles finalist at Wimbledon.

And two further world class sportsmen whom Prince Edward School would be proud of in the past pupil category were two brilliant golfers, namely Nick Price, who would go on to be crowned world champion and Mark McNulty, ranked 7th in golf's world rankings in 1991.

From Mondays through to Fridays the *Rhodesia Herald* newspaper was delivered around 5.00 a.m., being thrown onto the verandah of our hostel just outside our bedroom window by the passing newspaper roundsman (the *Sunday Mail* arrived even earlier on weekends) – intended reading material for the housemaster and hostel staff. If awake early enough I donned my dressing gown (in winter) and went onto the front verandah to read the papers from cover to cover before anyone else in the hostel had even stirred. This saved me a visit to the school library during the half hour break period between 10.30 a.m. and 11.00 a.m. each weekday where competition to read the *Herald* was always great, there being only one copy of the daily paper subscribed to by the school library despite several dozen eager readers waiting in line.

When teachers availed themselves of long leave this usually implied that they were away for an entire three-month term (semester). In instances like these, "reserve" teaching staff (usually retired teachers) were recruited for the period in question. This happened to our class during 1949 when one of our more popular teachers went away for a well earned rest and his replacement turned out to be a very grumpy and ill mannered old man whom we took to be in his early eighties – a character definitely from the "old school brigade". No doubt long retired from his teaching career, he gave us the unmistakable impression that he was far from happy to have had his retirement rudely disturbed in order to help out, and he made it quite clear to us from the outset that he blamed our class for inconveniencing his normal routine and keeping him away from his carpet slippers and retirement!

Within the first week the entire class had come to the conclusion that this individual was by far the worst teacher whom we had ever had the misfortune of encountering during our school career. We unanimously agreed that he was obviously way past his "sell by" date. We also calculated that his teaching career would probably have spanned from the late nineteenth century to around 1940 or so, and we sympathized with all those pupils whom he had taught over that period of time, which might well have included some of our fellow classmates' parents and possibly even a grandparent or two!

We suffered a week of non-stop verbal abuse, in which he berated almost each and every member of our class for being a "complete idiot" (his favourite expression). He also assured us that "NONE of us would EVER amount to ANYTHING in life, for he had NEVER encountered such a group of USELESS louts" sitting under one roof! This, he shouted, "thoroughly convinced him without even the SLIGHTEST doubt that we were ALL heading straight for the scrapheap". This became his daily mantra, and we were sick and tired of hearing it. He taught us nothing whatsoever during the entire first week, neither did he bother to hand out any homework. And he gave us the unmistakable impression that he had no intention of teaching us anything either during the weeks that were to follow. Although none of us relished homework, we realized that at this rate we would miss out on an entire semester's geography lessons, the subject that he was ostensibly there to teach. And with the usual vitriol still spewing from his drooping jowls at the commencement of the second week of this twelve week session, we came to a decision. Come what may, something drastic needed to be done to rid us of this tyrant. And the sooner the better!

The desk he sat at was perched atop a raised platform facing the class. Whilst slouched in his chair behind the desk, he was oft in the habit of suddenly leaning forward. This in turn caused his obese belly to push against the desk as he shouted words of scorn and derision at us. For good measure, he often thumped the desk with his right fist to emphasise his point. And we noticed that every time he did this, the desk moved fractionally forward towards the front of the platform ... Thus a plan was hatched!

The following morning two of the pupils arrived earlier than usual in the as yet empty classroom. They moved the desk slightly forward, so that the two front legs were placed somewhat closer to the platform's edge. Lessons, or shall we say pithy comments from our "geography teacher", continued throughout most of the 40 minute session. It became obvious that he seemed to be completely unaware of the fact that his desk had been moved closer to the platform's edge. After the lesson ended and he had departed the classroom, the desk was replaced in its usual position in the centre of the platform, prior to the arrival of the next teacher. The day thereafter the same procedure took place, except that this time the desk was moved further forward than it had been on the previous day. It was now positioned barely a few inches from the edge. Having not noticed how much closer the desk was from the edge compared to the previous day, would he now notice an even closer proximity some twenty-four hours later? We sat and waited ...

He gave no indication of having noted the change and flung himself into his chair, glaring at us with his beady little eyes. Would our little scheme come to fruition today? And in order to see it through to its hopeful conclusion, one of the boys proceeded to ask him a particularly dumb question which, as we anticipated, evoked a hearty thump on his desk. As expected, the desk moved forward to within a fraction from the platform's edge. One leg was now perched right on the edge, and our hearts began to pound, for we were convinced that a further movement on his part would send the desk spilling over the edge and onto the floor.

Obviously still incensed by the absurdity of the question, he now proceeded to shout at the questioner, telling him just how stupid he was and emphasised his words with another hearty thwack of his hand! And that did it! The desk tilted over the edge and toppled over onto the classroom floor amidst the sound of splintering wood as first one front leg and then the other gave way, dragging with and then depositing our teacher onto the floor in front of thirty goggled eyed boys. And there he lay, spread-eagled and seemingly unconscious to the world! A deathly hush prevailed, no one spoke or moved for what seemed like an absolute eternity.

Had we actually killed the old bugger?? That had certainly not been our intention. Our purpose was that he be removed from our classroom somehow or other and convince him to remain permanently retired. This way we hoped he would be replaced by another teacher who would at least show some interest in teaching us, enabling us to pass our forthcoming examinations, which, if present circumstances continued, we clearly had no hope of doing.

A few of us rose from our seats and approached him gingerly. Somebody felt his pulse – it was still beating as far as could be ascertained. Likewise, he appeared to be still breathing. So far so good! And with that our classroom door burst open and a teacher from the class next door ran in to see what had caused the almighty crash that had emanated from our classroom moments earlier. Solemnly, and in grave tones, we expressed our shock at this most unfortunate occurrence ... and that we were totally puzzled as to how this disastrous accident could have happened ... It was decided to let him lie comatose on the wooden floor for a few minutes, surrounded by the splintered wreckage of his desk, so that he might get his breath back and regain his composure. Thereafter, he was hoisted onto his feet and, gently supported under both arms, he was able to shuffle out of the classroom. He was taken along the verandah and into the school office, where he was deposited into a chair and left in the hands of a very startled looking secretary! During this whole episode he never uttered a word, just kept mumbling quietly to himself, and we all hoped that, with a little bit of luck, the incident may have caused him no more than a slight and temporary concussion. All being well, he would recall nothing of this event!

Thankfully we need not have felt apprehensive, for everything worked according to plan. He never showed up at the school again, and no doubt went back into retirement, possibly this time for good. And thankfully, the effort involved soon paid dividends, for a few days later, a young, keen and caring teacher was sent in as a replacement and, what's more, made geography lessons enjoyable! And for once we even appreciated the homework that went with it!!

Field Marshal Lord Wavell, hero of the British Army's World War II campaign in Burma, paid Rhodesia a visit and we as boarders congregated at the Drill Hall parade ground one Sunday morning to see him take the salute at a march past. Thereafter he addressed both the troops of the Rhodesian Army as well as the public after an impressive military parade had been staged in his honour. Apart from columns of troops marching past the rostrum, a military band led the parade, followed by armoured cars.

Sporting events attained a peak in Rhodesia in 1949, when, for the first time ever I actually managed to both appreciate and enjoy the game of cricket! Seated in the stands of the Salisbury Sports Club in early February of that year we were privileged to see England's M.C.C. in action when they played Rhodesia in a three day international. We witnessed such all time greats as Len

Hutton (who scored 79) and Denis Compton batting, plus ace bowler Alec Bedser take six wickets for 17 runs. During the course of their visit to Salisbury both Len Hutton and Denis Compton addressed a large audience of schoolboys and teaching staff in the Prince Edward School Beit Hall.

And continuing with cricket, later in the year, after the touring Australian cricket team had trounced Rhodesia in Bulawayo, the Aussies were matched against a South African XI in Salisbury. Once again we were encouraged to attend. We were most impressed by the Australians, under the captaincy of all time great Lindsay Hassett, supported by fast bowler Ray Lindwall and other top players. They turned out to be convincing winners in a somewhat one sided victory over the South African side, whose team included two Rhodesian players. An estimated 20,000 spectators in all watched this two day match which set an attendance record for Rhodesian cricket. On that particular Saturday afternoon at the Salisbury Sports Club, well over 10,000 cricket fans showed up.

I was thrilled one weekday afternoon to receive an unexpected telephone call from my mother to tell me the good news that my father had finally purchased his long awaited motorcar – a new British built 1949 Standard Vanguard four door sedan. The car, grey in colour, was purchased from Vulcan Garage in Gatooma for the sum of £618 (six hundred and eighteen pounds sterling).

The owner of the garage had clinched the deal by promising that he would personally provide a series of driving lessons for my mother – but unfortunately failed to keep his promise thereafter! Allocated the registration number H 2940 (the "H" standing for Hartley, Gatooma being the administrative "capital" of the Hartley district). As the prefix "G" had already been allocated to the town of Gwelo many years earlier, the Gatooma prefix became the letter "H" – but I am digressing! The Vanguard served us faithfully for several years and I learnt to drive in it, obtaining my driver's licence in 1952, aged 17. Now that he possessed his own transportation, my father found it far easier to venture further afield. By paying regular visits to the rapidly expanding gold mining town of Que Que, some 45 miles from Gatooma, he obtained many new clients for his expanding accountancy practice.

In July 1949 "rugby fever" gripped the country when the New Zealand "All Blacks", touring South Africa at the time, paid a visit to Rhodesia for two matches against the home side. The powerful visitors met Rhodesia in Bulawayo on Wednesday 27 July, and much to the surprise of all concerned the magnificent Rhodesian team achieved the pinnacle of success when they scored a close but well deserved 10-8 victory over the Kiwi side.

The return match was scheduled to be played in Salisbury just three days later, and the question was – could the Rhodesians pull off another win? We looked forward to the match in eager anticipation – it became a non-stop topic of conversation. That Thursday evening, two days' prior to the game and a few moments before "lights out", we were sitting on our beds discussing the forthcoming match when we were interrupted by a loud clattering. It sounded like numerous pairs of studded boots dashing up the concrete staircase, when suddenly our dormitory door burst open and a dozen burly men dressed in full rugby kit and boots suddenly filled our dormitory. It was the All Blacks rugby team – come to pay us a visit! We couldn't believe our eyes!

To say that excitement ran rife would have been the understatement of the year, as we had had no inkling whatsoever of this most unexpected visit. And neither for that matter had the New Zealanders! It transpired that the team were partaking in an evening training session at the nearby Old Hararians rugby ground, having arrived by train from Bulawayo earlier in the day. One of the local rugby administrators, who must have possessed a soft spot for Prince Edward School boarders, invited the visitors to pay us an impromptu visit, which they very sportingly agreed to do! News travels fast and within moments of their arrival, dozens of boys from the other dormitories descended on the scene. We had a lively question and answer session with the team for around thirty minutes, it was truly awesome to have players like Bob Scott, Peter Johnstone and skipper Freddie Allen sitting on our beds chatting with us! The evening proved truly amazing and a most unexpected treat for all the boys. Classmates and teachers simply refused to believe us the following day when we told them that the All Blacks rugby team had paid a special visit to Jameson House the night before!

Saturday 30 July found all roads leading to Old Hararians Rugby Ground filled with cars, pedestrians and well over a thousand schoolboys neatly dressed in school uniforms and blazers. Salisbury schoolboys were most fortunate, bloc bookings having been arranged well in advance by the various schools through the offices of the Mashonaland Rugby Union, and we filed directly to our seats without first having the inconvenience of queuing in order to purchase tickets. Close on 13,000 spectators managed to squeeze themselves into the stadium – the largest concentration of people ever to have gathered in Rhodesia in one place up to that time. And after a memorable afternoon of thrilling rugby the final whistle saw our valiant Rhodesian team hold the All Blacks to a very creditable 3-3 draw – a remarkable performance by the underdogs. We trooped back to our hostels in the strong belief that not only had we just witnessed a great game, but at the same time had possibly seen the strongest Rhodesian national rugby side fielded since the Rhodesian Rugby Football Union had been formed in 1895, over half a century earlier.

Cigarette cards – so popular in Britain during the first half of the 20th Century – never appeared to have had a following in Rhodesia. I had certainly never come across any issued locally. There were of course many well known local brands of cigarette on the market – *Gold Leaf* (the most popular), *C to C* (Cape to Cairo), *Gold Flake* and *Flight* are others that come to mind. These were all to international standard yet competitively priced – a box of 50 sold for only 2/6 (two shillings and sixpence – the equivalent of twenty-five cents). At the lower end of the market a packet of *Tom Tom* containing 10 cigarettes could be purchased for a fraction of the cost. The latter were priced, if I am not mistaken, at 1d. (one penny) per packet of 10. Although smoked mainly by Black Africans, they were also purchased by many aspiring young smokers, for even financially strapped schoolboys could afford a single penny – and receive no less than ten cigarettes in return – a bargain few could resist! Many young smokers in Rhodesia commenced his or her possible descent into throat cancer via the humble *Tom Tom* cigarette!

A sizeable number of people smoked several boxes of cigarettes a week (they were sold in boxes of 20s and 50s as a rule),
some managed to chain smoke their way through a box of 50 a
day. Cigarette advertisements in various magazines portrayed
medical doctors recommending certain brands healthier to
smoke than those offered by the competition! Many film stars of
the time appeared in cigarette advertisements and innumerable
actors and actresses lit up cigarettes on the big screen. It was the
expected thing to do and those few men who steered clear of
cigarettes very often took to smoking pipes or the odd cigar as
an alternative. Tobacco was grown in Southern Rhodesia on a
vast scale and had become a major earner of foreign revenue. It
was very definitely considered "cool" to smoke! Unfortunately, or
shall I say fortunately, I had been put off smoking by my uncle
Jul's enforced smoking session several years earlier and, although I tried the odd cigarette from time to time, enjoyment was
entirely lacking. I therefore found no difficulty whatsoever in
becoming a life long abstainer, much to the surprise of many of
my friends.

But back to cigarette cards – the nearest to these cards that I
recall seeing were the ones issued in boxes of Kellogg's Corn
Flakes. These cards depicted a series of forty makes of post-war
British motorcars. It was fortunate that I enjoyed corn flakes and
my consumption of this product increased considerably for the
duration of this particular sales campaign! No boxes of bran
flakes or rice crispies were purchased for several months, it was
just corn flakes, corn flakes and more boxes of corn flakes that
were consumed! We traded cards amongst ourselves and eventually I managed to collect the entire set. These were then pasted
into a special booklet issued by the manufacturers of Kellogg's
Corn Flakes. My favourite car at the time happened to be the
new Sunbeam Talbot 90 Sports saloon and I placed the Sunbeam card into my wallet, where it remained for many years.

One Sunday morning, as we sat relaxing and chatting over our
second cup of tea in the school dining hall, following a leisurely
breakfast, a junior ran into the hall and breathlessly announced
that an aircraft had "crashed onto the school grounds"! We all
streamed out and headed for the "crash site" – one of the sports
grounds situated behind the hostels. On arrival we discovered

that the term "crashed" had been somewhat exaggerated – for we found a small single-engine amphibian flying boat that had fortunately managed to clear the trees surrounding the sports field and had landed on the grass. It had fortunately rolled to a halt just short of a row of tall and imposing trees bordering the field, thus preventing any damage to the aircraft.

The pilot and his passenger stood in front of their rather unusual aircraft – an American built single-engine four seater Republic Seabee amphibian. They had hardly departed Belvedere Airport when the aircraft suddenly developed an engine problem. Having not yet gained any significant altitude at that stage, the most likely landing ground appeared to be Prince Edward School's sports fields, so the pilot made an emergency landing on the nearest one available. The aircraft was later loaded onto a large trailer and towed away, the following morning no trace remained of this unexpected visitor to our school!

Now that our family were the proud owners of a motorcar, Judy felt that it was high time that one of her unfulfilled ambitions in her life should be fulfilled – namely that we should venture out of town to some quiet little spot in the countryside and have a picnic! Judy, by now an avid reader of Enid Blyton stories, had read time and again of parents taking their children on idyllic sounding picnics in the English countryside, and she longed for the day that our family should follow suite! Proud owner of a toy tea set given to her on the occasion of a recent birthday, she had fed her dolls endless cups of tea and crumbs of cake in the confines of our garden, but now she wanted to experience the real thing ...

It took some time for my father to be talked into this venture, he was not a "picnic enthusiast" – and preferred to eat all his meals, cooked and served hot, in the comfort of a dining room. Furthermore, he disliked sandwiches! As he also just happened to be the one and only member of our family in possession of a driver's licence, the final decision whether or not to go on a picnic very obviously rested on his shoulders! But after a fair amount of pleading from his young daughter, plus some back up support from our mother and myself, he found himself out-voted, and finally agreed. A date had to be set – and one Sunday afternoon a few weeks hence was chosen for her big moment. Judy appeared satisfied with the arrangements and proceeded to work out what food should be prepared and taken with on this historic occasion – the very first picnic of her young life!

The agreed upon date finally arrived and, around four o'clock on the day in question we climbed into the car and set off in the direction of Chakari, travelling along the ubiquitous strip road leading to the little mining village situated some 25 miles north of Gatooma. Everything required for the picnic had been carefully placed in a basket – some bottles of cold lemonade, a flask of hot tea, sandwiches, a freshly baked cake, cups and saucers, cake plates, and a blanket to be spread onto the ground for us to sit on. Even Judy's favourite doll had been invited to accompany us, so that she too could partake in the joys of a picnic in the Rhodesian countryside! As expected – the doll accepted the invitation and accompanied us, perched on Judy's lap!

It was my father's intention to drive just a few miles along the Chakari road and find a suitable picnic spot as soon as possible, a spot preferably located under a shady tree to protect us from the rays of the still hot afternoon sun. After several more minutes an appropriate looking place hove into sight so we slowed down and drew to a halt. But on opening the car door I realized immediately that this would not be the best venue to hold a picnic, for the truly overpowering stench of cattle dung assailed us! It would appear that cattle had recently been herded along this very stretch of road and had probably been tethered at this site for a suitable "toilet stop"! So, on we on drove in search of another suitable locality ...

We drove on for a further few miles before arriving at an appropriate looking tree on the roadside. This one looked as if it might provide us with enough shade, and so our father pulled up alongside it.

The Chakari Road ran through a concentrated farming area. Farms extending on either side of the road were well fenced and in close proximity to the road, leaving little space between fence and road. Passing traffic threw up a fair amount of dust in their wake, resulting in a dust cloud hovering in the air for a few minutes. However, time was marching on and it was decided that the picnic would be held under that tree, never mind the inconvenience of dust clouds descending on us at regular intervals.

The blanket was carefully laid out over a section of gravel and the crockery placed thereon at somewhat uneven angles, the Chakari Road not being very conducive for holding picnics. It was whilst we were pouring our first cups of tea that we noticed a number of young poorly dressed children congregate around us, they literally appeared from out of the blue and as soon as we brought out the sandwiches and cake they put out their hands and started begging for something to eat. We handed out several sandwiches and before these had been consumed a further group of raggedly dressed children appeared. They too began demanding food. It was then that we noticed that we had parked close to a farm road and several grass huts. This was quite obviously not the ideal spot to hold a picnic. We gathered the remaining food and crockery, shook out the blanket to get rid of the accumulated dust and set off for hopeful greener pastures – once more heading north towards Chakari!

Unfortunately this time no suitable shady trees hove into sight and it was decided that we stop wherever the verges were wide enough to provide just that little additional space to park the car. No such luck – the road retained its unfriendly attitude towards prospective picnic-goers no matter how far we drove, the narrow width between the sides of the strips and the farm fences never seemed to vary. So it was decided that the picnic would be held within the next mile or two come hell or high water, the only condition being that there were no farm roads in the vicinity that might attract another batch of uninvited onlookers ... And, as the afternoon shadows lengthened, we now no longer needed a tree for shade.

A few moments later we pulled up at what looked like another suitable spot. It also became obvious that if we were to continue on our journey much longer we may well find ourselves in Chakari, and it had certainly never been our intention to travel quite that far afield! So we pulled up at the side of the road close to a large ant hill prominently situated on the other side of a farm fence. Out came the blanket, followed in turn by cups and saucers and the food. We settled down to drink the by now luke-warm tea and the no longer ice cold lemonade. At some stage I noticed that cake crumbs had spilled onto the blanket and so flicked them off onto the ground. Shortly thereafter I noticed a long line of large black Matabele ants heading directly for us and what was more, a number of these ants had already clambered onto the blanket and were heading straight for the food!!

That was it! Hastily we jumped up, gathered up the crockery, shook out the blanket to ensure that no ants remained thereon and placed everything into the trunk of the car. Judy, who had earlier insisted on pouring out the tea for all of us, had had hardly any chance to enjoy this picnic, which after all had been staged for her entertainment. She was given time to finish drinking her lemonade and eat her sandwiches whilst standing next to the car, thus keeping well clear of the marauding ants that had now invaded our abandoned picnic ground. We in turn were now seated in the car and keeping a wary eye on a crestfallen little girl, plus the odd car or truck that clattered past! I think my little sister realized there and then that picnics staged in the African bush were worlds apart from those cosy little picnics described so delectably in her beloved Enid Blyton story books!!

Judy never again requested that we should stage another picnic and, for that matter, no offer was ever made to repeat the experience! I later read that where there were ant hills constructed by white ants there were very likely to be colonies of black ants in close vicinity that preyed upon their white cousins. I don't know if this is true, but I can vouch for the fact that on that particular Sunday afternoon on the Chakari Road, local black ants had a real picnic – at our expense!!

Major fires seldom occurred in Gatooma, but despite that, a well trained volunteer fire brigade had been formed after the war ended. Members, all volunteers, consisted largely of younger men, many of whom had seen active service. Many of the newer residents to the town originated from Lancashire in the United Kingdom and were employed by the Cotton Spinning Mills, Gatooma's largest single employer of labour. Most volunteered their services and joined the fire fighters. The brigade were called out from time to time, usually in order to extinguish veld (grass/bush) fires which, if not kept under strict control, might prove to be a threat to nearby houses. A major fire occurred when the McDonald & Poley departmental store in Rhodes Street, a two storey building situated next door to the old post office building, caught fire. The departmental store was largely gutted – many folk were hoping that the post office, with its creaking wooden floors and limited space, would have gone up in flames as well! I missed seeing this particular fire by a few hours, having returned to Salisbury earlier that day after spending an exeat weekend at home.

However, a minor fire occurred some weeks later. Mrs Parris was busy cooking supper in her small kitchen behind the shop in Union Street, the very shop from where I used to purchase American comics. It appears that one Sunday evening she spilled the contents of a saucepan onto the stove that resulted in a rather large flame, followed by a plume of acrid smoke. She apparently panicked and ran to the front of the shop yelling "fire, fire". In the process, perhaps hoping to save some of her stock from the expected blaze, she opened the front doors of the shop wide open. She then proceeded to throw various items from her shop out into the centre of Union Street, a street which ran parallel to the shop frontage. Unfortunately, in her haste to save some of her stock she tossed a number of large glass jars containing sweets into the street. These glass jars quite naturally shattered upon impact with the road, spraying thick sharp fragments of glass in all directions. No one appeared to have stopped her doing this (her husband, the only other person on the property at the time, was probably busy dousing the mini-fire on the stove). It being practically dark at this stage and with the apparent danger over, the front door of the shop was locked for the night, and the couple went to bed. And, seeing that no damage had been sustained apart from probably a mark on the stove, neither Mr or Mrs Parris bothered to report the incident to either the police or the fire brigade as to what had happened in their kitchen.

The fun began the following morning when traffic began to move on Union Street just prior to eight o'clock, when most shops and offices opened for business. Motorists first became aware of the dangers of driving past Mrs Parris's shop when their car tyres omitted loud crunching sounds as they drove over shards of glass from the shattered remnants of sweet bottles. The glass promptly sliced right through the tyres and in so doing punctured and shredded the rubber tubes (tubeless tyres were not yet in general use at that time), thus forcing the air to escape with a loud hiss. Some cars I was told had had all four tubes/tyres ruptured, others managed to escape with only one or two punctures. By the time that the glass had belatedly been swept away, well over a dozen automobiles had been affected and Union Street was for all purposes blocked off to traffic. Cars were left as they stood as the irate owners had to walk (or telephone from shops – no cell (mobile) phones invented as yet – except for Dick Tracy's wristwatch phone!) to various garages around town and request that tyres and tubes of various sizes be delivered to Union Street. The mechanics delivering replacement tyres first had to strip the shredded tyres from the marooned vehicles, a somewhat messy job in the circumstances.

Garages in town had a field day – never had they sold so many tubes and tyres in a single day! As there were only a few garages in Gatooma at that time, the smaller establishments soon ran out of tyres and both Duly's and Wilson's Garages remained with depleted stocks! It took some hours before Union Street was again open to traffic. The name of the person who had caused this minor calamity soon became known and Mrs Parris became a very unpopular person in the eyes of those motorists whose vehicles had been affected! For the following few weeks many of them slowed down to a crawl when driving past her shop, casting a wary eye on the road ahead to make sure that she had not jettisoned another few bottles into the road without warning! But to the garage owners of Gatooma she became a brief symbol of profitability, and I am sure that this resulted in many a chuckle over the next weeks whenever this incident was recalled over a glass of beer!

Gatooma continued to expand at a steady rate as new residents continued to stream into the country, mainly from South Africa and the United Kingdom. That there was an acute shortage of housing throughout the country became increasingly apparent. To help alleviate the problem it was therefore decided to construct individual homes known as "pise houses" to accommodate immigrants in most of the country's urban centres. The pise house was a fairly compact low cost type of house that was constructed of special bricks, the building was given a thatched roof and designed to last for a maximum of nine or ten years at most, as it was the intention of the authorities to demolish all pise houses after that period. It had been calculated that sufficient permanent housing would have been made available to satisfy the housing market within this ten year period. It turned out however that the pise houses were, in the majority of instances, so sturdily constructed, especially those in the Gatooma scheme (which were largely built in Godwin Road) that many of these houses remained occupied for almost thirty years, although in the end most were in fact demolished as they had by then outlived their useful lives well beyond everyone's expectations.

I often visited friends who lived in these houses. Although these look-alike homes often tended to blend scenically on the exterior, their individually designed interiors were well finished and one never had the impression that these homes were intended to be of a temporary nature only. Nevertheless, most residents moved out of pise accommodation as soon as they managed to either rent or purchase a conventionally constructed house or apartment in other parts of the town.

Current roads, mainly in the residential areas, were busily being widened and upgraded. Many gravel roads were now surfaced with asphalt in order to prevent them turning into virtual quagmires during the rainy season, whilst at the same time new roads were being hacked out of the bush as expansion in all directions took place. The Gatooma municipality's old and oft used steam roller was put to constant use during the construction of these roads, and some of my friends and I spent time during school vacations watching the vintage roller in action. Clanking and crunching its way forwards and backwards over the new road surfaces, its grimy funnel emitted puffs of black smoke which tended to hang in the air. At the same time the very pungent smell of fresh asphalt assailed our nostrils as the glistening black mixture was poured onto the road surface from a tractor towed bowser. Incidentally, the steam roller was expertly driven by a man who possessed only one hand, for his left arm ended in a stump at the wrist, the wrist being encased in a round leather mitten. We surmised that his hand had been lost in an accident at some stage, but despite this handicap he made good use of his truncated arm to effortlessly change gears whilst turning the large and heavy steering wheel with his good hand. We found him a remarkably cheerful and friendly person and often chatted to him at the end of his day's shift.

Participating in life's cultural aspects was encouraged by the school authorities and this included taking ballroom dancing lessons. Friends who had signed up for a course persuaded me to join them. Thereafter, one afternoon a week, we walked to a large hall in Jameson Avenue, it might well have been the Athenaeum Hall, where a number of boys from other schools joined our contingent from Prince Edward. We all lined up on one side of the hall and, facing us on the opposite side, were girls from Queen Elizabeth, Girls High and the Dominican Convent. A professional dancing teacher and her assistant demonstrated the various dance steps and eventually we were requested to choose partners with whom to practice these steps. Initially, this involved a little bashfulness from many of the boys and coyness from numerous girls, but eventually we selected partners to dance with and couples took to the floor. Sometimes girls turned out to be the taller of the couple dancing together, which caused further embarrassment, but these moments likewise passed once everyone had got into the swing of things.

After learning the basic steps we were taught the quickstep – slow-quick quick-slow, followed in turn by the waltz – one-two-three, one-two-three, and later the foxtrot. These dances we found reasonably easy to comprehend, although at times we appeared to possess two left feet, especially when negotiating sudden turns! Once the steps had more or less been mastered to the teacher's satisfaction, we were introduced to the rumba, the samba and the tango, but unfortunately not everyone proved proficient enough to dance these successfully. The music was furnished by 78 rpm ten inch records played on a gramophone, at the end of the record the gramophone required manual winding up. The majority of these records featured Victor Silvester and his Ballroom Orchestra and, when I now close my eyes, I can once again hear the strains of *Brown Eyes* (quickstep), *Always* (waltz) and *Stranger In Paradise* (foxtrot) played over and over again in my mind – and always by Victor Sylvester and his Orchestra! These dance lessons proved valuable in our future social life, for ballroom dancing still featured prominently at the time – and for many years to follow. In those days, when attending dances, dancers were issued with blank dance cards to which stubby little pencils on a string were attached – used for filling in the names of respective dance partners for the evening's duration. Double bookings for individual dances could prove most embarrassing – and no one wanted to be left sitting alone at a table when all their friends were gliding around the dance floor!

The 1949 school boxing championships were drawing near and I once more entered my name in the competition. I had, not unexpectedly, gained some weight (and thankfully also a little height!) and now found myself competing in the welterweight division, one weight division up from that of the previous year. I was sparring much bigger boys now which made one wary of getting hit on the whiskers, so decided to concentrate a little more on self defence, meaning that greater emphasis was now placed in slipping and ducking away from an opponent's blows. After all, this sport was known as the "noble art of self-defence" and I intended to keep my current visage intact if possible! I sparred a number of times with fellow Jameson House boarder Robin Hein, a member of the school boxing squad and a particularly hard puncher. Robin usually pulled his punches during our sparring sessions which was just as well, thus ena-bling me to keep my teeth in the position where they rightly belonged!

I was drawn against a boy whose surname was Smith, I do not recall his first name. A day scholar whom I had not met before and who, not surprisingly, had a height advantage over me, for I was still on average much younger than most pupils in Form Three. Despite the discrepancy in height, this did not prevent me from punching him at every opportunity and we went at each other hammer and tongs throughout the entire contest, pausing only for a brief minute's rest between rounds. I felt quite elated when the final bell rang, as I was convinced that I had earned the decision. To my utter surprise the verdict went against me and Smith was declared the winner. The Jameson House supporters, including quite a few members of the School boxing team, were all emphatic that I had deserved to win, but refrained from booing the decision. For the referee, the sole arbitrator of the bout, happened to be a teacher at the school. My supporters were of course all pupils, and pupils were strictly forbidden to show any disrespect to members of the teaching staff – especially by showing their dissatisfaction and venting their displeasure at what they all felt was a poor decision! As I have always maintained – you win some, you lose some!

Unfortunately, this was the last time I boxed in an actual contest, for the following year (1950) the boxing championships were cancelled due to an inopportune outbreak of measles throughout the school. The year thereafter, my last year at Prince Edward, I was busy studying for the forthcoming final examinations so could not devote sufficient time for training. However, my interest in boxing continued to grow and it was during the year in question – 1949, that I first subscribed to the weekly British magazine *Boxing News* – and have remained a subscriber to this well respected journal (established 1909) – to this very day. In later years, a number of boxing articles authored by myself were printed in *Boxing News*, as were various articles submitted to other international boxing magazines.

A friend and fellow boarder at Jameson House, who likewise hailed from Gatooma was Ken Barton. He too travelled on the school train at the beginning of each term. He later played rugby for the Prince Edward First XV and also boxed for the school team in representative matches. However, his mother originally had aspirations for her son to play the violin, and Ken dutifully took his violin with him on the train in order to study music in Salisbury. Unfortunately, Ken was not really interested in learning to play this instrument. On one of the train journeys his violin case "accidentally" slid off the top bunk of his compartment and flew out of the open window onto the tracks below – never to be seen again! No replacement violin appeared the following term, and Ken found to his relief that he now had a few extra hours each week that he could devote to additional sports training – far more to his liking! Ken eventually became Head Prefect of Jameson House and a school prefect to boot, but never a musician! To this day I still count him and his wife Sheliegh as good and kind friends.

When it was announced that the 1949 South African Amateur Senior Boxing Championships were to be staged in the open air at the Salisbury Drill Hall grounds during the month of October, I was elated. It would be the first time that these prestigious championships were to be held in Rhodesia's capital city. This meant that many of the top boxers from one of the world's strongest amateur boxing nations would be displaying their wares in Salisbury, and boxing fans throughout the country were delighted to hear the news. Boxers from both Southern and Northern Rhodesia competed annually in these championships, so their participation proved an added attraction. As most of the previous year's 1948 South African Olympic Games team members had already turned professional (they had garnered no less than two gold, one silver and one bronze medal in the previous year's London Olympics) this signified that the majority of South African boxers competing in Salisbury would showcase the exciting new generation of post-war amateurs emanating from that country. As the 1950 Empire Games (now known as the Commonwealth Games) were due to be staged in Auckland, New Zealand early in the following year, these championships would without a doubt also provide an excellent guide for the South African team selectors – and the boxers were well aware of this added incentive now placed on them.

The eagerly awaited championships finally arrived and I managed to see several of the preliminary bouts prior to finals night. Boxing fans amongst us attended the finals on the Saturday night, viewed by an appreciative crowd of some 5,000 fight fans, probably the largest number of spectators to have witnessed amateur boxing in Southern Rhodesia, period. It turned out to be a thrilling occasion, featuring many exciting contests. Marcus Temple of Natal won the flyweight title, Johnny "Smiler" van Rensburg (Transvaal), at the very tender age of 17, won the bantamweight crown in brilliant style. Rhodesia's own Andy Vercieul triumphed at featherweight, Transvaaler Paul Karam won the lightweight title, Peter Galleymore (Natal) won the welterweight crown. Teuns van Schalkwyk was crowned middle-weight champion, J. Hattingh became the light-heavyweight title-holder and the much fancied Lou Strydom (Transvaal) won the heavyweight title with a crushing first round knockout over his outgunned opponent.

Several of the new titleholders were subsequently chosen to travel to New Zealand where Johnny van Rensburg and Teuns van Schalkwyk won gold for South Africa and Andy Vercieul won silver for Rhodesia. A number of these boxers later joined the professional ranks and some fought for and won South African national titles. The most successful of the lot turned out to be the precocious Johnny van Rensburg, who went on to win British Empire titles in both the lightweight and welterweight divisions, in addition to South African titles at the same weights.

As my parents had not taken a vacation since arriving in the country some ten years earlier, apart from having spent a few days at the Victoria Falls at some stage during the course of my father's military service, they now decided they would take a trip to the seaside. However, due to the fact that they both worked full time in the now rapidly expanding accountancy practice, it was decided, for practical reasons, that the office should not be closed and, as no additional office staff were employed at that stage, they agreed to take separate holidays on this particular occasion. Not by any means an ideal situation but practical in the circumstances, especially as they had diverse plans as to where to spend their respective holidays!

In November 1949 my father caught the train to Cape Town, a two and a half day journey by rail, and there he spent a three week long vacation, staying at the Marine Hotel. He savoured the sights of the city that he had last visited some ten years earlier when the *Ussukuma* had docked whilst en route from Hamburg to Beira. So much had happened during that intervening period, it was quite incredible. He returned to Gatooma both rested and refreshed, stating however that the next vacation he undertook would be with his entire family!

Meanwhile, rail bookings had already been made for my mother, Judy and I to travel to South West Africa (now Namibia) to visit relatives Hans and Ruth Isenberg and their children, Eve and newly born Mark David. They lived in Windhoek, the country's capital. We were also booked to spend two weeks in

Swakopmund, situated on the Atlantic seaboard. All very exciting and a vacation to look forward to with great anticipation.

A few days after my return from boarding school in early December, the three of us boarded the Rhodesia Railways Salisbury to Bulawayo passenger train. It was midnight when the train pulled out of Gatooma, and I remember waving farewell to my father, a lone figure standing on the deserted and poorly lit platform, until his image disappeared from sight. Shortly thereafter we settled ourselves in the freshly made bunk/beds in our reserved compartment and managed to sleep soundly despite the somewhat narrow bunks. We awoke just as the train pulled into the Bulawayo station, alongside what was reputed to be the world's longest railway platform at the time. It was a little after 6 a.m. and already there were throngs of people milling around waiting to welcome and collect passengers alighting from this regular overnight train, which had departed Salisbury some nine hours earlier.

We now had several hours at our disposal and carried our overnight cases with us. The larger suitcases had been booked to travel directly from Gatooma through to Windhoek in the guards van, which alleviated the necessity of keeping them with us. We alighted and made our way to the Bulawayo station bathroom facilities which, for the bargain price of two shillings and sixpence or thereabouts, provided modern baths and shower facilities with unlimited hot water, toilets and all other mod cons. We took our time, luxuriating in our individual hot baths, for we had a fair amount of time to kill prior to boarding the south bound passenger train later that morning.

We arranged to meet at the entrance of the station restaurant and, having selected a table next to a window, enjoyed a leisurely breakfast. Our train for South Africa was only due to depart around midday, so we decided to take a walk into Bulawayo itself. After having placed our overnight cases into a safe-deposit locker, we set off down the road leading into the city. The distance to the city centre turned out to be far shorter than had been anticipated, and before long we were spending our time window shopping. Many of the larger shops turned out to be branches of Salisbury departmental stores, with which we were already familiar. We enjoyed an ice cream in a little tearoom and

then set off to walk back to the station. Upon arrival, we found
dozens of people milling around attempting to read typewritten
lists of names which had been pinned inside a glass fronted
notice board situated on the station platform. The names were
listed alphabetically and alongside them were the coupe or
compartment numbers that had been allocated, followed by the
passenger coach numbers. One compartment had been allocated to Mrs I Sternberg and her two children, and after collecting
our overnight cases, we made our way to our passenger coach.

We settled ourselves into our compartment, eagerly anticipat-
ing the journey ahead. A short while later the locomotive's
whistle emitted a loud blast and the train began to pull out of the
station, heading for Bechuanaland (now Botswana). Before long
we had left Rhodesia's second largest city behind, and some 60
miles further down the track the train pulled to a halt at
Plumtree, a little town close to the Bechuanaland border. Only a
short stop here, and not long thereafter we crossed the border
and into the neighbouring country. Francistown was the first
station we stopped at and within moments the passenger coaches were surrounded by dozens of beggars, including many who
were physically disabled. Most of the beggars were dressed in
tattered and unkempt clothing, their gnarled hands clutching
begging bowls which were thrust up at us. It was a sight I had
never experienced before and passengers were taken aback at
this abject display of poverty.

Many of us reached into our pockets and threw Rhodesian
coins into the outstretched bowls, hoping that the beggars could
make use of this (to them) foreign currency. Other passengers
leant out of the windows and handed sandwiches to some of the
impoverished looking children. And further down the carriage a
few teenagers threw a number of coins well over the heads of the
beggars standing next to the train, then taking a perverse delight
in watching several of the smaller children scramble for the few
coins lying half buried in the dust. We were most relieved when
the train finally pulled out of the little station, for the sights that
we had witnessed were most depressing.

Further stops included Palapayi Road, Gaberones and Lobatsi
and arrival at Mafeking meant we had crossed into South Africa.
Here the Rhodesia Railways Garrett locomotive heading our

train was uncoupled to be replaced by a South African Railways locomotive, after which the journey continued. The next stop of any consequence was Vryburg and later that day we found ourselves in Kimberley, South Africa's major diamond mining city. Here we were due to have a fairly lengthy stop. Rather than whiling away our time at the somewhat grimy looking railway station, we decided to take a stroll into town. I must admit that we were not overly impressed by either the shops or the general surroundings. We came across an old cinema screening a matinee, and, more to avoid the heat and dust of Kimberley's streets, decided to see a movie for the next hour or two. After having paid for our tickets at the box office we were shown a door leading into the auditorium, and were then left to grope our way in the pitch dark towards the general direction of the seats that had been allocated to us. There were no torch bearing usherettes to be found. We failed to locate the allocated seats in the dark and lowered ourselves into the first available seats we could make out in the Stygian gloom! In any event it made no difference as to where we sat, for there appeared to be only a handful of patrons in the old "bioscope" on that hot afternoon!

We had not noticed the poster advertising the film that was being screened, and were somewhat surprised to see that *A Night At The Opera* starring the Marx Brothers turned out to be the feature film! At that stage I had only heard about the Marx Brothers but had never seen any of their films, and this movie (released originally in 1935) proved to be somewhat different to anything I had seen before. A lot of their weird humour was, not surprisingly, lost on my young sister that afternoon! To this day she has had an aversion to viewing old movies and the Marx Brothers in particular, claiming that this particular film could be blamed for that! In any case, my mother decided during the interval that we had better return to the train station to enable us to arrive well in time to catch our train, so we never got around to seeing the second half of this movie!

We took our places for dinner in the train's dining saloon – an enjoyable experience. We were shown to a table covered by a crisp white tablecloth, starched white napkins perched on china plates, and a printed menu was handed to us by a smartly dressed steward. I recall being offered soup, a portion of fish, entree of beef or chicken with vegetables, followed by dessert and coffee. The service was excellent and we thoroughly enjoyed our meal before heading back to the compartment. The bedding attendant had already made up our beds with freshly laundered sheets, firm pillows and warm blankets, all with the South African Railway logo embossed thereon. After a long day, a very unexpected and crazy Marx Brothers' movie, followed in due course by an excellent dinner, we were all ready for bed. Not long after we turned in, virtually falling asleep as our heads touched the pillows!

During the night I awoke with the sensation that our passenger coach was being shunted around, and I gathered that we must have arrived in De Aar in the northern Cape Province. This is where the railway line branched off to South West Africa. Whilst all the other coaches with their slumbering passengers continued on to Cape Town, the coach that we were in had been uncoupled from the south bound train and was now in the process of being coupled onto the north bound train, bound for Windhoek. I opened the compartment door and stood in the corridor watching a number of locomotives shunting around this large marshalling yard, whilst dozens of spotlights atop large overhead pylons illuminated the scene with their dazzling beams. Great clouds of steam hissed out from under the locomotives, only to immediately evaporate into the night air. Once our coach had been coupled onto the Windhoek train matters quietened down, so I returned to our compartment and soon fell asleep.

We awoke a few hours later to be greeted by the sun streaming into our swaying compartment and to a frenzied puffing sound which gave the distinct impression that the locomotive heading this train was experiencing some difficulty in making headway, for we seemed to be crawling ever so slowly along the track. On looking out of the compartment window, and whilst the train was negotiating a bend, I caught sight of our locomotive which appeared to be a very small one, hence the slowness of travel and the continuous breathless sound of its non-stop puffing. However, despite its lack of size this locomotive managed to belch more smoke than I had ever encountered, whilst at the same time emitting large quantities of soot, most of which found

its way into the passenger coach compartments. This left a layer
of grimy coal dust all over the seats and floors, likewise over any
food which had not been well covered, plus over our reading
material and last, but not least, over the passengers themselves!
We hastily closed the windows but soon found that in so doing
we soon began to swelter in the heat, so were compelled to open
the windows once more to let in some "fresh" air, if one could
call it that!

Eventually we pulled into Upington, the border town linking
South Africa and South West Africa, and shortly thereafter
crossed the Orange River on the longest railway bridge that I
had ever travelled across – a bridge almost 3,000 feet in length
which separated the two countries. The Orange River was one of
South Africa's major waterways. Despite the parched looking
countryside we had earlier travelled through, the land in the
vicinity of the Orange River appeared to be most fertile and large
areas were lusciously green in colour.

Before long it was not only the soot from the locomotive which
proved to be a nuisance – we were now travelling through a
section of the Kalahari Desert and clouds of sand began to blow
through the open windows of our compartments. So once again
the windows were closed and we sweltered – and this was only
9 a.m. – with a blistering hot day still to follow! In the end we
compromised – the windows were left open but the shutters were
pulled down, which allowed us to breathe in equal quantities of
hot desert air and fine gritty sand, mixed with a portion of coal
dust from "Puffing Billy" up ahead!! And of course we could
smell and virtually taste the clouds of black smoke which swirled
around the train both day and night and, like the soot, was
mercilessly sucked into the compartments to torment each and
every passenger travelling on the "Süd-West Express" ...

In total this rail journey was a five-day one, of which no less
than three days were spent on the De Aar to Windhoek section
of line. This must surely vie for being one of the most tedious
and boring railway journeys on planet earth. There were neither
baths nor showers aboard, nor was there a dining saloon
attached. We seemed to be permanently covered in layers of soot
and sand. No matter how much sand and grime one managed
to shake off, in no time further layers had accumulated on one's

skin and clothing and, during the night, on and into one's bed sheets. On a scale of between one and ten, this journey figured to be a minus five in my humble estimation ...!

On and on the train chugged, brief stops were made at a number of small stations en route – Keetmanshoop, Mariental, Tsumis, Rehoboth. We simply had to be getting closer to Windhoek. The luxury of a hot bath, a sand free bed and some freshly ironed clothing to wear lifted our spirits in anticipation. And, in the end, we finally did make it – the train pulled into Windhoek's colonial era railway station and our uncle and aunt, Hans and Ruth, were there to greet us. It was a considerable relief to have finally arrived and it was just as well that the hot water geyser in their house was a large capacity one – for three of the deepest and hottest baths were thoroughly enjoyed by three very weary and soot covered visitors!

Hans and Ruth lived in a very comfortable and modern house in one of Windhoek's newer suburbs and we were made to feel right at home. We were soon introduced to a number of their friends who came over to meet us, including Val and Isa de Jongh, teenage daughters of Hans's business partner. Val and I soon struck up a good friendship which has lasted to this day. Hans owned one of the town's major butcheries plus a meat canning factory and an outlying farm. He was very tied up with all his ventures, and would be absent from home for days at a time. Val invited me over to her house and she soon became my unofficial tour guide, showing me around a town steeped in history with a plethora of historical buildings. The languages spoken in the country were Afrikaans, English and German and one could not fail to notice the stately Herero women walking by, dressed in lengthy skirts of a bygone era. Barely thirty years had elapsed since control of German South West Africa had been wrested from the "Fatherland" following World War One, and the country thereafter had become a protectorate of South Africa, its neighbour to the south.

Windhoek proved to be an interesting city with modern buildings nosing their way skywards, invariably surrounded by older buildings dating back to an earlier era. Hans and Ruth proved to be most generous hosts, and we were ferried around, introduced to an endless number of their friends and shown numer-

ous places of interest. After a week of continuous social life we
once again caught the train, this time for an overnight journey
to Swakopmund, situated on the Atlantic coastline. There we
checked into the Hansa Hotel. The small seaside town of Swakopmund consisted largely of 19th and early 20th century German
designed buildings and a handful of modern ones – the town
appeared to me as if it had been largely caught up in a time
warp.

Swakopmund is situated at the mouth of the waterless Swakop
River. The bed of the river usually remained dry for years, then
suddenly flooded should heavy rainfalls occur, usually many
miles upstream. This I was told, happened fairly infrequently.
Originally established as a German military base in 1893, some
120 troops encamped there and were then joined by some 40
German civilians. A harbour was constructed, which incorporat-
ed a long wood and iron jetty. The harbour had since disappeared and only the jetty remained, utilised by fishermen, and
those wishing to take a bracing walk along its creaking planks
to witness the waves breaking down below. This encampment
and the immediate surrounding area was proclaimed a town in
1909 and the Herero name for the area was "Otjozondjii" – the
place of sea shells.

Swakopmund is, to a great extent surrounded by the Namib
Desert and many large sand dunes stretched for miles into this
arid land. We were warned not to walk on or even get close to
any of these dunes – for many of them consisted of loose and
shifting sand which had garnered a treacherous reputation. Just
a few years earlier, in April 1947, whilst attending a picnic near
the Swartkop River, a sandbank collapsed, burying five young
schoolboys. Other picnickers managed to dig out two of the boys,
but it took an hour to dig out the other three. These unfortunate
boys, two aged 11 and one aged eight, had been suffocated.
Needless to say, we made sure that we heeded that bit of advice!

One day, literally out of the blue, it started to rain whilst we
were walking in the Swakopmund main street. It was not by any
means a heavy downpour but enough to send us seeking shelter
under a shop canopy. Imagine our surprise when dozens of
children, including a few adults, dashed out into the street,
laughing and shouting whilst in the process of getting them-

selves wet! The rain however soon stopped and I wondered what
had caused people to run out into the rain. It was then explained
to me that as it only rained every few years in that area, many of
the younger children had possibly not encountered rain before –
hence the novel experience for some of them to actually be able
to feel and experience rain for the first time in their lives!

We paid a brief visit to Walvis Bay, a small harbour town,
situated a few miles south of Swakopmund. We travelled in a
friend's car, carefully following a sandy road. This road was
marked every fifty metres on either side by disused 44 gallon oil
drums. This was done in order to keep the driver and his vehicle
on the "straight and narrow", for this so-called "highway" led
through the desert, and without the drums to act as guides,
drivers could quite easily lose track in the featureless terrain and
drive off into the desert! The visit to Walvis Bay, which had
replaced Swakopmund as South West Africa's principal harbour,
turned out to be quite a nostalgic one for it was here in 1939,
some ten years earlier, that the *Ussukuma* had docked. Aunt
Ruth had come to visit us on board, and at the time had wished
me a belated fourth birthday. I had to admit (not surprisingly)
that I no longer recalled her visit to the ship at that time! Many
memories were rekindled between my mother and her sister
regarding their earlier meeting in Walvis Bay, and it was amazing to realise how much had happened to both our families over
the past decade.

Whilst in Swakopmund we took daily walks alongside the
promenade and enjoyed the fresh and bracing Atlantic sea
breezes blowing in from the ocean. We swam as often as
possible in the fairly cold water and from time to time visited a
small amusement arcade situated near the beach. Amongst the
amusements on offer were a number of archaic slot machines,
relics from a bygone era – even by 1949 standards! First, a
penny coin (the current value of a one cent piece) was inserted
into these ancient contraptions. After waiting for the coin to
noisily rattle its way down into the machine's innards, an interior
light then came on. One then leaned forward and peered into a
slot, at the same time turning a handle attached to one side of
the machine. Very primitive black and white cards sprang to life
in jerky movements, flipping over in rapid succession (depending

at the rate one turned the handle). This gave the cards the impression of movement. The duration of the film averaged about a minute, then the light inside the machine abruptly went off and the "film show" came to an abrupt halt. One could choose from a number of titles – *What The Butler Saw*, *The Arrival of the Train* and *Girls Dancing* were typical examples, and one's pennyworth always seemed to run out at a rather riské moment in the storyline! Invented in 1894 by Thomas Edison, the "Kinetoscope", as it was then named, was originally installed in penny arcades so that people could watch these short and primitive picture cards in motion – it was in fact the forerunner of the cinema. Today these antiquated machines can virtually only be found in museums – but in 1949 they still remained part and parcel of the entertainment scene in Swakopmund – as Ripley would have stated – "Believe it or not"! No wonder that I was under the impression that this little town had somehow been caught up in a virtual time warp!

Our seaside holiday came to its inevitable end and we caught the train back to Windhoek, where we spent the last week of our vacation. Whilst we had been in Swakopmund, Uncle Hans had purchased the latest radiogram complete with all the bells and whistles – which included a powerful radio capable of picking up stations worldwide. Sufficient capacity was included to eliminate the usual atmospheric interference still so prevalent at that time. On the night of 24 January 1950, British titleholder Freddie Mills was due to defend his world light-heavyweight boxing title in London against American Joey Maxim, and I was very keen to listen in to the fight. As the contest was due to be held at a fairly late hour I would somehow have to keep awake, for everyone had already retired to bed by 9 p.m. I was advised on how to locate the BBC overseas service, and to make quite sure that the radio was switched off immediately the broadcast had ended, for the large wooden radiogram cabinet tended to overheat if left plugged in for too long. Instructions duly noted, I settled down on the sofa and commenced reading my book, carefully checking the time at regular intervals to make sure that I would be ready to switch on just before the broadcast was due to commence.

At long last the time arrived and I managed to pick up the broadcast loud and clear. Despite a large number of fans willing him on that night at Earls Court Arena, crowd favourite Freddie Mills was steadily out-boxed. In the tenth round of this scheduled fifteen rounder he found himself on his knees, both dazed and utterly exhausted – and was duly counted out. By this time I was pretty exhausted myself, firstly for attempting to remain awake for seemingly hours on end, then followed by the excitement of the fight itself. When the broadcast finally ended I was only too happy to close the radiogram doors, stagger off to the kitchen to make myself a cup of cocoa and then headed straight for bed. It had without doubt been a long and tiring night ...

I awoke somewhat later than usual the next morning, and in due course joined the rest of the family at breakfast in the dining room, which room adjoined the lounge. Whilst about half way through my cereal I remembered having left a magazine in the lounge the previous evening, one that I had intended to take to bed with me. I briefly excused myself from the table and went through to the lounge to retrieve the magazine that was lying on top of the radiogram. As I approached the radiogram a distinctive smell of burning assailed my nostrils. Picking up the magazine, I was startled to find its covers distinctively warm to the touch! When I felt the top of the radiogram and it wasn't just warm – it was downright HOT! I immediately realized that, due to my drowsiness following the late broadcast, I had obviously forgotten to switch off the radio itself, and had only closed the cabinet doors! There and then I switched off the radiogram, thanking my lucky stars that I had been the one to discover this potentially disastrous oversight, and that no one else had – as yet! I sincerely hoped that the lounge would not be utilized until the radiogram had had a chance to cool down. My prayers were answered, for we all set off for town right after breakfast and the radiogram thankfully remained undisturbed. When it was again switched on that evening (not by me, for I decided to steer well clear of it) it performed flawlessly and the wooden top showed no trace of the ordeal that it had been subjected to the entire previous night! Whew!!!

A few days later our vacation came to an end and we found ourselves once again at the Windhoek station, this time to catch the train back to Rhodesia. A most memorable and enjoyable vacation had been spent in a country which appeared, in my opinion, to differ greatly in many respects from that found in Southern Rhodesia. And yet I had only seen a fraction of "South West", as its inhabitants affectionately called it. As the saying goes – "travel broadens the mind" – and I felt that I had greatly benefited from this visit to what I considered, in many respects, to be a "foreign land". Yet surprisingly, South West Africa bordered partially onto Southern Rhodesia.

Our generous relatives furnished us with a food hamper overflowing with both well chosen and extremely delicious "padkos" (Afrikaans for food and drink for a journey), and we literally wined and dined our way through this bountiful fare during the course of the following five day rail marathon. This certainly helped in alleviating the return journey, a repeat of the same tedious landscape, sand, heat and nauseating smoke that the small locomotive heading our train belched out nonstop. We finally pulled into De Aar, where the small locomotive was thankfully replaced by a larger, more powerful and faster one!

Never were we so pleased to arrive back in Gatooma and were greeted at the station by my beaming and happy father, who was delighted to have his family back again! As expected, we had a lot to relate and over the next few days we talked incessantly! The school term had already commenced, and soon I found myself on a train once again, this time heading for Salisbury. As none of my school friends had ever been to South West Africa I spent the next few weeks relating my experiences, whilst also attempting to catch up with a fortnight's missed schoolwork due to my late arrival back in the classroom!

I had managed to see a great selection of films during the 1949 year, which included *Morning Departure* (John Mills), *The Third Man* (Orson Welles), *Kind Hearts and Coronets* (Alec Guinness), *Twelve o'Clock High* (Gregory Peck), *Champion* (Kirk Douglas), *White Heat* (James Cagney) and *Neptune's Daughter* (Esther Williams) – the latter film featured that year's Academy Award winning song *Baby It's Cold Outside*, a very catchy song indeed. Once again I could not complain that I was letting the world of cinema pass me by whilst attending boarding school!

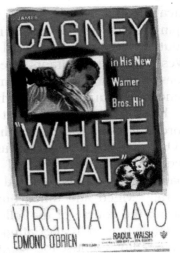

Interior Belvedere Theatre

Peter and Eva

1950

Entering Form Four (Form 1V) elicited a number of benefits – we were now acknowledged to have transcended to senior pupil status and were accordingly allocated a dormitory on the ground floor. This move possessed the twin advantages of firstly no longer having to climb a set of stairs in order to enter ones sleeping quarters, and secondly we were also now in closer proximity to bathrooms, showers and toilets, all of which were located on the ground floor. Not a big deal, but a convenient improvement nevertheless.

Around this time a measles epidemic swept Salisbury and many schools were affected. Numbers in classes dwindled daily as pupils caught the dreaded rash and were forced out of circulation for a week or longer. On waking one morning I too found myself covered in a rash and was promptly dispatched to the school infirmary, a mini-hospital now bursting at the seams. This infirmary was under the care and ever watchful eye of the matron, Sister Freda Thompson, who was assisted by a couple of orderlies. Sister Thompson proved to be strict in manner, but she was also kind, helpful and pleasant. She also required all of her skills, tact and expertise to keep a full complement of young schoolboy patients under control!

We listened diligently to the popular hospital's request programme titled *Look For The Silver Lining* which was broadcast from the Southern Rhodesian Broadcasting Corporation Salisbury studios on weekday mornings. This programme was heralded in by its theme tune of the same name, and presented by the popular young radio announcer June Tobin. Friends and relatives sent in requests for songs and music to be played for patients in hospital and for those recovering at home. I was delighted one morning to hear the announcement "And the next request is for the song *Always.* It is being played for Peter Sternberg of Prince Edward School with best wishes for his speedy recovery. With all her love, Eva". The song and the message proved to be an excellent "get well" tonic! Needless to say, I took a considerable amount of ribbing from my fellow patients following that message!

With good nursing care, a somewhat superior hospital diet and plenty of rest, most of us were up and about before long, much to our collective relief. We faced a hard scholastic year and all felt that missing out on lessons would not be in the least beneficial to us.

We were allowed to visit the Belvedere Theatre one weekday evening to see a play produced by the Salisbury Repertory Company. This was a rare treat, for boarders were as a rule "confined to barracks" during midweek evenings. Salisbury Reps, by which name the city's leading amateur company was known, took over a small theatre, situated in the Salisbury Show Grounds, from the recently departed Royal Air Force. The building had initially been constructed by the RAF during the war years for the purpose of entertaining the many airmen stationed in and around Salisbury at the time, screening movies and staging theatrical productions. After revamping the building, Reps staged productions in this newly found "home" from 1947 until 1959. Thereafter they moved to their magnificent newly constructed theatre in Second Street in 1960, where they remain to this day. This repertory company was formed in 1931 and produced many wonderful stage productions, many of which I had the pleasure of attending in the years that followed. Unfortunately I cannot recall the name of the play we saw that particular evening in 1950, but it certainly helped nurture in me a growing love for the theatre.

To our great regret, the much respected and admired E.J. "Jeeves" Hougaard, housemaster of Jameson House, who had been on the teaching staff of Prince Edward School since 1925, was transferred to another school. To our dismay, he had been promoted to become the first headmaster of a newly constructed high school for boys in the city. Situated on the then outskirts of Salisbury, the school had recently opened its doors under the name of "The Eastlea Boys' Secondary School". This somewhat unimaginative and lacklustre name was not to the liking of its newly appointed principal, who, unbeknown to anyone, wrote directly to no less a personage than Winston Churchill, Britain's illustrious war time leader, and boldly requested his permission to name the school "Churchill". Much to his surprise and delight, the great man agreed to this request, hence the name Churchill School came into being. However, having sidestepped bona fide channels regarding this proposed name change, "Jeeves" Hougaard was now compelled to follow the official path and in due course received a reprimand from the "men in the ministry" for having breached procedure. For Winston Churchill himself replied to the then Rhodesian Minister of Education that there was no need to ask permission for a second time in order to use his name, as he and Mr E.J. Hougaard had already settled the matter between themselves! As "Jeeves" Hougaard later commented, "When a man gets a sound idea, he must push on regardless"! That was "Jeeves" Hougaard in a nutshell! And "Jeeves" proved to be a wise and astute founder-headmaster and set this new high school onto a good footing.

When "Jeeves" Hougaard retired as headmaster of Churchill School at the end of 1961, his successor turned out to be no other than John Simpson, former headmaster of Jameson High School in Gatooma from 1945 to 1961. John Simpson likewise proved to be an excellent head of Churchill, and remained in that position until 1968.

The person who eventually replaced "Jeeves" as housemaster of Jameson House in 1950 was a newcomer to the school. Let us call him "Spooky", for that is the name we soon dubbed him. He duly settled into the housemaster's quarters with his family. Initially all went well, but our attention was soon drawn to the hostel notice board. For it began to rapidly fill up with newly promulgated rules, regulations and notices. These new regulations were far in excess over the previous number of rules and regulations that had sufficed perfectly well over past years. The new housemaster was obviously a stickler for rules – everything was now expected to be followed "by the book" and there was to be no deviation from the straight and narrow.

Initially, these inflexible rules were shrugged off with a laugh – we knew they were virtually impossible to follow, as many of them were quite impractical. It started off with "lights out" in the evening. The lights in our dormitory were to be extinguished by

9.30 p.m. – SHARP! And NO talking whatsoever after lights out – under any circumstances! This rule could possibly be applied to boisterous First Form pupils who needed some sort of discipline – which was in effect a prefect's duty to enforce. In the circumstances we felt that many of these rules were not intended to apply to the hostel's senior pupils. We were soon to find out however that we were highly mistaken in our assumption!

"Spooky" though intended to stick to his new rules, come hell or high water! A few nights later, virtually on the stroke of 9.30 p.m. he suddenly appeared – virtually like a silent spook (ghost) at the entrance of our dormitory and demanded to know why the lights were still on. He brooked no excuses and personally switched off all lights, leaving several boarders still in the showers. He insisted that they find their own way into bed in the dark – no lights were to be switched on under any circumstances! He issued a dire warning that, should anyone in the future be caught in the showers after lights out, they would be punished.

The twenty or so schoolboys in our dormitory, who had been a happy and relaxed bunch of kids at the beginning of the term, became, within a short space of time, both angry and frustrated. And we could not even discuss our gripes in the gloom of the now darkened dormitory for, in order to enforce this new "no talking" rule, "Spooky" kept up a constant patrol outside our bedroom windows that evening and for many evenings to follow, no doubt hoping to catch out a transgressor ... We were aware of his constant prowling around the entire hostel for many weeks. With all the lights out he could indeed flit around the darkened building like a spook. What was this man up to?

He next targeted visiting parents who had come to collect their sons on weekday afternoons for various reasons, be it a social visit, medical appointment or on other grounds. The pupil intending to depart the school property would have to notify "Spooky" well in advance as to the justification for his parent's visit, provide him with the date of the visit and the exact time that he would be collected. The pupil was strictly forbidden to leave the school grounds prior to the time stated. Should parents unexpectedly arrive a little earlier than originally planned, they were still barred from collecting their son prior to the original time declared. This ruling angered and frustrated parents and pupils alike and helped escalate the ever increasing tension in the hostel.

New rules and regulations were pinned onto the hostel notice board on almost a daily basis. "Spooky" would turn up at the most unexpected times and locations in order to ensure that none of these rules were broken. No pupils were spared his wrath, for he would single out and punish both juniors and seniors alike. In his zeal he also commenced to pick on and reprimand a number of the hostel prefects. This both embarrassed and angered the prefects no end, especially when "Spooky" reprimanded them within earshot of junior pupils. Punishments were liberally meted out for even the slightest infringements, and any modicum of respect we might initially have shown towards this housemaster had by now evaporated. For many of us, this was probably the first time that we had come up against people who today are probably referred to as "control freaks". "Spooky" may well have been the first person of this nature whom I had personally encountered. In later years however I met up with a number of these individuals, usually finding them very unpleasant people to deal with.

Whilst rules stated that we were expected to wear our standard weekday uniforms (khaki shirts and shorts) in the school grounds from Mondays through to Saturdays, we were permitted to wear coloured shirts on Sundays, provided we remained on school property. This had always been the rule, providing us with a little relief and variation from the humdrum all khaki attire of the other six days. However, it so happened that one of the Jameson House boys, for whatever reason, happened to be wearing a multi-coloured shirt one Saturday morning – a whole 24 hours before wearing this shirt would have become legal! As can be expected, the poor lad was promptly spotted by our ever vigilant housemaster!

One would have thought that a misdemeanour of the worst kind had been committed, judging by "Spooky's" hysterical reaction! The poor lad was given a major dressing down right in front of his friends, the reason given for wearing this shirt was not accepted, and he was promptly barred from wearing another coloured shirt for the remainder of the school term. An over the top reaction, but that should have been the end of the incident. However, "Spooky" was not finished yet, not by a long chalk. The pupil was then accused of "deliberately trying to undermine the housemaster's authority" by wearing this shirt on a Saturday (instead of a Sunday). And for good measure was also "gated" (confined strictly to within the school grounds) for the remainder of the school term, which still had a few weeks to run. And all this for having worn a coloured shirt on the "wrong" day! The following morning a notice appeared on the notice board stating very clearly that anyone found wearing a coloured shirt on any other day other than Sunday would immediately be "gated" (confined to barracks).

The whole matter came to a head when one of the senior pupils decided to test this rule. Donning a brightly coloured shirt the following Saturday morning, he paraded around the hostel in full view of all, including the housemaster's quarters. "Spooky The Vigilant", ever on the lookout for infringements, spotted the law breaker and called him over. Needless to say, after a severe dressing down, he too was "confined to barracks" for the remainder of the term (semester).

Word of this incident got around the hostel in minutes, and a plan of action was put into place. This plan had obviously been hatched in advance, no doubt having been discussed and formulated by some of the Form V and VI boarders over the past week. The majority of boarders had been kept in the dark about this plan, rumour later had it that some of the teaching staff residing in the school hostel were part and parcel of this scheme. If so, proof was never furnished nor names named. All Jameson House boarders were immediately requested to don a coloured shirt, and if any did not possess one, they were provided with a colourful example by a fellow boarder who had a spare. This request was readily complied with and the brightest of colours were chosen!

We then formed up and walked in groups of half a dozen past the housemaster's apartment, in order to deliberately provoke him to come out and berate us. Not unexpectedly, a few fellow boarders disagreed with this plan and declined to take part in our "protest march". However, the great majority participated without any qualms whatsoever. It now boiled down to some seventy boarders pitting their combined will against the machinations of one extremely unpopular housemaster!!

We walked right up to his office, dressed in a multitude of rainbow colours, and awaited his reaction. We did not have to wait for long. He came charging out of his office door, having noticed us walking past his window. He stood transfixed on the office steps, obviously not believing what he was seeing. He was about to open his mouth when to his amazement, the second group of colourfully garbed youngsters arrived, followed by a third and then a fourth group. We had him virtually surrounded by what was surely the largest and most colourfully dressed group of boys ever to have assembled on the lawns of Jameson House! "Spooky" stood motionless as he faced the sea of shirts. Unsmiling, our arms folded, we stared back at him. Up to that point not a word had been uttered. Which party would be the first to break the silence?

We thought the man was about to have an apoplexy, for he looked absolutely livid. He attempted to speak, but words failed him ... After waving his arms in the air a few times, he swung around and retreated into his office, loudly slamming the door behind him. There was silence. We decided to wait, fully expecting him to re-emerge at any moment and read us the riot act. Nothing happened. His door remained firmly closed. Eventually we dispersed, and, returning to our respective dormitories, we changed back into our everyday khaki shirts. We had made a statement, – a most emphatic one at that!

The next morning we scanned the hostel notice board with just the slightest hint of trepidation, fully expecting the entire complement of Jameson boarders to be on the "banned and gated list". But no such list appeared. We waited for a monster "dressing down" to be sprung on us during the day, where in most likelihood we would be accused of having instigated a mutiny against authority. But nothing happened. By Tuesday it finally dawned on us that our housemaster must have realized only too well that we had decided to call his bluff. Should he have carried out his threats he would no doubt have become the laughing stock of the entire school over such a trivial and petty matter. "Spooky" somehow managed to avoid showing his face for the next few days. What is more, he proceeded to remove the majority of his typewritten rules and regulations from the hostel notice board, thus leaving us to get on with our daily lives without his constant and annoying interference. Even the unpopular "lights out" rule was scrapped and a sense of normality slowly returned to hostel life. As far as I recall, "Spooky" never resorted to his gimmicks again, or at least not during the remaining period of my stay at Jameson House. Whether or not our housemaster had really changed for the better I could not tell, but at least, for the moment anyway, he appeared to have been kept in check ...

Our class was given the opportunity of writing the Rhodesian School Leaving examinations during the year and most chose to write this exam. Although we were scheduled to write the Cambridge School Leaving examinations in due course, I felt that it would do no harm to obtain an additional certificate along the way. This examination was a very straight forward one and required little preparation. As far as I know we all passed this examination with little difficulty.

The annual cadet camp for boys' high schools in Rhodesia was held at the end of the second term, over a ten day period. The venue was Inkomo Barracks, situated some twenty miles north of Salisbury. Cadets arrived from all four provinces of the country. Salisbury (Mashonaland Province) provided Prince Edward School, Saint George's College and Allan Wilson High, Umtali (Manicaland Province) sent cadets from Umtali High School. Gwelo (Midlands Province) provided Chaplin High School. The three Matabeleland schools were Milton Boys High School and Technical College from Bulawayo and Plumtree Boys High from the border town of Plumtree. Those eight schools represented all boys' high schools in Southern Rhodesia at the time. Although Churchill School had recently been established, they appeared to not yet have become involved in the cadet corps and so did not send a contingent. Two of these schools, namely Chaplin and Umtali, were in actual fact co-ed schools. Girls however did not participate in the cadet movement.

We were billeted under canvas tents, each accommodating six cadets. We slept on reasonably comfortable camp beds, and were awoken each morning by reveille played on a bugle, almost home from home for the hostel boarders present! Marching and rifle drill took up a good part of the morning's activities and a Bisley Shooting competition took place between various school teams. Lectures on various military topics were given. Much emphasis was placed on sport – a school cadet athletics (track) meet was held and we had the pleasure of seeing the majority of the top junior athletes in the country competing against each other. An inter-school boxing competition was held which produced an evening of excellent and hard fought bouts.

Meals were served in the mess hall – a large canvas tent – where we were seated at long trestle tables and supplied with enamel plates and mugs. The food was good, wholesome and plentiful, which turned out to be just as well for appetites had been whetted by all the open air activities that we were subjected to! A well attended open air concert was staged one evening and it was amazing to see how much talent various schoolboy cadets from around the country possessed. A number of evenings feature films were screened, I recall seeing one movie, *West of Pago Pago* which turned out to be such a poor movie that many of us left half way through its screening. We returned to our tents, where we fell asleep long before the film had come to an end!

One Saturday morning we all set off on a route march, being kitted up to the hilt. The day turned out to be an exceptionally hot one, and soon many of us had consumed all the precious liquid in our water bottles. This was serious as the march never seemed to come to an end and most of us felt absolutely parched. On and on we tramped, the hot sun beating down on our aching backs, already strained under the weight of a hefty backpack. Eventually some cadets started to stumble, a few proceeded to drop out of the march altogether. They sat down at the side of the route, trying to find some shade from the blazing sun, and hoping to be "rescued" by the medical orderlies who were following up in the rear. A few cadets actually fainted and were assisted back to camp. Wearing heavy army boots made it additionally tough going – I could not wait to get mine off! Nevertheless, we soldiered on, for there just had to be an end to this seemingly never ending march ... we hoped!

But all things do come to an end, – even route marches! We arrived back at camp, forming up on the parade ground. After a brief address by one of the Staff Corps officers, we were thank-fully dismissed. Most of us headed straight for the canteen where we purchased bottles of ice cold Coca Cola, downing them with great relief. To this day no cold drink has ever tasted as good and refreshing as it did that Saturday morning! Next stop was the showers to wash off the accumulated dust, grime and perspi-ration. After lunch we made our way to our tents, where we flopped down onto our camp beds to rest our weary bodies and aching feet!

Later in the afternoon, I took a stroll to visit some friends in another section of the camp. Never will I forget the incredible sensation I experienced that afternoon whilst wearing my com-fortable and soft pair of shoes – compared to the heavy boots I had worn earlier. For I had the distinct feeling – which seemed quite uncanny, most surreal – that I was walking, indeed floating – on air! The shoes felt so unbelievably light that I could hardly feel them! The sensation wore off after a time, but I am still reminded of it to this day!

The cadet camp experience proved to be an interesting and enjoyable one and at the end of the ten days we were transport-ed back to Salisbury, where, shortly thereafter I caught the train back to Gatooma and a well-earned school vacation. I could not wait to sleep in a little later in the mornings and thankful that I was not going to be woken up at 6 a.m. by a bugle call! Those were my plans for the vacation that now lay ahead ...

But my parents sprang a surprise by informing me that I had been offered a "vacation job" by one Sigi Weber, one of my father's clients, owner of Elite Outfitters, a recently opened gents outfitters. He required a cashier/counter hand who could be entrusted to handle money as well as sell clothing. The pay offered was 10/- (ten shillings) a day which was considered good and, despite my "late lying in" plans having now been scuppered, I happily accepted the job. Working hours were from 8 a.m. to 5 p.m., with an hour off for lunch, Mondays through to Fridays, plus Saturday mornings.

Business turned out to be fairly brisk, and funds in the till tallied at the end of the day, as they were of course expected to do. However, by the end of the first week, I had already made a mental note that shop keeping was not really a profession I wanted to get involved with on a permanent basis, for I found the work involved neither stimulating nor challenging. Selling socks and underpants, watching prospective customers agonize over whether to choose a yellow shirt over a pale green one (neither colour appealed to me) did not exactly help! Other would be customers tried on endless pairs of shoes to while away their time (and unfortunately mine too). They often promised to return the next day to try out further styles and colours - but most never did. Despite these minor irritations, I must admit that on the whole I enjoyed my stint serving behind the counter. I was asked to come back during further school vacations, which as a rule I did, for the wages earned always came in useful!

With the December 1950 school vacation approaching I received a request (via my parents) from Harry Malkow (another client of my father's) - the proprietor of Battlefields Trading Company, a general dealers store situated in Battlefields. Battlefields was situated on the railway line between Salisbury and Bulawayo, approximately half way between the towns of Gatooma and Que Que. It was a small rail siding which served the numerous farms and mines in the area. The buildings in Battlefields consisted of a small police station, a railway goods shed cum office, a post office, half a dozen houses - and a single shop which traded under the name of Battlefields Trading Company. Harry Malkow, a bachelor at that time, had requested me to help out in his shop during the two week period leading up to Christmas 1950. Remuneration offered was good, certainly to a 15 year old schoolboy, and I promptly accepted his offer.

In order to travel to Battlefields so as to arrive in time for the eight o'clock shop opening, I needed to be on the Gatooma station platform by 7 a.m. to catch the goods train from Salisbury. This train stopped briefly in Gatooma, unloaded the day's *Rhodesia Herald* newspapers, then proceeded on its way to Que Que, followed by Gwelo, until it finally arrived in Bulawayo, its destination. Being a goods train, it stopped at most rail sidings en route. Most people in the country have never heard of Battlefields, and when they discover its existence, frequently enquire which battles took place there to warrant such a name. The answer is that no battles appear to have taken place there at all. For some reason, many of the pioneering farmers, who settled in that area around the turn of the century, named their farms, all hewn out of virgin bush after much effort and sweat, after well known European battles of yesteryear. The names included Agincourt, Blenheim, Trafalgar and Waterloo. With so many farms, and a number of mines in that area also named after prominent battles, the Government decided to name the newly constructed post office built to service this area "Battlefields" and that is how the place name came into existence!

Travelling on the goods train entailed sitting in the small three seat coupe/compartment (2nd Class) of the guards van, coupled onto the rear of the train. Most days I was the sole occupant. No facilities were provided – if one needed to heed the call of nature it was a case of waiting for the next halt and then jumping out of the van and sprinting off into the surrounding bush. Then clambering back, as soon as possible, prior to the train setting off, without bothering to wait for its lone passenger! This very nearly happened to me on one occasion! Thereafter, I made sure to advise the guard that I would be "in the bush" for a few minutes and would he please confirm that I was back in the guards van, before proceeding to wave his green flag to the engine driver at the other end of the train!

Battlefields Trading Company catered for the local farming and mining community and stocked a large variety of goods – from foodstuffs to cycles, farming equipment to clothing, cigarettes to furniture, in other words, a great variety of merchandise. Selling all these items kept me on my toes and locating some of the goods requested by customers often took up a major amount of time, for the items on offer were not particularly well laid out and many of the goods were difficult to locate. But I soon learned to cope!

Early in the week that led up to Christmas the shop became so busy that I missed my late afternoon train connection back to Gatooma and was compelled to spend the night at Harry Malkow's house. The house was situated in fairly close proximity to the shop. Harry, as mentioned earlier, was at that stage still a bachelor and he employed a cook (or "cook-boy" in the language of the day) who prepared all his meals, from nutritious mealie-meal (maize-meal) porridge and scrambled eggs at breakfast to delicious thick soups, sumptuous steaks and roast potatoes for dinner in the evenings. In the line of duty I thereafter decided to spend the rest of the week leading right up to Christmas Eve in Battlefields, as we were frantically busy in the shop. During that week I probably gained a few kilos in weight after consuming dinners of this magnitude, but one must accept the good with the bad!

Harry invariably retired to bed early and I was left reading on my own in the lounge. But the light tended to attract numerous beetles and moths, most of which managed to fly or flutter in through various holes in the gauze window screens or crawl in from under the door. After some time I usually abandoned the lounge and took a bath (piping hot water always available – even in the bush ...), after which I headed for bed. I always checked that the screens fitted to the bedroom windows were properly fixed in place. I lowered the mosquito net over the bed and carefully tucked in all sides beneath the mattress. Mosquitoes thrived in outlying areas like Battlefields, surrounded by bush, farmland and dams filled to the brink. The month of December fell well into the rainy season and one could hear the non-stop croaking of frogs throughout the night. This indicated that there was plenty of water around – ideal conditions for mosquitoes to breed in. A small bookcase in the lounge yielded several old and dusty detective novels and I remember reading Agatha Christie's vintage crime thriller *Mystery of the Blue Train* whilst lying under the mosquito net at night. I used to pause after having read a few pages to flick off *creepy crawlies* and various flying insects that had settled on the outside of the net. For most were trying their best to make their way under and into the net in order to join me for the night ...

But what I recall most vividly about my fortnight's sojourn in Battlefields was working alongside a young man in his early twenties. He seldom uttered a word, which was perhaps not surprising, for his command of the English language was virtu-ally non-existent. He also appeared to be of a very nervous disposition and kept glancing over his shoulder every few min-utes. He carried a packet of sandwiches around with him which he kept in one of his trouser pockets. Every now and again he would pull out the packet, open it, stare at the contents and then replace it. This was repeated on numerous occasions, but I don't recall him ever eating a single sandwich. Harry had told me he was a person who needed rehabilitation and more or less left it at that, no further details were furnished, and I refrained from asking further questions. Although he also resided in Harry's house, he only joined us at meal times, otherwise he kept himself confined in his bedroom.

A few days later the weather proved to be exceptionally hot, and those employees wearing long sleeves rolled them up in an attempt to keep cool. This also applied to the young man who happened to be working right next to me at the time. He passed me something and I caught a glance at his arm – and I promptly froze. For clearly tattooed on it were a row of numbers which could have mean only one thing – that he had been an inmate in a concentration camp. He was the first former inmate I had ever met. I had of course seen the dreaded tattoo in photographs, in documentary movies and read about them – but here, right in front of me, was the real thing.

In a flash the whole puzzle became clear – this poor victim's obsession with keeping a packet of food on him at all times of the day – and quite possibly night, was due to the fact that he needed some sort of guarantee that he would never again experience the pangs of starvation, and that some food at least would always be available to him whenever he needed it. Was his continual glancing around in all directions still a reminder of being traumatized by murderous Nazi guards threatening to beat him up or kill him on a whim? His reluctance to mix with others – was this possibly due to withdrawing from life in general after no doubt losing both family and friends in the most brutal of ways imaginable?

I immediately felt a great deal of compassion towards him and at the same time realized that he had quite possibly been affected mentally by his experiences, despite five years having elapsed since he was freed from the concentration camp. What a horrific price to have had to pay for his current "freedom" – a freedom alive with memories that would remain with him and haunt him till his dying day. I realized then that there must also be hundreds of thousands of other former concentration camp victims scattered throughout the world, whose entire lives had probably been shattered, mentally and physically, by beatings, torture, incarceration and starvation. Many, like this person, were probably reduced to a hollow shell of their former selves. I felt quite helpless in the circumstances – but why had Harry not told me of this person's condition from the outset? Thereafter, I made a concentrated effort to befriend him and tried to coax him to talk to me, but he remained utterly withdrawn. I learned a few weeks later that his employment had been terminated and that he had left the country.

To this day I have never forgotten how distressed I felt when I met up with an actual survivor of one of these dreaded camps. I felt grateful and extremely humble to realize, once again, how fortunate we had been to escape from Germany in time. I think I matured that day when I realized just what could well have befallen us if we had failed to flee Germany – a scant eleven years earlier ...

During school vacations, dances were often arranged by various ladies' organizations – usually by the members of the Women's Institute. These were arranged for the benefit of the town's teenagers, to hopefully keep boredom at bay. The most popular venue for these events was the Women's Institute Hall in Newton Street, next door to the library. From time to time the Gatooma Sports Club would also hold a dance for the town's teenagers. These dances were usually well patronized, not only by the locals but by teenagers who lived on many of the outlying farms and mines throughout the widely spaced district. For aside from going to the local cinema, visiting friends, or listening in to the radio, there appeared little to do to attract our attention after nightfall. Television in the early 1950s was practically confined to audiences in the United States of America. It was only a phenomenon that we had read about and were unlikely to see in Africa for very many years to come ... This indeed proved to be the case.

Junior tennis tournaments were organized by members of the Gatooma Sports Club during vacations, and tournaments were also staged by the Hartley Sports Club, situated some 20 miles away. As expected, the local swimming pool proved most popular, especially during the summer months. The Royalty Theatre screened three different films each week, and on Saturday nights the Cam & Motor Recreational Club in Eiffel Flats also screened a movie – but usually a very dated one. As always, the library proved a popular venue for the readers amongst us. Those were also still the days when (mainly) boys collected postage stamps as a hobby! Soap box derbies were becoming popular worldwide, and a few teenagers in Gatooma began to construct soapbox racers, usually with the assistance of their technically minded fathers. However, a few years were still to pass before the first soapbox derby became an annual fixture in our town.

We celebrated the festival of Chanukah during the month of December, lighting the requisite number of candles each evening over the eight day period that this festival lasted. Judy and I had received some great presents from our parents over the years, and each year I had likewise bought Chanukah gifts for my family out of my pocket money. Having earned my first wages from vacation jobs, I could now afford to spend a little more on the gifts I gave them and distinctly recall what a good feeling it gave me to see these presents being enjoyed by my family. Chanukah, the festival of lights, has, to this day, remained my favourite festival and continues to remain a solid reminder of the happiness and security that we experienced within our home.

 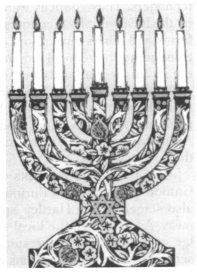

1951

Having passed the end of year examinations in December 1950 I, together with the majority of my classmates, moved up to Form V. For many in my class, 1951 was scheduled to be our final year at Prince Edward. We were all due to write the University of Cambridge School Certificate examination at the end of the year, and of course we all hoped to pass well.

Our teachers recommended that we pair off with a fellow pupil who would also be writing the Cambridge examinations at the end of the year. The idea behind this being that the two pupils spend as much time as possible revising all set works and testing each other's knowledge on various subjects due to be written. I paired up with fellow Jameson House friend and classmate Wrex (Wrexford) Tarr. We spent approximately an hour each weekday morning – Mondays through to Fridays – revising and tossing questions at each other. Rising most mornings at 5.30 a.m., we headed for the prep room, a prefabricated building situated behind Jameson House. However, in the process of testing each other's academic knowledge during those early morning sessions, it was difficult not to be inveigled into spending a good amount of time listening to Wrex's endless array of jokes. I attempted, often futilely, to suppress my laughter in order not to disturb other pupils, who were likewise attempting to study in the prep room. Wrex possessed an endless array of jokes, which he related with gay abandon. Where he got them all from, goodness knows! Nevertheless, despite our early morning joke sessions, we managed to spend most of our time studying, which in due course paid off.

In later years Wrex, who in 1978 was awarded the President's Medal for rifle shooting, went on to become a leading member of the victorious Rhodesian team in the World Series. He competed in the 1988 Olympic Games in Seoul, South Korea, at which games he represented Zimbabwe at archery. At one stage of his working career he joined the Rhodesian Broadcasting Corporation as a prime-time news reader. During the 1970s he became Rhodesia's top musical entertainer and comedian following the release of his *Chilapalapa* recordings which he personally presented on radio, television and on stage.

I was never particularly happy in French classes, partially due to differences I experienced with the French master from time to time. Halfway through my final year, I elected to drop French as my foreign language subject and chose German to take its place. That of course was the language that I had initially grown up with, but of course had switched over to English upon arrival in Rhodesia. I felt confident that I would still be able to muster sufficient German to see me through the Cambridge examinations, despite the fact that I had virtually not spoken the language for the past twelve years. Unfortunately, no member of the Prince Edward School staff taught German, Afrikaans and French being the only foreign languages taught at that time. Despite that, I stuck to my decision and dropped French as a subject.

In order to bolster my chances of success in passing the German examination, I decided that additional revision in the subject would be necessary. I approached my good friend Margot Stiefel and enquired whether she would be prepared to provide me with an hour's tuition per week in order to brush up on my knowledge of the language, especially on aspects of grammar. This she readily agreed to do. Margot in fact proved to be a most competent teacher, and through her efforts I managed to obtain a distinction in the subject at the end of year examinations.

By the late 1940s and early 1950s newly styled American and British cars began appearing on Rhodesian roads with increasing frequency, replacing most of the pre-war automobiles that had been soldiering on since the 1930s. The majority of the older cars now landed up in junkyards or on used car lots, where they were often sold, as the expression was: "for a song". Britain at this time was vigorously promoting its post-war export sales campaign in cars and manufactured goods – "Buy British" and "British Is Best" were the slogans in most common use. At that time, the major portion of Britain's annual automobile production was geared for export and many of these new cars could now be found on local roads. Motor showrooms throughout the country were filled with these new vehicles. In Gatooma, being an agricultural centre, local Ford dealers Duly & Company showcased their latest Fordson tractors displayed between the new Ford Consuls and Zephyrs, in addition to their larger American Ford passenger cars and pickup trucks. Although the vast majority of British cars imported into Rhodesia were the familiar Austin, Ford, Morris and Vauxhall ranges, many autos now sported newly designed bodies, and it was interesting to find entirely new British models such as the Armstrong Siddeley Typhoon, Austin Sheerline, Austin Atlantic, Triumph Renown, Jaguar XK120 and Jowett Jupiter appearing on local roads, many fitted with rakish and attractive bodywork. My favourite amongst these new cars was the 1951 Sunbeam 90 saloon, (a car formerly known as the Sunbeam Talbot). An example of such car was driven by the parents of a Jameson House boarder, and I set my sights on one day owning a similar model. As was to be expected, by the time I finally managed to earn enough to purchase this car, the Sunbeam 90 was long out of production. However, in 1958, seven years after having initially set my sights on owning Sunbeam, my dream was fulfilled when I purchased, from Vulcan Garage, the local agents in Gatooma, my first ever car, a sparkling new 1958 Sunbeam Rapier Series II two door hardtop coupe. It had been well worth the wait, and proved that dreams can come true!

The second term of the year heralded the rugby season and I was elated at being chosen to represent Jameson House in the Inter-House rugby championships. I had previously played in the eighth man position but in 1950 the coach decided I should switch over to full back. This move worked out well and I remained in that position thereafter. After a number of good wins our team advanced into the finals of the school championship. At this stage a number of our team members, myself included, were replaced by Jameson House players who throughout the rugby season had been regular members of the Prince Edward School First XV team. The rules stated that regular first team members were not eligible to play in the preliminary rounds of the Inter-House rugby competition, but could participate once their particular Sports House team had reached the finals. Jameson went on to win the 1951 school rugby championship and I was happy in the knowledge that I had contributed towards the winning of the Inter-House trophy.

The 1951 season saw the Prince Edward 1st Rugby team score five wins, net one draw and suffer three defeats against various Rhodesian high schools. However, to the delight of their supporters, the team scored a fine win over visiting St Andrew's College from Bloemfontein, South Africa. Witnessed by hundreds of cheering spectators, the home side scored a resounding 21-0 victory in front of ecstatic schoolboys, parents and staff over the very popular and fancied South African touring side.

Fellow Jameson House boarder Marty Timms (1st team cricket captain) and a regular 1st team rugby player, later went on to represent Rhodesia at rugby, and in 1955 played for his country against the British Lions.

I decided not to participate in the annual boxing championships in 1951 for I felt it wiser to devote any spare time that I might have had available on revising school work rather than get involved in training sessions. I did however play social tennis on Sunday mornings on the school courts, enjoying tennis far more than I had initially done a year or two earlier. There were an endless number of players to compete against and I regretted not having taken up tennis as a regular sport, realizing that I had missed out on some expert coaching over the past few years. Prince Edward School had a long and rich tennis tradition – many former pupils represented Rhodesia in the Davis Cup Competition and provided winners in numerous prestigious overseas tournaments.

My interest in aviation was compounded by events which occurred during the year. Firstly, in March 1951 the Southern Rhodesian Air Force received its first squadron of Supermarine Spitfire Mk.22 fighters. These were the latest and virtually the last in the line of British piston engine fighter aircraft of which we had heard and read so much. These Spitfires, equipped with more powerful Rolls Royce Griffon engines and capable of reaching speeds of well in excess of 400 miles per hour, initially took off from a base in Britain. Flying down the length of Africa in stages, they landed at Salisbury's Cranborne Aerodrome, a former World War 2 R.A.F. training base, one Thursday afternoon. This prevented me from being present upon their arrival, for Cranborne was situated several miles out of town. In due course these sleek fighter aircraft took to the skies over the city and we witnessed several thrilling formation and individual fly pasts during the months that followed.

During the course of the year we were most privileged to be addressed by no less a personage than Air Commodore Sir Frank Whittle, who spoke to the senior boys about his experiences in the Royal Air Force over the years. Sir Frank, British inventor of the jet engine, provided a most fascinating talk on this new form of propulsion. His address was delivered in an easy and understandable manner, which we greatly appreciated whilst listening in rapt attention to one of the great inventors of the 20th century. Many questions were put to him after his talk, which were readily answered. Having recently been given an autograph book as a birthday gift, I made sure of obtaining Sir Frank's autograph as a matter of priority immediately following his address!

I read in the daily press that four R.A.F. de Havilland Vampire single seat jet fighters – accompanied by two de Havilland Mosquitoes, would be spending a few days in Salisbury following their visit to South Africa, and would be landing at Belvedere aerodrome the following afternoon. This was great news and I immediately approached the master on hostel duty and asked his permission to visit the aerodrome in order to witness this historic event. For this would be the very first time a jet aircraft would be landing on Rhodesian soil, or shall I say, tarmac! To my amazement he emphatically refused to sanction my request, stating that if he would grant me such permission then there may well be the possibility that other boarders would also want to go along. He saw no reason for anyone to pay Belvedere Airport a visit, it was after all, just another aircraft, and whether or not it happened to be a jet aircraft should surely be of no particular interest! He emphatically warned me not to be foolish enough to disregard his decision, for there would be consequences to pay should I choose to ignore him ...

Needless to say, I duly arrived at the small Belvedere airport terminal the following afternoon, consequences or no consequences, joining twenty or so fellow aviation enthusiasts who had likewise read about the jet's arrival in the previous day's *Rhodesia Herald*. We waited patiently. Arrival time was fast approaching and our eyes were riveted in the direction of South Africa from whence aircraft from "south of the border" normally made their appearance. Occasionally a spectator called out that they could see spots approaching on the horizon, these "sighting" however amounted to no more than wishful thinking. Minutes went by and these "spots" (if there had indeed been any) never appeared to venture any closer ...

Eventually another two "spots" materialized on the distant horizon and to our relief these "spots" actually increased in size. We could hear the sound of aircraft approaching and they soon came into view – four finely synchronized Merlin engines approaching at speed. For that is exactly what they were, two twin-engine de Havilland Mosquito light bombers, flying in our direction in close formation. What a thrilling sight they made as they flew directly overhead, banked, then made another low pass in perfect unison over the control tower, before finally coming in to land. What a fantastic aircraft this famous "wooden wonder" appeared to be, an aircraft that had been acknowledged as probably being the finest all round aircraft to come out of the Second World War.

The two Mosquitoes taxied in and parked fairly close to where we stood. We watched eagerly as the crew disembarked and made their way into the airport building. The two lead aircraft had now arrived, but where were the Vampires? We patiently waited, whilst studying these two beautifully designed aircraft from a fairly close range – probably the first time any of us had seen this famous aircraft in the flesh. Years later I discovered to my surprise that a Mosquito had been compelled to force land near Que Que, a town fairly close to Gatooma, a few year's earlier. We continued to wait for the jets to arrive and a few of the less patient spectators once more began scouring for tell tale "spots" on the horizon!

Suddenly, and without prior warning, a loud "whoosh" thundered directly overhead. We swung our heads in the city's direction, for none of us had either seen or heard an approaching aircraft, neither had we expected one to approach from that direction. Its pilot had certainly taken us by surprise! We gazed in all directions, trying to trace this aircraft, which now appeared to have vanished from sight as suddenly as it had arrived. Seconds later, and again without warning, another tremendous "whoosh" erupted over our heads. The second Vampire, apparently coming from the direction of the control tower, screamed over our heads. Craning our necks, we managed to follow this now rapidly climbing aircraft before it too managed to disappear, possibly into cloud. Moments later another Vampire flashed overhead from yet a third direction, and this jet was followed seconds later by the fourth and final machine which also whistled loudly over our heads, likewise at an extremely low altitude. What a truly fantastic introduction to this new method of jet propulsion! We all stood there with wide grins, and I am sure that no one present there that afternoon would have missed those truly magic moments! Welcome to the jet age!

The four Vampires regrouped, and after flying a few circuits, proceeded to land one after the other. We could clearly hear them taxiing in our direction and noted the unfamiliar whine of their jet engines, a sound still alien to our ears but one that we would grow accustomed to in the years that followed ...

And the aftermath of my visit to witness the arrival of the jet age in Rhodesia? Later that evening, one of the prefects summoned me to "pay him a visit" in the prefects' study, situated on the first floor of the hostel. There I was informed that he had been instructed by the master-on-duty to administer "suitable punishment" for having blatantly ignored the "curfew" that had been imposed upon me. The prefect in question happened to be a friend of mine, and had been so from the day that we had simultaneously arrived at Jameson House, almost five years earlier. We looked at one another and smiled. Silently, he motioned me to move aside. He picked up a cane, positioned himself, then proceeded to enthusiastically whack a small leather cushion that lay on a couch in the study! He administered four good whacks of the cane onto that innocent little cushion! The caning, I might add, sounded most convincing! Four of the best, and justice was heard, if not actually seen, to be done! This little charade, I might add, was no doubt played out for the benefit of any snoopers who might just have been inclined to congregate on the other side of the study door to listen in on punishment being administered. There were always a few sadists around who seemed to derive great pleasure from hearing the whack of a cane being administered on someone else's backside, and it is quite possible that my friend might well have satisfied a few sick minds that evening. On this particular occasion however, it was at no discomfort to me! Thank you, Brian Watkins!

With Rosh Hashanah (the Jewish New Year), falling on Monday and Tuesday 1st and 2nd October 1951, my parents, out of the blue, offered me a ticket for a flight on the recently inaugurated Central African Airways (CAA) Midlands "Beaver" Service. This for a flying visit to Gatooma to spend this major religious festival at home. Was I interested? This question could elicit only one possible answer – a very positive YES!! Not only would it be great to spend four days with my folk, but I would finally get to realize my long held dream of flying. I could hardly wait to climb into an aircraft which would actually take off – and take me with!!

This route plied between Salisbury and the smaller Midlands Province towns of Gatooma, Que Que, Gwelo and Fort Victoria. These high winged, all metal monoplanes, designed and built in Canada, seated some six or seven passengers in a single cabin. The Midlands service had been introduced to enable people from the above mentioned areas to catch early morning flights to Salisbury, complete their business on the same day and be in a position to fly home again that afternoon. Passengers would thus be saving themselves the expense of having to stay overnight in a Salisbury hotel, in addition to spending many hours behind the wheel of their cars driving on strip roads that were still in common usage. Although the Beaver Service initially proved popular, the strip roads were eventually replaced by modern highways and the demand for the Midlands Service fell away. Flights decreased until the service was eventually terminated a few years later.

However, that was still in the future and right now I was in my seventh heaven and about to embark on my first ever flight. It was hard to concentrate on my schoolwork during the days leading up to the flight, but the big day finally arrived – Friday, 28 September 1951.

Fully dressed in school uniform complete with tie, long grey flannel trousers and blazer (it was mid-summer – the hottest time of the year) and carrying my suitcase – I set off on foot towards the direction of Belvedere Airport, a few miles distant. There was no bus service that took one to the airport, certainly not from the area where the school was situated. I also had no intention of spending several weeks' pocket money on a taxi fare. Besides, I had ample time to get to the airport, and the thought of the forthcoming flight kept me moving at a brisk pace.

Arriving at Belvedere Airport with time to spare, I walked into the departures hall and checked in my small suitcase, had my ticket scrutinized and immediately recognized two of my fellow passengers who would, like myself, be flying on to Gatooma. Both were lawyers who operated the town's two legal practices, and we exchanged greetings. Dressed in suits despite the intense October heat, they had no doubt attended court cases in Salisbury earlier that day. Shortly thereafter the remaining passengers arrived and when everyone was present the flight was called. The pilot, who was smartly dressed in white shirt, shorts and long white stockings, led us to the gleaming aircraft which was parked on the tarmac in front of the terminal building. He proceeded to assist us up a small ladder into the aircraft's cramped cabin. Once seated, we were asked to strap ourselves into our seats and he thereafter checked that all buckles were securely fastened. Two passengers sat in the rear, three in the centre row, myself in the middle, and one passenger sat up in front, next to the pilot. It was hot in the somewhat cramped confines of the fuselage (no air conditioning or temperature control) and hardly any room to move our arms and legs. The aircraft's single door having by now been securely shut, we sweltered away in the confines of the cabin, whilst the pilot conversed on and off with the control tower. Before long we were all perspiring freely and wondering when permission would finally be given to depart!

After what seemed like ages the pilot informed us that he had been given the all clear for take off. The whirling propeller blades glinted brightly in the afternoon sun through the windscreen directly ahead of us. The chocks in front of the wheels were pulled aside and we taxied towards the runway en route for takeoff. This, I told myself, is what I had been looking forward to ever since I had avidly watched all those training aircraft take off from Gatooma airfield, and had fervently wished at the time that I too would be given the opportunity to fly. And now, finally, this wish was about to be fulfilled!

The aircraft trundled along until we eventually reached the main runway, where the pilot positioned the aircraft for take off. A few moments later, after further words with air traffic control, the engine omitting a muffled roar, the entire fuselage vibrated and the little Beaver commenced its take off run. Being fully laden on this hot summer afternoon, the aircraft required a goodly amount of runway before it finally rose into the air. The pilot set course for Gatooma and we began to climb, but being a relatively short flight of around forty minutes, we did not fly at too high an altitude. The ground remained in sight throughout the flight and at times I managed to distinguish cars travelling on the roads below.

Thermals (rising currents of hot air) were usually at their worst during the fiercely hot summer months and the little aircraft commenced to bounce around in the sky. These air pockets were acutely felt, and we were advised to remain securely strapped into our seats. Being dressed in a school blazer and tie did not help, and I continued to perspire with a vengeance. Although I managed to take off my tie, I found I could not remove my jacket, for I was too tightly wedged between my fellow passengers. Literally sweating it out, I had no choice but to keep the blazer on. I felt somewhat nauseous, and fervently hoped that I wouldn't become airsick in this confined space. The aircraft appeared to hit every air pocket in the vicinity, which caused it to leap in all directions – upwards, downwards and sideways without any let-up.

Could matters get worse? Yes, they certainly could! The passenger to my right was rather plump, therefore managing to obscure much of my view. This was a little frustrating, for I had hoped to be able to see the sights below. But that turned out to be a relatively minor problem in comparison to what was going on with the person on my left. For, soon after we become airborne, a distinct smell of alcohol assailed my nostrils, giving me the strong impression that my fellow passenger may well have spent considerable time in the airport bar prior to boarding the flight. Although he showed no signs of being intoxicated, both his breath and perspiration appeared to contain a fairly high alcohol content! Within ten minutes or so after departure, he began to wriggle and squirm in his seat. Much to my dismay, he produced a hip flask from the inside of his jacket which he then placed to his lips. Soon the entire cabin seemed to reek of alcohol. I gathered that it was brandy, and, each time he un-screwed the flask, which happened frequently, he managed to spill some of its contents onto his jacket and, for that matter, mine as well! This flight had become nothing more than a wild ride through the heavens instead of the sedate and enjoyable maiden flight that I had envisaged!

It seemed a miracle that none of us actually became airsick on this flight, for had this happened the outcome could have been truly appalling. For periods of time all I could do was sit and grit my teeth, willing myself to keep the contents of my stomach where it belonged, and it was with great relief when the pilot announced that we would shortly be landing in Gatooma. I had by now ceased attempting to peer out of either side window at the countryside below, as I had been spending most of my time trying to keep my distance from the flask's spout on its numer-ous journey's twixt coat pocket and lips. When I felt the wheels touch down I breathed a great sigh of relief! We taxied in and came to a halt next to the windsock. I could not wait to exit the aircraft in order to breathe in some fresh country air. The door to the small hold in the fuselage was opened by the pilot and my suitcase handed to me. My father had come to collect me in the Standard Vanguard. After warmly greeting me he enquired whether there had been an air hostess aboard dispensing alco-holic drinks to schoolboys – as he could quite clearly smell alcohol on me!! Even before my suitcase could be placed into the trunk of the Vanguard, the pilot had climbed back into his seat, gunned the engine and was already taxiing the Beaver towards the runway for the next stage of its flight to the town of Que Que (now renamed KweKwe) – a mere 40 miles away. My first flight was over – and never to be forgotten! A truly memorable experience!

I spent a most enjoyable four days at home and, for the first time ever, appreciated the secure feel of "terra firma" underneath my feet! As usual my father led the congregation in prayer, assisted at times by Ezra Hasson, a local shopkeeper. Due to the fact that the congregation was small in number, much effort needed to be put in place to ensure that sufficient members of the community were available to attend services in order to form a minyan (quorum) of ten men. Despite the fact that the majority confirmed that they would be attending, it frequently happened that one or two congregants failed to arrive on the day in question. Likewise, a few of those who had promised to be there invariably arrived late, to the distinct annoyance of those who had arrived on time. The service on both days of the New Year was scheduled to commence at 8 a.m. and due to conclude only at around 1 p.m. (a full five hour service). Therefore delays in starting were not appreciated by those who had made the effort to be there on time ...

My journey in the Beaver had a sequel. Following my flight, my Aunt Marta, who, with my uncle Julius, had now settled in Que Que, where they had opened their own butchery, was told of my recent flight to Gatooma. This was mentioned during the course of a telephone conversation a week or so later by my mother. What she obviously failed to mention to her sister in Que Que were the consequences of flying in a light aircraft in Rhodesia during the intense summer month heat at low altitude. The bumpy part of the ride had obviously not formed part of the discussion!

Having been made aware of my flight, Aunt Marta decided that she too would like to make use of the Midlands Beaver service. During a visit to Salisbury she decided there and then to fly back to her home in Que Que, rather than catch the train. She booked a seat and caught the afternoon flight out of the city. The weather was still extremely hot. So hot in fact, that, when the aircraft landed in Gatooma, she felt she had suffered sufficient trauma in the air! Disembarking immediately once the aircraft had rolled to a stop, she point blank refused to step back inside the Beaver and fly on to Que Que, this being the next scheduled stop. Obviously, she had no intention of facing a further stressful 20 minutes in the air! She was quite emphatic about her decision. She was NOT going to get back into that confounded little aircraft, under any circumstances! Finding it futile to argue with her, the pilot climbed back into the aircraft and took off, now one passenger short!

Aunt Marta managed to obtain a ride from the aerodrome straight to my father's office. On arrival, she immediately telephoned her husband in Que Que, requesting him to drive to Gatooma and collect her! She was going to complete the remaining 45 miles of this journey by road, and vowed there and then never to fly in a Beaver again! Knowing my Aunt Marta, it was probably not long before many of the locals in Que Que would have heard of her recent flying experiences. And the chances are that quite a number of potential Beaver passengers from that town were unnerved after listening to her experience, and were quite possibly persuaded into believing that road and rail travel were far better options to take when intending to travel to Salisbury!

During school vacations I managed to see a number of films and of these, enjoyed the Alfred Hitchcock thriller *Stranger's On A Train* Starring Farley Granger, Ruth Roman and Robert Walker it turned out to be a thriller of the first degree and one of my favourite Hitchcock movies.

As the dates for the crucial end of year examinations drew nearer, most boarders scheduled to write Cambridge examinations decided to relegate Sundays to additional revision – going out for the day to visit friends took a definite back seat. Finally, the first day of the examinations arrived – these exams were to be held over an approximate two week period. We had been handed our timetables earlier and these set out the various subjects, days, dates and times of writing. Some days we were due to write only one examination, on other days two, in which case one exam would be written in the morning and one in the afternoon. On a few intermediate days, no examinations were due to be written at all. This gave some of us a "free day" to concentrate on additional revision, which we certainly took full advantage of. The fortnight now ahead of us was expected to be very stressful. We wished each other the very best of luck – and many of us felt we certainly needed all the additional luck we could get!

The examinations were held in the school's Beit Hall, named after Alfred Beit – a great Jewish humanitarian, philanthropist and staunch ally, friend and supporter of Rhodesia's founder, Cecil John Rhodes. Beit funds had helped construct not only this hall but countless other school halls, swimming pools and other amenities throughout the country. The Prince Edward School Beit Hall, venue to countless weekday assemblies, theatrical productions, lectures, debates, film shows, dances and boxing tournaments, now took on a more serious tone as we filed to our allocated individual desks, set out in neat rows, covering most of the available floor space. Each desk contained an inkwell topped to overflowing, we in turn supplied our own blotting paper, pencils, erasers and rulers. Although steel tipped wooden pens were still in use, many of us used our personal fountain pens, which were thankfully permitted. The recently developed ball point pen, still fairly new to the market, was not permitted for examination use.

We seated ourselves and were given a briefing by the teacher-in-charge regarding the etiquette, rules and regulations appertaining to the examinations. Thereafter we were handed examination papers which were carefully placed face down on our desk, and which were not allowed to be turned over until all papers had been handed out and the teacher had returned to his table. We had been warned that during examinations we were strictly forbidden to talk, whisper or make signs to other candidates, pass notes or throw pieces of paper around, in fact, we were not to get involved in any possible "funny business"! Cheating was strictly "verboten" and any culprit caught doing so would instantly be thrown out of the examination room. Any infringements committed would be treated in the strictest possible manner.

I knew that there had been a handful of "wise-guys" who, a few days earlier, had discussed a system whereby they intended to assist each other should answers elude them. Whether any of them actually managed to obtain any benefit from this scheme was afterwards neither disclosed nor discussed! Other teachers on duty were tasked to patrol up and down the line of desks to ensure that examination papers were not turned over until permission to do so was given. Once permission was granted we were allowed five minutes in which to peruse the instructions and questions set out on the exam paper. When this brief period was up it was announced that we could now begin writing. "Commence writing and good luck" we were told, to which I added silently "and let the best men win!"

The two week exam period went by without incident. I recall the frenzied squeaking of a hundred pens scratching away on paper day after day. This sound never seemed to let up. Algebra, Geometry, General Mathematics, Biology, General Science, English, English Literature, Geography, German and History papers were written, in no particular order. I found the majority of question papers posed no particular problems, having been well prepared for them. But in one particular examination paper, we encountered various problems. One of our classmates laughed out loud upon hearing of the difficulties that had beset us. He arrogantly informed us that this particular examination had posed no problems to him whatsoever, and could not understand why we had experienced problems. We were a little dismayed by his comments. Why had he found all the questions so simple and straightforward when we in turn had struggled with a number of them?

Several weeks later, and following the release of the results, our fears were laid to rest — we had passed that particular paper but our confident classmate had managed to fail the examination in question!

Once candidates had completed writing their Cambridge examinations they were free to go home for the holidays. This applied equally to boarders and day scholars, despite the fact that the school term was not yet over. For many of us the term, the year — and for that matter one's entire school career had finally drawn to a close and it was now a case of waiting (somewhat anxiously!) for the examination results to be released around mid-January of the following year. This entailed a wait of several weeks, for the examination papers, having been set in England, would likewise be marked there. Apart from those having written the Cambridge examination and the Higher School examination, the rest of the school continued to function, as pupils in the junior and middle classes were still busy writing their own end of year examinations. A week or so later the entire school shut shop for the annual six week December 1951 – January 1952 school vacation.

Whilst still in the throes of writing examinations I had noted an article in the *Rhodesia Herald* of Friday 30 November 1951 informing sports fans that a number of top ranking professional boxers from Europe would be appearing in Salisbury on Saturday 8 December at the Raylton Athletic Club Grounds, a prominent sports venue and home ground to Raylton Football Club, then situated at the junction of Manica Road and Fifth Street, a short walk from the city centre. To me this was exciting news and the timing could not have been better, for I was due to finish writing my final exam a scant few days prior to this event taking place. Although it had been my intention to head for home immediately the last examination had been written, I decided there and then to change my plans. Rather than travel home, I decided to prolong my stay at the hostel for an additional few days and take in the boxing event on the Saturday night.

This being only the second professional fight card to be staged in Salisbury since the Second World War, and having missed out on the first one which had taken place in May 1949 (during the school vacation), I had no intention of missing out this time! And as for the boxers appearing on the bill, I could not have wished for more, for they were truly top class performers. Firstly there was Luis Romero, the reigning bantamweight and featherweight champion of Spain and former European bantamweight champion, who had recently lost a 15 round decision to Vic Toweel in Johannesburg on 17 November when unsuccessfully challenging the unbeaten Toweel for the world bantamweight title. Romero's "opponent" in a scheduled six-round "exhibition bout" was former French bantamweight champion Georges Mousse who had been outpointed in a 10 round non-title bout by reigning world champion Vic Toweel in Port Elizabeth in November. Since that defeat the Frenchman had out-pointed South African flyweight champion Marcus Temple in the latter's home town of Durban – barely a week prior to his (Mousse's) now scheduled appearance in the Salisbury ring.

Also appearing in an "exhibition contest" and very optimistically billed for six rounds, was former European heavyweight champion Jo Weidin (Austria). The Austrian had recently demolished two top South African heavyweight prospects, namely the unbeaten "white hopes" Lou Strydom and Johnny Arthur, both within the space of five weeks in Johannesburg. He was now billed to appear against another South African "prospect", one Eddie Theron, a near novice to the professional ranks. From Theron's point of view, he could count himself fortunate indeed that this was not billed as a "real fight"! In addition, a light heavyweight bout between South Africa's Freddie Vorster and Jack Krynauw was scheduled over the six-round distance, and additional "supporting bouts" had been announced. These additional bouts however failed to materialize on the night, despite being advertised on posters displayed around the city.

The Meteorological Department predicted a dry week ahead and fight fans made their way to Bain Brothers, a leading sports shop situated in First Street, to reserve their seats. It was during the course of that week that I completed writing my examinations, my mind already well focused on the forthcoming boxing event. Life was looking up!

The examinations finally over, I proceeded to enjoy a few days of relaxation, the pressures of schoolwork having now taken a backseat as I packed my metal trunk in preparation for it to be dispatched back to Gatooma. I saw a film or two in the city during the course of the week, a luxury I had seldom allowed myself during my five year sojourn at boarding school.

Saturday finally arrived and during the latter part of the afternoon I found myself at the Raylton Sports Club grounds. Officials and helpers were busy placing chairs around the open air ring and my offer to assist was accepted. I also offered my services as a programme seller during the course of the evening, this too was accepted. With that I obtained free entry into the grounds and to the tournament!

In due course spectators began to arrive and I, together with a handful of other programme sellers, did a fairly brisk trade. Acting as ushers, we showed fight fans to their seats. The crowd that evening numbered around 2,000 which the promoters were very happy with. In the opening bout, Jack Krynauw outpointed future South African light-heavyweight champion Freddie Vorster in a hard fought contest. Shortly after the bell rang for the opening round I forsook my programme selling role and found myself a good seat close to ringside – I was not going to miss out on any of the action! This fight was followed by the exhibition contest between Weidin and Theron. Within a few minutes it became obvious that Theron was completely out of his league, and although the unbeaten South African flung punches with gay abandon, Weidin's exhibition of ducking, weaving and general ring-craft left the South African mostly hitting thin air. By the fourth round the crowd, tired of seeing Weidin very obviously pulling his punches, pleaded with him to finally hit Theron. He proceeded to do just that, and launched a half hearted attack. A few good blows found their mark and, with Theron now virtually out on his feet, the referee rescued the outclassed South African boxer.

Now came the "exhibition" contest that everyone had paid to see, two experienced and highly ranked boxers who, unbeknown to me and probably 99 per cent of the local fight fans present, had already fought each other twice, in Paris and Barcelona. Mousse had won their first encounter on points and Romero, four months later, avenged this defeat by knocking out the Frenchman in two rounds in Barcelona. This time they would be trading punches in far off Africa, but with this contest merely billed as an "exhibition" bout, no one expected to see fireworks but simply a slick exhibition of boxing staged by two experienced artistes of the ring.

This may have been the perception that evening, and Georges Mousse might have had similar thoughts, but knock out artist Louis Romero appeared to have adopted a different outlook. Hardly had the bell sounded for the first round when he launched himself at his former opponent, throwing dynamite laden punches to the Frenchman's head and body. An extremely surprised Mousse back pedaled in great haste to avoid Romero's vicious blows.

In round two Romero continued his frenzied attack and had Mousse not been an experienced and crafty boxer he would surely have been driven on to the canvas. The crowd soon realized that this so called "exhibition bout" had turned into a real contest as Romero punched away at the retreating Parisian. Halfway through the round Mousse finally managed to hit back, his slick punches penetrating Romero's almost non-existent

defence. The crowd loved the action and the faster and six
pounds heavier Mousse managed to keep away from the Spaniard's bombs, making him miss time and again, but could never
afford to relax, even for a second. The delighted crowd witnessed
a magnificent contest and cheered both boxers wildly throughout the entire six rounds. When the final bell rang to end the
"fight of the night", I immediately vacated my seat and headed
straight for the dressing room in order to obtain the boxers'
autographs.

Unsure whether I would be permitted to enter the dressing
room, I was most surprised to find that my entrance was neither
barred, nor for that matter, even queried. After knocking I walked
straight in to find Jo Weidin lying flat on his back on a rubbing
table, looking extremely relaxed. He greeted me without moving
from his supine position and quite happily signed my proffered
autograph book.

With that, the door burst open and in stormed a very angry and
distraught Georges Mousse, followed in turn by manager Bobby
Diamond. Mousse was gesticulating and complaining very loudly in French, whilst the small and rotund Diamond made every
effort to placate him. A few moments later Romero entered the
room, and closed the door behind him. Mousse continued to
remain in a very voluble mood, complaining to his manager
(Diamond was one of the world's leading boxing managers of the
day) that Romero had tried to knock him out instead of treating
the bout as an exhibition contest as had been advertised. He
gave the distinct impression of wanting to pick a fight with the
Spaniard, right there and then in the confines of the dressing
room.

Romero however appeared to treat Mousse's tantrums as a big
joke, whilst Weidin remained prone on the table, laughing loudly
at the antics going on around him. I could not believe what I was
witnessing, much less the fact that no one was taking the
slightest notice of me! Here I was, a complete stranger to all of
them, and they allowed me to stay around to witness their antics!
When the shouting had finally died down, I hastily pulled out my
autograph book for the second time that evening and requested
both Mousse and Romero to sign – prior to bidding them all

good night and making my exit. It had certainly been an evening to remember, but for me the night was not yet over ...

I now made my way to the railway station to board the goods train that departed Salisbury around midnight every night of the week, arriving in Gatooma at approximately 7 a.m. Having purchased my ticket, I was accommodated in the guards van (this was the same train that I had caught from Gatooma to Battle-fields the previous year) and, as expected, I was the only passen-ger that night. I made myself as comfortable as I possibly could on the hard green leatherette seat, and attempted to sleep whilst the hard working Garrett locomotive chuffed its way through the warm summer night. However, I was not yet ready for sleep as my mind was still churning with the excitement of the Mousse-Romero fight and the confrontation which had taken place thereafter in the "privacy" of their dressing room.

This goods train, as expected, stopped at every halt and siding in order to allow northbound trains to pass, then continued at its leisurely pace in the direction of Bulawayo. However, each stop brought on board swarms of mosquitoes, despite the win-dows being kept tightly shut as a preventative. Much slapping and swatting followed every stop − there seemed to be hundreds of the little pests! I found sleep virtually impossible and at every one of the frequent stops one could clearly hear the loud croaking of frogs in the damp and sodden undergrowth which adjoined the railway tracks. We waited patiently for the oncom-ing train to arrive, a distant whistle in the night air signalling its approach before it eventually thundered past in a swirl of steam, smoke and noise.

I dozed off intermittently and was relieved when dawn broke shortly after 5 a.m. This enabled me to examine my arms, legs and ankles for mosquito bites − and there were many to be found! The train pulled into Gatooma on time and I stepped out of the guards van and onto the platform with my small suitcase. I purchased a *Sunday Mail* which had just been unloaded by local newspaper vendors, thereafter walked the fairly short distance to our house in Smith Street. It was good to be home after a somewhat hectic school year.

However, the exciting news had been broken to me some weeks earlier that my parents had booked a seaside holiday for the entire family at a resort in South Africa called Strandfontein, commonly referred to as The Strand, and situated fairly close to Cape Town. This being the height of the holiday season, both in South Africa and Rhodesia, many families flocked to the more popular coastal holiday destinations of Cape Town, Durban, Port Elizabeth and Muizenberg, plus a number of other seaside towns and cities. A friend however had recommended a hotel at The Strand, a smallish town which boasted a beach almost five miles wide in extent and which offered excellent swimming facilities. This town was situated four miles from Gordon's Bay, another popular resort, and was within easy reach of Cape Town by commuter train. This was a most practical way to travel, considering that we would not have a car at our disposal, having chosen, as the majority of holiday makers from Rhodesia did at that time, to travel to South Africa by train.

A week prior to our scheduled departure for South Africa I felt a little "off colour", and awoke one morning with a sore throat and a slight chill. I was advised to stay in bed and as a result our family doctor was called in (yes, virtually all doctors made house calls in those days)! I was assured by him that I would be fit and well by the time we were due to depart for the coast, and was duly treated with a prescribed medicine obtained from the local Phelps Chemist. A few days of bed rest were recommended.

It so happened that a newcomer to Gatooma by the name of Mrs Zuckerwar, arrived the following day to pay my mother a social visit. This lady was in fact a medical doctor, but had last practised in her home country of Poland pre-war, and was not registered to practise in Rhodesia. The bedroom I occupied was adjacent to the lounge and, when I heard Mrs Zuckerwar (a.k.a. Dr Kastellan) announce herself at the front door, I called my mother into the bedroom and implored her that, under no circumstances whatsoever, was she to mention my condition to her visitor. I did not fancy a visit from Dr Kastellan and her undoubted enquiry into my condition, for she possessed a very thick East European accent which, on the few brief occasions I had met her, I could not understand. I also suspected that, should my condition be mentioned, she would not only request to see me but would wish to examine me, and I really did not fancy an examination by this lady!

Judy, aged nine at the time, was keeping me company and we were playing a board game when we heard Dr Kastellan enter the front door. Soon we could hear her strong accent filtering through from the adjoining lounge. Invariably we joked about her accent, for we knew that our mother experienced great difficulty in understanding her visitor's diction. It did not take long before we began to chuckle at the problems our mother must be facing. We both began to mimic the doctor's speech, then proceeded to crack a few silly jokes. Kids can be cruel ...

Without warning, I developed a coughing spell, unfortunately continuing to cough without let up. After what seemed ages, I finally managed to get the cough under control and lay back with my head on the pillow, attempting to regain my breath. But the damage had been done. Dr Kastellan had heard my paroxysm of coughing and decided to come in to investigate. Ascertaining from my mother that I was resting in the next room whilst recovering from a sore throat, Dr Kastellan rose to the challenge and marched straight into the bedroom without even bothering to knock, much to my surprise and chagrin. There was nothing for it but to greet her and hope that she would not launch into a torrent of questions about my condition. However, no questions were asked. Without even a greeting, she simply uttered the following three words – "OPEN YOUR MOUSE"!

It was the worst possible thing she could have said. My sister immediately dissolved into torrents of laughter and fled the room. I lay stunned for a moment, then it was my turn to burst out laughing. My laughter almost verged onto hysteria, for I simply found it impossible to control myself following a request such as that! It became quite clear however that Dr Kastellan was not in the slightest amused by my conduct. She glared at me, then abruptly turned around and flounced out of the bedroom, slamming the door behind her. Bidding my mother a curt farewell, she left the house, never to set foot in it again! Mrs Zuckerwar had arrived at our house to pay a social visit, but it was Dr Kastellan who irately stormed out. As for my mother, after we had explained to her what had inspired us to laugh, she too joined in!

The following day I had recovered, bed rest having served its purpose. A friend called in during the course of the morning and brought me the latest *Outspan* magazine, a then leading South African weekly publication which I enjoyed reading. A regular item in the magazine featured a page of jokes entitled "Laugh – And The World Laughs With You". A good laugh was described therein as being an excellent tonic for one's health and personal well being, and I most certainly had had my share of "medicinal laughter" the previous afternoon during the course of the doctor's visit! Perhaps there really was some truth in that saying! Was it possible that Dr Kastellan had been partially responsible for my recovery – without her even being aware of it?

We caught the midnight passenger train to Bulawayo a few days later and after arrival in Bulawayo relocated to the Cape "mail train". The two and a half day journey itself was fairly uneventful. We enjoyed the daily meals partaken in the dining saloon with the tables neatly covered by crisp white tablecloths, starched napkins and solid cutlery immaculately laid out for each and every sitting. At one station in Bechuanaland we passed a freight train heading north in the direction of Rhodesia, transporting over a dozen new Studebaker Champion and Commander automobiles with their distinctive "bullet nose" design, all lashed down firmly on flatcars. Our train travelled on the same railway line that we had taken when journeying to South West Africa two years earlier, except that at De Aar our train continued on its journey southwards to Cape Town instead of changing locomotives and branching off north to Windhoek. Awaking in our compartment on the last day of the journey we found ourselves surrounded by the spectacular scenery of the Hex River Valley, while the train snaked its way along a lush green mountainside with the Hex River flowing alongside us in the valley below. Viewing the same breathtaking scenery a little later through the large picture windows of the dining saloon, whilst breakfasting in style on stewed fruit, maize meal porridge, kipper and eggs, toast and coffee was even more enjoyable!

Our train pulled into Cape Town's main railway station around midday and shortly thereafter we transferred to a local train. With brief stops en route at Bellville, Eersterivier and Van der Stel, we pulled into Strandfontein station. After alighting we made our way to the Strand Hotel where we were to spend the next few weeks. It appeared to be a pleasant enough establishment and after unpacking we all set off for a walk along the beach front, prior to returning to the hotel where a good dinner awaited us.

Not having a car at our disposal limited us to walks along the beach and through the small town of Strandfontein. Or, we simply relaxed at the hotel and caught up with all the accumulated reading material that we had brought with us from home. Whilst my mother and Judy both enjoyed swimming and sunbathing, I decided to curtail my time in the sun as I had no desire whatsoever to catch another dose of sunburn. My father and I spent time relaxing on comfortable veranda chairs on the hotel balcony and caught up with our reading material. Although I enjoyed daily swims in the ocean I made sure to avoid sitting in the sun for too long. My father, a non-swimmer, often accompanied me to the beach, and despite only walking ankle deep in the water, he still managed to get his lower legs sunburned! Over these few weeks I was privileged to spend a lot of quality time with him – well before that expression had even been coined! He was one of the most sensible people I have ever met, always remained calm, seldom raised his voice and always planned things meticulously in advance. He was very knowledgeable, and I recollect that over the years many people called on him for advice on a multitude of concerns, both private and business related. He was steeped in Judaism, founded the town's Hebrew Congregation and led the local Jewish community for many years. He became, as far as I know, the first and only designated (former) "enemy alien" to be elected onto a Rhodesian Municipal Town Council and what's more, served as Mayor of Gatooma on no less than three occasions. He served on the Gatooma Public Library Committee for over forty years, several times in the role of Chairman, and at one stage in the 1960s served on the committee of Southern Rhodesian Prime Minister Sir Edgar Whitehead's (United Rhodesia Party) personal "think tank". A Rotarian of long standing, he served as President of the Gatooma Rotary Club a number of times. He was a very public spirited man and an excellent after dinner speaker. But I have jumped the gun a little, for many of these activities were yet to take place in the years that followed.

To return to our Cape holiday. Amongst the books we had brought with was Herman Wouk's newly published novel *The Caine Mutiny* which won the author the Pulitzer Prize. Although I normally read non-fiction books in preference to novels, I found this tale extremely gripping and thoroughly enjoyed its almost 500 pages, finishing the book in record time. As an aside – in 1956 I paid my first ever visit to London and the first West End play I chose to see was *The Caine Mutiny Court Martial* – which featured Lloyd Nolan in the central role of Lt-Commander Queeg. Nolan, a fine actor, had played the same role on Broadway prior to his London engagement. In 1954 a film was shot for the big screen which starred Jose Ferrer, Van Johnson, Fred McMurray and Humphrey Bogart in the role of Queeg. It turned out to be a top rate movie and I had become thoroughly hooked on Herman Wouk's masterpiece – I kid you not!!

We boarded the commuter train to Cape Town on a number of occasions and explored the city and its sights, visiting art galleries, museums and other places of interest. We walked up and down the length of Adderley Street, Cape Town's premier shopping thoroughfare. The city boasted many fine departmental stores, Stuttafords, Garlicks and Cleghorns come to mind, and when one exited these buildings the majestic outline of Table Mountain was often there to greet one. This provided a most spectacular backdrop to the city skyline and a reminder that one was visiting a unique part of the world. We visited the busy harbour and admired the Union Castle liners that plied the busy South Africa – United Kingdom run. On one of our visits to the harbour the Cunard luxury cruise liner *Caronia* lay at anchor and we admired her lines. Despite getting on in age this graceful ship still embarked on annual world wide cruises, many of her passengers were elderly American millionaires who spent a great deal of their time cruising the world's oceans in the absolute lap of luxury.

We booked seats on a tour bus which drove along the coastal road from Cape Town to Cape Point, where the cold Benguela current of the Atlantic Ocean meets the warm Agulhas current of the Indian Ocean. At times the bus journey reminded me of the ride from Umtali up into the Vumba Mountains, with the road itself precariously carved out of the cliff face on one side and with the usual sheer drop on the other. However, this time, instead of a steep drop into a lush green valley, there was a spectacular view of the ocean down below with waves pounding onto the jagged rocks.

We stopped for a lunch break at Cape Point – and hardly had we pulled out our sandwiches and packed lunches then we found ourselves surrounded by dozens of chattering monkeys and baboons.

We had all been warned in advance not to feed these apes, likewise to ensure that all bus windows were kept securely closed. A few passengers chose to ignore these warnings and within seconds they were surrounded by these chattering creatures which tended to become quite aggressive when denied food. Trying to ignore the apes, we were shown around the area by the tour guide and viewed the interesting lighthouse. We were informed that in the earlier part of the century icebergs originating from Antarctica could occasionally be spied from Cape Point. On boarding the bus for the return journey to Cape Town, we left both monkeys and baboons lying in ambush for the next bus load of visitors to hopefully provide them with further titbits!

BUTCH BURMAN

81 Rissik Street headquarters for Nat Fleischer's world famous boxing publications and Record books, has opened a branch at

12 WANDERERS STREET, Corner of Plein Street,

where he will be pleased to reserve your copy of RING, FIGHT, BOXING NEWS, IRON MAN, WRESTLING MAT, STRENGTH & HEALTH, YOUR PHYSIQUE, MUSCLE POWER, VIGOUR, BODY CULTURE, and all American periodicals. Stocks of books on BOXING, WRESTLING, JUDO, BASEBALL, CRICKET, SWIMMING and other sports always on hand. Mail orders promptly handled.

BUTCH BURMAN'S
B o o k   S t o r e,
81 RISSIK STREET,
and
12 WANDERERS STREET,
JOHANNESBURG.
Phone 33-7578

Our Cape visit drew to a close and we found ourselves on the train once more, this time heading in a northerly direction – destination Johannesburg, a city we had not visited before. Rooms had been reserved at the Hotel Victoria in Plein Street, in the heart of South Africa's largest city. After booking in and depositing our suitcases, we set out to explore the area surrounding the hotel. It was here that I took my first ride on a tram, a novel experience. I made my way to Butch Burman's Book Store, at that time situated at 12 Wanderers Street, which specialized in sporting books and periodicals, with special emphasis on boxing material. Whilst the rest of the family explored the "City of Gold", I spent a most enjoyable afternoon paging through the myriad of boxing books and magazines in this most fabulous of sporting book shops.

The following day, after breakfasting in the large dining room, we were making our way out of the hotel lobby when we found the doorway virtually obstructed by a man sporting the most enormous pair of shoulders that I had ever seen. His upper torso alone seemed to take up the entire width of the doorframe! As I had just read about him in the newspapers, I had no trouble in recognizing him – for he was none other than the current holder of the Mr Universe title, namely Reg Park of South Africa. My autograph book was whipped out and a smiling "Mr Universe" appended his signature therein, to which he added "Best Wishes"! My day had virtually been made before it had even begun!

The last port of call on my list was Laurie Stevens' Sports Shop, situated in Rissik Street, and here I met one of South Africa's most prominent boxers, the great Laurie Stevens himself. Winner of the Olympic lightweight title at the 1932 Los Angeles Games, he became the country's most popular boxer of the 1930s, and now, after retiring from the ring, ran a successful shop in the city centre. Another autograph was added to my collection!

Regretfully, our short visit to Johannesburg drew to a close, and we found ourselves at the Johannesburg station boarding the mail train for Rhodesia, a journey of approximately a day and a half. As one would say in Afrikaans – it had been a "lekker" (enjoyable) holiday but now the time had come to head for home. We departed Johannesburg mid-morning and the train made its way north, headed by a powerful steam locomotive. After an uneventful journey, we pulled into Bulawayo late the following afternoon. That evening we boarded the Salisbury passenger train.

An approximate six-hour journey culminated with the train conductor rattling on our compartment door while the train was in the act of crossing the Umsweswe River bridge, announcing that we were due to arrive in Gatooma in fifteen minutes. We arose from our comfortable bunk beds, hurriedly dressed, gathered our belongings and at around 4 a.m. or so we were back in Gatooma. We alighted on the familiar station platform, during the course of the train's brief four minute stopover. The Standard

Vanguard awaited us, having been parked there the previous afternoon by one of my father's office employees, the keys handed in at the station master's office for collection. Our suitcases, having been unloaded from the guards van, were placed into the trunk of the car by the obliging railway porter. We drove the short distance home through a few rain washed and deserted streets and were greeted by our loudly purring cat, only too delighted to welcome us home!

The following day we paid a visit to the building site to review progress on our new house and suite of offices which were under construction at the time. Work on these premises had commenced some months earlier, but, due to a severe nationwide shortage of building material, progress had been both slow and erratic. Cement was at a great premium, as were bricks, roofing tiles, plumbing supplies together with most other essential materials. Rhodesia was experiencing an unprecedented building boom and builders spent more time attempting to locate elusive building materials in hardware shops and brickyards than time spent on building sites!

Both house and offices would eventually be completed in April 1952. The large airy offices, together with a walk-in strong room would afford all the space required at that time, and the combination of these offices and adjoining modern residence proved to be a most eye-catching and practical design.

However, we were now well into the month of January 1952 and all schools had already re-opened. Within a day of arriving home from our South African vacation I was busy packing clothing into my now well travelled tin trunk. For I had agreed to return to Prince Edward in order to await the results of my Cambridge School Certificate examinations. These results usually arrived during the latter part of January. At that stage I had no idea whether or not I had passed the examinations, and felt it was best to return to school, in case I would be required to re-write any of the subjects that I might not have passed.

We had just sat down to breakfast on the very day I was due to depart for Salisbury when the telephone rang. My mother answered the call and after a few moments returned to the table. With a wide smile she informed me that Mrs Tilly Cohen was on the line and requesting to speak to me! Why would Mrs Cohen want to speak to me, I wondered, as I picked up the receiver. "Congratulations on passing, Peter," she said in her distinctive and clear voice, "you did well in the examinations". And then it dawned on me. The Cambridge Examination results had obviously been received and released by the Ministry of Education to all high schools, and likewise to the national newspapers.

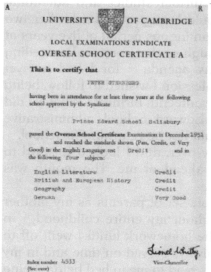

Examination results now filled two full pages of the country's major newspapers – the *Rhodesia Herald* and the *Bulawayo Chronicle*, both with a nationwide circulation. This was the custom at the time, enabling reader's access to the results of all examinations recently written by high school pupils throughout the entire country. Pupils' names were listed, the categories of examinations they had written (Cambridge School Certificate, Higher School Certificate, etc), the number of passes, credits and distinctions obtained by each and every individual pupil – and woe betide if one's name did not appear on the list, for that clearly indicated that the pupil in question had failed their examinations. Many readers made it their express purpose to carefully check who had passed and who had failed these recently held examinations. At that stage in time the country still consisted of a reasonably small and closely knit community where many people personally knew families whose children had sat for these examinations. Many additional copies were printed on "exam results day" and newspaper sales greatly increased throughout the land, turning this edition into what was probably the most popular and best selling one of the entire year!

Our telephone continued to ring for most of the day as further congratulations came in from friends and classmates. Likewise, I telephoned many of my fellow-classmates, but only after I had briefly slipped out to purchase a copy of the *Herald* in order to read the results for myself. Just to be sure!

My mind seemed to be in somewhat of a whirl – but overjoyed with the news just received! I had been adamant all along that, should I pass these examinations I would leave school, and was determined to keep with that decision. An alternative would have been to go back to school for further studies and additional examinations. However, that would have entailed a further two years of schooling and, after a continuous period of five years at boarding school, I had had enough of that routine. Proceeding on to university was not on my agenda – for I had not yet decided as to what career or profession I wished to follow, being just over a month short of my seventeenth birthday. What we did do was telephone the Prince Edward School administrative offices to advise them that I would not be returning to school.

My school days were officially over, and I looked forward to facing the world that now lay ahead of me. The month was January 1952.

In fact, I feel I had a remarkable set of parents as my mother was always there for me throughout my entire childhood – in times of illness, to assist with the homework (until I went off to high school), tasty meals were always served on time and in my younger days stories were always read to me in bed before being tucked up for the night. And she was a mother one could TALK to and discuss matters with. She and my father loved each other deeply throughout their lives and I consider myself most fortunate to have had parents of this calibre.

Our new home.

Kalley

#0062 - 061118 - C0 - 210/148/15 - PB - DID2353648